AF324894

JAPAN ON STAGE

Kawatake Toshio

JAPAN ON STAGE

*Japanese Concepts of Beauty
as Shown in the Traditional Theatre*

Translated by
P.G. O'Neill

3A Corporation

Tokyo, Japan

Translation and publication supported by a grant from The Japan Foundation.

Originally published in Japan as *Butai no Oku no Nihon* 'Japan on Stage' by Toshio Kawatake. © Toshio Kawatake 1982, published by TBS-Britannica Co., Ltd.

JAPAN ON STAGE

©by 3A Corporation
Shoei Bldg., 6-3, Sarugaku-cho 2-chome, Chiyoda-ku, Tokyo 101, Japan

Translated by P.G. O'Neill

First English Edition published 1990

Printed in Japan

Photographs: Courtesy of Toshiro Morita, Heibonsha, TANKŌSHA
Co., Ltd., the head of Kanze school and Hinomisaki Shrine.

ISBN 4-906224-62-8 C1074

Translator's Introduction

This book is many things. It is first, as the title indicates, an account of Japanese attitudes to beauty, illustrated mainly by examples from the traditional theatre; but in giving this account, the author has ranged widely over other aspects of Japanese life and culture and has throughout made illuminating comparisons with the west.

The result is a book that is also valuable for its treatment of Japan's drama as a whole, her general cultural background and, in addition, many other aspects of modern Japanese society, for the country preserves the old when she takes on the new. This produces, in the author's phrase, 'any number of streams flowing side by side but with waters of different colours,' and makes Japan to an unusual extent the product of her past.

In drawing his material mainly from the Japanese theatre, the author describes its development from ancient court music and other early entertainment forms, through the Nō and Kyōgen of the medieval period, to the Kabuki and puppet theatre of pre-modern times and the rise of newer forms after the Meji Restoration of 1868. As he does so, he makes comparisons with western forms ranging from Greek drama to Ibsen and *Hamlet* in modern dress. What is most interesting in his account, though, is the common ground he shows to exist for such seemingly different forms as the aristocratic, restrained Nō and the plebian, colourful and spectacular Kabuki.

His comparisons also take in many other aspects of life and culture in Japan and the west. Since these include artistic traditions and their transmission, attitudes to nature, landscape gardening, flower arrangement, colours, food and housing, there can scarcely be a reader who will not in future look at some or all of these with new eyes.

The author's treatment of dramatic themes inevitably leads him to deal too with human emotions and the problems arising from them. The harsh realities of feudal Japan, with its continual conflicts between the individual on the one hand and the demands of authority and the expectations of society on the other, for centuries provided playwrights with rich material. The book's analysis of love, loyalty, cruelty and death as portrayed on the stage offers insights into some of the fundamental characteristics of modern Japan.

For the western reader, one of its appeals must be that it was written by a Japanese for the Japanese, and therefore gives a private view, as it were, of how a cultured and cosmopolitan writer sees his own country and its people. His credentials for the authorship of this book could hardly be better: the great-grandson of the greatest Japanese playwright of the nineteenth century and the son of a famous scholar of traditional drama, he himself has made a lifelong study of comparative theatre; and while his travels abroad have reinforced his pride in being Japanese, they have also enabled him to see his country and its unique features more clearly and within a world setting.

This book is thus as many-sided as Japan itself. It has been interesting and enjoyable to translate it, and I feel privileged to have played a part in bringing it to a wider readership.

London, July 1990   P.G. O'Neill

Contents

Chapter One   THINGS JAPANESE
[1]

Chapter Two   FREEDOM OF TIME AND SPACE
[39]

CHAPTER THREE   PLASTIC BEAUTY AND A SENSE
OF SOUND
[83]

CHAPTER FOUR   EMOTIONS AND LAMENTATION
[119]

CHAPTER FIVE NATURE'S EMBRACE
[169]

CHAPTER SIX THE AESTHETICS OF "BEAUTY IS TRUTH"
[205]

CHAPTER SEVEN THE LIVING TRADITION
[243]

PHOTOGRAPHS

PREFACE

This publication of an English translation of my book *Butai no Oku no Nihon* 'Japan on Stage' gives me great pleasure.

The first reason for this is that, although I have published more than sixty books beginning with *Nihon no Geinō* 'The Performing Arts of Japan' in 1953, this is the first one that has been fully translated into English. There are other works of mine in foreign languages—*Engeki Gairon* 'An Introduction to Drama' has been translated and published in Chinese, and those in western languages include *The Traditional Theatre of Japan*, *Kabuki on the World Stage*, and *Das Barocke im Kabuki—das Kabukihafte im Barocktheater*—but these were written from the outset for foreign readers, being very specialized pieces of research, for example, or talks given for the overseas service of the Japan Broadcasting Corporation. This is my first book written in Japanese for the general reader which has been published in a complete English translation.

The second reason for my pleasure is that I wrote this book for Japanese readers but, deep down, hoped that it might be read by foreign people too. Fortunately, it has had many readers in Japan and has now gone through four printings since its first publication in 1982. It won an award at that time from the Tokio Marine Kagami Memorial Foundation as the book of the year, and Gregory Clark, a jury member who is a professor at Sophia University, stated in his recommendation that it was a book which should certainly be translated and made available to foreign readers. I was happy that what I had had in mind received this recognition, but it was quite impossible to tell whether or not it would ever be realised. That it has been, and in such an attractive form, naturally pleases me very much.

My third and main reason for the pleasure I feel is that I have had an eminently suitable translator in P.G. O'Neill, a Professor Emeritus in the University of London and a leading figure in foreign research on the traditional theatre and culture of Japan. We do not have the opportunity to meet all that often, but he is a contemporary of mine, known to me for many years, who is also one of my foreign friends I hold in the highest regard. It is twenty years ago now, but I remember him attending a lecture I gave on Japanese drama at London University as if it were yesterday.

I am well aware from my own experience how difficult is the work of translation. In 1954 I translated and had published a Japanese version of *Playwright at Work* by the American dramatist John van Druten: this contained quotations from wartime and post-war American plays which were not known in Japan at the time, and I had to go to endless trouble searching out this and confirming that before I could even translate their titles.

This kind of thing must have been even more true of this book which, dealing as it does with traditional Japanese drama, is full of unique elements, many of which are nowadays unknown even to Japanese. Being far better acquainted with Japan's drama and traditional culture than many Japanese, Professor O'Neill was indeed an ideal translator. He wrote to me directly on several occasions to query or confirm small points of doubt, and in the course of this correspondence I became impressed by his deep interest in the book and his work on it, and strengthened in my belief that it would turn out to be an outstanding translation. It has, in addition, had a final careful check by Professor Tsuchiya Motoko of Tōyō Women's College, who has throughout been closely concerned with the undertaking and given it every support as it progressed.

There can surely be no more ideal situation in which to produce a translation.

In realising the publication of this book, I have enjoyed all manner of kindness from other quarters too, including Professor Gregory Clark and Professor Donald Keene, a friend of many years renowned for his studies of Japanese literature and drama, who were good enough to write recommendations for it; the Japan Foundation, for its grant towards the cost of publication; Toita Yasuji, the drama critic, and Fujinami Takayuki, director of the National Theatre, who kindly recommended such a grant; Fukumoto Hajime, president of the 3A Corporation, whose good offices made publication possible; and Morita Toshirō for supplying the excellent photographs in the book.

Having already written about the aims of the book in the introduction to the original Japanese edition, I will not repeat them here. I will just say that although this book takes its material from drama, it is neither an exposition nor a study of Japanese drama, but something unique among my published works in that it goes beyond drama to consider the particular features of Japanese culture and concepts of beauty among the Japanese from the viewpoint of comparisons between Japan and other countries. It might be called the fruit of my forty years of comparative study of drama and contemplation of culture.

As it happens, a Chinese translation of this book is even now being prepared, but if this English version is read by a large number of people in different parts of the world and serves as a bridge to help an understanding of Japanese culture and of Japan itself, then as its author I can think of nothing that would give me greater pleasure.

Tokyo, October 1990   Kawatake Toshio

Introduction to the Original Japanese Edition

Born a Japanese in Japan, I have now lived for more than fifty years. Having had my first opportunities to travel to the west exactly a quarter of a century ago and then, three years later, to go with the Kabuki troupe for its performances in America, I have lived and travelled in various places.

They were of course working trips made when I could take time away from my main duties in Japan, and so there was nothing particularly special about them as far as personal experience goes. Even so, having found myself in the midst of various cultures and ways of life in different parts of the world, I realize what a small, distinct, parochial country Japan is. When I think about this, I also feel very deeply that there is no other country so good and so blessed by nature.

In this book, I have tried to see where Japanese beauty is to be found or, to put it rather more grandly, to look at the special features of Japanese culture. I have done this from a comparative viewpoint, insofar as I am able, to give them a setting within the world at large. Everything, though, has its good and bad sides, and it has never been my intention to insist that the traditional beauty of Japan is the finest there is.

I have tended simply to try to recapture those 'Japanese things' which are in danger of dissolving and disappearing in the flow of modern and contemporary life, while authenticating them as graphically as possible by what I myself have seen, heard, or experienced. This may also be described as giving answers to my own questions.

My main material has been the theatre, or stage arts. This is because that is my special field, but it is also because, to paraphrase Shakespeare, 'A play is a mirror truly reflecting its country and time.' One can hardly go astray, I feel, to look for a country's culture and sense of beauty on its stage.

It was from this idea that the title of the book, *Japan on Stage*, happened to come to me.

Such were my feelings when I wrote this book as the spirit guided me, making it a kind of personal record or essay. It is neither a formal critique nor a thesis. For me, it is the first book of its kind.

It could, though, perhaps be described in one sense as an interim statement of my research so far because, presumptuous though it may be, my ultimate aim in doing comparative work is to make clear the special features of Japan's drama and culture, and to give them their place within mankind generally.

April 1982   Kawatake Toshio

EDITORIAL NOTES

Japanese names appear in the Japanese order, with the family name given first and followed by the personal name.

Book and play titles and the like have been given in italics throughout and, where appropriate, translated on their first appearance.

Japanese words not commonly used in English have been given in italics and translated or explained on their first appearance only.

Japanese titles and words which occur in the text more than once are translated or briefly explained in the Selected Glossary at the end of the book.

Long vowels in Japanese are shown by a macron over the vowel, except in a few well known words such as Tokyo and Judo.

Stage sides, left and right, are referred to throughout from the viewpoint of the audience.

CHAPTER ONE

THINGS JAPANESE

KABUKI GOES TO AMERICA

The Beginning of the Story

On 27 May 1960 a Kabuki group flew off from Haneda for New York on the first-ever visit to America.

I was one of that party, and in my role as literary adviser I was responsible for such things as general consultancy, explanatory material and audience surveys. Not yet a full professor, I was thirty-five at the time.

The group was made up of sixty-three people. In recent years, of course, with the international exchange of such things as opera and orchestras, numbers running into three figures are not all that unusual, but in that period when the world was only just at peace again, it could well be called an undertaking on an unprecedented scale.

However, there were no more than twenty-four actors among that number, led by the most eminent performers of the time: Nakamura Kanzaburō, Onoe Shōroku and, as the leading player of female roles, Nakamura Utaemon. Why, then, was there such a large company of more than sixty people?

The reason is that Kabuki is a multi-faceted "composite drama" which requires not only the lines and actions of the players but all kinds of other elements such as music, special effects, large-scale sets and scene changes. Therein lies one of the main characteristics of theatre in Japan and of the concept of beauty among the Japanese revealed in their theatre, which I propose to consider in this book; but before doing so I should like to cite one or two examples from pieces performed at that time.

First, *Chūshingura* 'The League of Loyal Retainers.' This is a work originally written for the puppet theatre (now known as Bunraku), and so it has to have the type of chanting called *gidayū*. *Kanjinchō* 'The Subscription List' and *Musume Dōjō-ji* 'The Maiden at the Dōjō Temple' have *nagauta* singing and musicians playing the flute and different types of drum ranged right across the stage on floor covering of scarlet cloth. Gidayū and nagauta have samisen (shamisen) players as well as chanters and singers, and so their contributions alone required eighteen people. When, in addition to these, there were for example a stage manager and assistants responsible throughout the stage performances for scenery, properties, costumes, wigs and the use of wooden clappers, as well as office staff, interpreters, and also a doctor in close touch with the health and morale of the company, the total inevitably came to more than sixty.

But the number of people was only part of it. Since even the scenery was all made in Japan and sent over by ship, and then carried across America from one place of performance to another by train and truck, these overseas performances were indeed a headache.

Naturally, the costs increased. The whole operation was mounted by the Shōchiku company, but it could not do it alone. Therefore, since this first visit of Kabuki to America was seen as taking place during the hundredth anniversary of friendly relations between Japan and the United States, it was finally achieved as a result of enthusiastic urging from America, the efforts of the Cultural Projects Section of the Ministry of Foreign Affairs, and help from the Kokusai Bunka Shinkōkai 'Society for International Cultural Relations,' the forerunner of the Japan Foundation.

Now my reason for bringing up the subject of Kabuki performances overseas is simply this: I feel that hidden within such things as the initial complications, the troubles experienced abroad, and the reception of the performances, there are clues to the problems I am going to consider below.

Where is the unique character of Japanese drama or traditional Japanese culture to be found? Do they have nothing in common with those of foreigners who have different languages and customs; that is, do they have no universality? And if we assume that they do, where is it to be found?

Such questions as these have already been discussed in various ways by many people, but I would like to consider them in my own way, on the basis of my personal experience. Although this type of comparative study, as it is called, has been of interest to me since I began work in this field thirty years ago, on thinking about it now, I find that what prompted me to take it up in a direct and positive way was this first visit of Kabuki to America. In which case, it can be said to have been for me a most valuable experience. Since it would be a waste to keep it all to myself, I felt that that was where I should start.

That was not, however, the first time that Kabuki had been abroad. The first time of all was a visit to the Soviet Union by Ichikawa Sadanji II in 1928, when public performances were given in Moscow and Leningrad. There were no more until after the war when, before the visit to America, performances were given in China on two occasions. These were in 1955, by the troupe of Ichikawa Ennosuke II (En-ō, the grandfather of the present Ennosuke), and in 1960 by the Zenshinza company immediately before the tour of America. This tour, though, was the first ever in America or any other western country.

Since it was only a short while since peace had been restored, there were all kinds of complications apart from the economic ones, but I shall give just one inside story, that of the fuss about whether or not to include a "harakiri scene" which arose at the stage of programme selection.

When *Chūshingura* was put forward and was eventually about to be officially confirmed, an objection came from the Ministry of Foreign Affairs: did we think that the scene in which the young lord commits harakiri was all right or should it perhaps be cut out? In this scene, Enya Hangan Takasada, a feudal lord from the province of Hōki who had been utterly humiliated by Kō no Moronō in the Pine Room in the shogun's palace, was ordered to commit harakiri because he had finally drawn his sword and wounded him. In fact, of course, these names of earlier historical figures are used as a transparent device to refer respectively to Asano Takuminokami and Kira Kōzukenosuke, the main characters in the contemporary incident concerned, and by this means avoid the displeasure of the authorities. As the appointed time arrives, the young lord plunges his dagger into his stomach before the supervisory official—whereupon the climax comes as the curtain at the back of the theatre is raised and, with a clatter of running feet, the lord's long-awaited senior retainer Ōboshi Yuranosuke (Ōishi Kuranosuke) rushes along the *hanamichi*, the passage-way through the auditorium, onto the stage.

Silence and bitter grief—a dark scene weighed down with sadness and full of tragic beauty and pathos. It is one of those typical situations, full of a uniquely Japanese type of grief, which I am going to comment on later. As such, it is so vital to maintain the atmosphere on stage that it has long been the custom, once the curtain opens, not to let any members of the audience enter until it is over. It is therefore called a "no-entry scene."

The worry in official quarters was that, if this scene were shown abroad, it might be mistakenly thought that harakiri was still to be found in Japan or at least that it was still admired here. It is not unusual for Japan to be unnecessarily con-

An overseas performance on Kabuki, at the Odeon
Theatre, Paris.

cerned about reaction overseas but, on this occasion, I felt that
they may well have been right. There were two reasons for
this. The first was that the memory of Kabuki revenge plays,
particularly this *Chūshingura*, having been prohibited immediately after the war was still fresh in my mind; and the second
was that I knew from what I had seen and heard while studying in America three years previously that the Japanese word
harakiri was pretty widely known there.

When all concerned were at a loss what to do about this,
it was Faubion Bowers who suddenly broke in to say that we
need have no worry and should certainly perform the piece.

This took place, I believe, in a room in the old Imperial Hotel. Bowers was a devotee of Kabuki and was not only a benefactor who had rescued it by removing entirely the severe restrictions on performances when he was a censorship officer with the Occupation forces, but was also someone who had proposed and promoted this Kabuki tour of the United States.

"Kabuki is a classic art," he insisted. "No American is going to think that present-day Japanese like harakiri because it is shown on the Kabuki stage." These words from one who was owed so much carried weight enough to reassure even the Ministry of Foreign Affairs, and the performances of *Chūshingura* were realised after all. What is more, far from it giving rise to any misunderstanding, this *Chūshingura* which at first sight might appear so undemocratic won the highest acclaim among all the seven pieces performed.

How was it that *Chūshingura* broke through the barrier of differences in language and historical and social background and moved foreign audiences? What was it, on the other hand, that brought a poor reception for pieces that had seemed acceptable? I shall go on to consider such questions on the basis of reactions from the audiences concerned, but I should just like to say a word beforehand here about the subjects and methods of the surveys.

I mentioned already that I have begun with an account of performances overseas in order to look for clues relating to the theme of this book as a whole, and it goes without saying that adequate data for this cannot be gained simply from performances in the United States. For any particular conclusion—for example, whether or not the harakiri scene in *Chūshingura* is moving or not—must be confirmed by a sufficiently large number of examples before a conclusion can be reached with any confidence.

It is also difficult to infer the reactions of foreigners in general from the reactions and praise of a few hardly typical individuals. Rather, there is the danger of arriving at a wholly wrong conclusion. It is a fact that foreigners who know Japan well and professional dramatic critics praise such pieces as *Musume Dōjō-ji* and *Kanjinchō* as being the ultimate expression of a uniquely Japanese beauty. They are not wrong in this, but on balance these plays were not well received by ordinary foreigners who saw them.

Foreign experts on Japan are captivated by its traditional beauty, and study and empathize with it more than we Japanese. Professional dramatic critics at least make serious efforts to study Japanese drama before they come to see it, aware that they must understand it and review it fairly. But what I would like to know is where, in all honesty, ordinary foreigners outside these special groups feel sympathy, disharmony and rejection.

Statistical methods based on an adequate number of cases: this is probably the one and only method of grasping objectively and scientifically mental behaviour which precludes artificial experiment and retesting, that is, cultural phenomena.

In that regard, I believe I can speak with confidence about the reactions of westerners to Kabuki for, on five occasions following the tour of America, six in all and over a period of some seven months, I was in constant attendance at overseas performances as literary adviser and thus had increasing opportunity to study the response to them. The six occasions were the United States in 1960 (New York, Los Angeles, San Francisco); the Soviet Union in 1961 (Moscow, Leningrad); the first performances in western Europe in 1965 (Berlin, Paris, Lisbon); England and Germany in 1972 (London, Munich); Australia in 1978 (Sydney, Melbourne, Adelaide); and western Europe in 1981 (Berlin, Paris, Reggio-Emilia, London).

Each night I sat among the audience and saw, heard and physically sensed the local people as they watched, yawned, gasped and, sometimes, wiped away a tear. What is more, at each place I distributed detailed questionnaires containing some twenty items and managed to collect large numbers of replies.

For example, in Europe, these amounted to 903 in Berlin, 1,107 in Paris, and 109 in Lisbon, for a total of 2,119 in 1965; 1,143 in London, and 138 in Munich, for a total of 1,281 in 1972. (The figures are roughly in proportion to the number of performances.) Only in the Soviet Union were we unfortunate in being unable to obtain permission for a survey.

But that as it may, the following description of the situation regarding audience reactions is the result of this kind of experience and data, and so I feel that I can talk and even generalize about it with assurance.

Japanese, All Too Japanese

Why Was Musume Dōjō-ji Not Well Received?

What kind of pieces would please foreigners seeing Kabuki for the first time?

Most people would probably answer "dance dramas" rather than ordinary plays, on the grounds that dances in which performers wearing beautiful robes simply move to a musical accompaniment—a world of pure colour, form, sound and movement—would be better than a textual play for foreigners ignorant of the language, and that those who knew neither the language nor historical background would be unlikely to understand dramatic pieces with a story-line.

In fact, the people concerned and I myself also thought that at first: with dancing, we would be on safe ground, and dancing by a female impersonator would surely be ideal. After all, most foreigners who would take the trouble to see Kabuki at the present time, even if they were not experts on Japan or drama specialists, would probably at least know that the female impersonator was its greatest aesthetic feature without a counterpart in the west. . . .

So it was that *Musume Dōjō-ji* was chosen. A Kabuki version of the Nō play *Dōjō-ji* 'The Dōjō Temple,' it is regarded as the very best of all the dance pieces for female impersonators and, what is more, the dancer was to be Nakamura Utaemon, the finest performer of the time. Our expectations, however, were woefully disappointed. When the beautiful young woman—a type of travelling dancing-girl known as a *shirabyōshi*—appeared on the hanamichi, the audience naturally held their breath and looked and stared as they asked themselves whether she really was a man. There were even gasps here and there at such unworldly beauty. Yet, somehow, the tension and concentration in the auditorium lasted a bare five minutes or so. The audience became bored, fidgeted with their programmes, whispered with their neighbours, or even began to doze off. This lack of enthusiasm continued until the end of the piece, which was then given only muted applause.

This did not happen only on the first tour, when we were in the United States. This same *Musume Dōjō-ji* was also given on our second trip, to the Soviet Union, and on the third, when the first performances were given in Europe, because it was thought that there might be different reactions in different countries and that we might do well to vary the way it was presented. In the Soviet Union it was danced by Utaemon again, and in Europe by Onoe Baikō, both first-class performers. We also tried a complete version of the piece rarely given even in Japan, right up to the 'Temple-bell' scene in which the shirabyōshi Hanago reveals her true nature as the vengeful ghost of the jilted village girl Kiyohime, in the form of a serpent. The result was the same, however, and in the end this famous piece was dropped from the repertoire of subsequent performances overseas.

In comparison, *Chūshingura* and *Shunkan*, which had been anxiously expected to suffer a bad reception as a feudal drama and a vengeance play, were highly acclaimed. Why should this have been ?

Now the first thing that comes into my mind about the poor reception of *Musume Dōjō-ji* is a doubt expressed by someone, probably a drama critic, who had been attentively watching a stage rehearsal in New York. "What I saw doesn't match the explanation in the programme," he said.

He was right: the programme had been produced on the American side, and when I read the explanation of the piece in question, it was very clear to me that, while great pains had been taken to make it easy for foreigners to understand, there was a place where it had been analysed a little too logically and missed the mark. The part in question begins:

> 'On the day a new bell is to be dedicated, a beautiful young woman comes to the temple and asks to be allowed to pray. The priests guarding the entrance refuse because, once in the past, a village girl fell in love with a priest and, when she pressed him to respond, he hid under the hanging bell at the Dōjō Temple. At this, she changed into a great serpent, coiled herself around the bell and turned it into molten metal, burning to death the priest inside.'

This far, it is all right: this is the story of the priest Anchin and the girl Kiyohime, a legend concerning the Dojo Temple in the province of Kii which still exists there. The problem was in the next part:

> 'She then pleads with them to be allowed to dance, and so they allow her into the temple. But while they are watching her dance, they feel there is *something strange* about her. As she dances she makes costume changes and, at this, the priests become more and more fearful. Then they suddenly remember that the great serpent too had cast off its skin, that is, the dancer's robes, to reveal its true form. . . .'

The man's question, then, was this: "This is what it says in the programme, but from what I saw she wasn't at all like a serpent and she didn't seem to be frightening either. What

The Kabuki *Musume Dōjō-ji*.

is in the dancer's mind, and every time she changes her costume
how much closer does she come to turning into a serpent?"

It was, I thought, an understandable question. He may well
have been quite happy if, as the programme indicated, there
had been a clear representation of a dramatic development as
the dancer underwent a psychological change.

The Nō *Dōjō-ji*, the source of this piece, has a clear dramatic development in which the vengeful spirit of Kiyohime
appears as a beautiful woman on the day a new bell is to be
dedicated, approaches the bell as she dances and, when the
priests are not looking, brings it crashing down over her. She
then appears in the form of a serpent, but leaves the stage having attained salvation through the prayers of the priests.

In the Kabuki version *Musume Dōjō-ji*, however, the story
in fact does nothing more than provide a setting. By various
costume changes and music and choreography which weave
all kinds of patterns to show the different aspects of a woman's
feelings, a single performer will subtly distinguish these in his
dance. The delicacy and colours of the design are truly a sight
to behold.

This does not mean, though, that there is any particular dramatic development in which there is a *gradual* change into a serpent. . . .

Such were my explanations, but the man did not seem to find them easy to accept.

In western drama, this 'dramatic development' has to take precedence over anything else. It is an indispensable element. Come what may, in the stage arts westerners seek to base their appreciation on the premise that they will be dramatic. Of course, what is dramatic is itself a very large question which sooner or later I must examine in this book by comparisons between east and west, but I will leave that for the moment. At any rate, western ballet, whether it be *Swan Lake* or *The Sleeping Beauty*, for example, moves forward along a line that, simple though it may be, is unequivocally dramatic. Or, if not, then like modern dance which uses the body itself as its medium, there will be a thorough exploration of form in fluid motion, with no reliance at all on literary elements or dramatic line. It is one or the other.

Kabuki dance, however, depends on samisen music accompanying a sung text and so it certainly has a story-line or literary content, but this is not the dominant element. Nevertheless, if one does not understand the meaning of the words, it is impossible to achieve full appreciation. Furthermore, not only are the physical expressions simply too delicate and lacking in variety in comparison with western dance, but they are also full of examples that are closely linked to the everyday life of Edo (pre-modern Tokyo). For example, in the *Koi no Te-narai* 'Learning about Love' scene famous as an 'emotional passage' (*kudoki*), the lines:

'In learning about love
I now know what it is
But who will there be to see this?
Such are my thoughts as I paint my lips

All from devotion to my lover. . . .
are accompanied by the actor making the movements of painting the lips; and at the lines:

'Is even a written pledge false?
A lie, or truth perhaps?'
the movement of writing such a pledge is made; but these are
simply gestures and movements, without any use of stage
properties. Similarly, *Musume Dōjō-ji* has written into it here
and there sequences containing the names of gay quarters, hills
and so on, and such things as references to special Edo customs,
ways of life and placenames from the Yoshiwara gay quarter
and the like.

Strictly speaking, is it possible to see and hear the fine dis-
tinctions in these things and to be enraptured by the charm
of it if one does not have the senses of a person living and
breathing in the Edo period (1603–1867) itself?

Human, All Too Human is the title of a work by the
philosopher Nietzsche, and we might then call this situation
'Japanese, all too Japanese.' It is a world of a special kind of
beauty which was perfectly matured and refined during the
long period of national seclusion; a distinctive world not easily
entered into nowadays even by a Japanese, unless he himself
does nagauta singing and traditional dance. Thus, I cannot
help feeling it only reasonable that it should be even less
accessible abroad.

A similar case is the one-act excerpt called *Kuruma-biki* 'Pulling the Carriage,' which was utterly rejected because of a lack
of understanding of the dramatic circumstances, even though
it is rich in the special beauty of its colour, form, sounds and
movement. Mention of the beauty of Kabuki immediately
brings to mind the violent scenes (*aragoto*) typified by striking *kumadori* make-up and dramatic poses (*mie*), which take
less than half an hour, have lively music, and backgrounds and
costumes overflowing with colour. As happened with *Musume*

Dōjō-ji, everyone thought that this *Kuruma-biki* would be a sure success—but the audience was at a loss throughout, as if utterly bemused.

The reason for this was that *Kuruma-biki* is a mere fragment of the long drama *Sugawara Denju Te-narai Kagami* 'Sugawara and the Secrets of Calligraphy,' and since there is no setting for it as an independent play, the significance and content of what was represented on the stage was lost on the audience. As a result, even though they may have held their breath for a moment as they stared wide-eyed at the strange make-up, vivid colours, and the dramatic poses, this reaction was not so very different from what might be produced by a painting, and to maintain this as dramatic emotion as time went on was just impossible.

Even though it was a dance drama, the audiences enjoyed such a piece as *Kagami-jishi* 'The Dancing Lion' which had clear-cut variations and plot, with the first half showing the grace of a lovely woman and the second half a male type of active beauty. There was also ready understanding of *Sumida-gawa* 'The Sumida River,' with its theme of the universal human emotion of grief, in this case, that of a mother who has lost her child; and with Utaemon playing the main role, it was very popular especially among women members of the audience from its first performances in London and Munich in 1972.

THE UNIVERSALITY OF HUMAN DRAMA

Why Shunkan and Chūshingura Were Well Received

Let us now look at pieces that did receive a good reception.

The comic dance item *Migawari Zazen* 'The Substitute in Meditation,' a Kabuki version of a Kyōgen play in which a henpecked husband's dalliances are discovered and lead to a great fuss, and *Tsubosaka Reigenki* 'The Miracle at Tsubosaka Temple' which has as its theme the marital love between the blind masseur Sawaichi and his beautiful wife O-Sato are examples of pieces which were more popular than had been expected. This was because they both have straightforward stories and tell of the love and jealousy between man and woman which can be found at any time and in any place.

The pieces which have made the greatest impression so far, however, are *Shunkan* and *Chūshingura* which I have mentioned already. *Shunkan* is the story of a senior priest of that name who, having been exiled to Kikai-ga-shima 'Devil's Island' for resisting the oppressive rule of Taira no Kiyomori, is left alone on that remote island when his two companions Yasuyori and Naritsune are pardoned and sail back to the capital. The first overseas performance of this play was in the Soviet Union in 1961, with the old Ichikawa Ennosuke (En-ō) as Shunkan and Danko, the present Ennosuke, as Naritsune.

The curtain opens to the rumbling thunder of waves from the big drum and, though there is as yet no one on the stage, this brings a kind of inaudible sigh from the audience. In Kabuki, this is known as *jiwa ga kuru* 'the coming of the emotional pause'; that is, the momentarily silent reaction of the audience when they are suddenly deeply moved. It was something completely unexpected and, the next moment, it was followed by enthusiastic applause.

A background of the open sea already known, perhaps, from Ukiyoe prints, and the noise of waves from the drum, were stylized but well understood. Through their combined effect the foreign audience had grasped intuitively the tragic plight of the exile on his remote and lonely island.

The dramatic tension lasted from the opening of the curtain until the very end. When the final curtain closed on Shunkan, high up on a rock, gazing motionless at the ship disappearing over the far horizon, there was literally thunderous applause. Before long the almost deafening 'Bravos' and 'Hurrahs' were joined by voices demanding an encore. . . .

In Japan there is no tradition of responding to applause by giving an encore in either Nō or Kabuki but, since this was a theatre abroad, the elderly Ennosuke who was in the main role drove his tired body to do so on those occasions. On average, he did so twelve times or more. Also, regularly every night, the applause after a while turned into handclapping to a regular beat. This kind of clapping is said to be peculiar to the socialist countries, but that does not mean that it always happens. In fact, even the Russian audiences did not show this kind of reaction to other pieces in the repertoire.

This overwhelming response was vividly captured in "The First-night Scene," a programme recorded by the Moscow Broadcasting Station for transmission to Japan. I have a tape of it beside me now. It was given to the present Ennosuke—then a fourth-year student at Keiō University—and he passed it on to me. I still often use it at lectures and the like to convince people through their own ears that my description of the response there is neither false nor exaggerated.

This kind of reception for *Shunkan* might be summed up by saying that it was the result of its universality and excellence as drama. The original of this piece, incidentally, was a play written for the puppet theatre under the title *Heike Nyogo-no-Shima* 'The Island of Heike Women' by the great playwright Chikamatsu Monzaemon (1653–1724), who is often compared to Shakespeare.

Shunkan has the humanity of its protagonist—for example, his love for others which led him to sacrifice himself by staying on the island so that his young companion Naritsune might return to the capital with his new wife, the pearl-diver Chidori—the tyrannical inhumanity of the despot Kiyomori which is in such marked contrast, the dramatic complications arising from the loneliness of the exiles, and completeness as a drama. All such aspects have enabled it to win unreserved approval from foreign audiences. It is for this reason that they have also been able to enjoy Kabuki's particular form of presentation and to accept it as being right for its purpose.

I cannot help feeling that the response to *Chūshingura* was due to the same kind of reason. I have already mentioned that there were discussions about the rights and wrongs of harakiri on the first visit to America, and if that scene alone had been performed, it would probably have ended either in laughter at such an anachronism and subservience to authority or, at least, in a morbid interest in the exotic nature of the act itself.

Chūshingura was performed complete, however, from the prologue (the inspection of the helmets at the Tsurugaoka Hachiman Shrine), to the third act in the Pine Room in the shogun's palace and the fourth depicting the harakiri and the surrender of the castle by the retainers. First, the prologue makes very clear, through the contrast between the villainy of Moronō and the stubbornness and quick temper of Wakasanosuke, that Enya Hangan, though a young samurai

The harakiri of the young lord in *Chūshingura*.

like the others, was a man of character, gentle and thoughtful. It is masterly in the way it does this, even if not all the text is understood. In the next scene, 'The Wounding in the Palace' in the Pine Room there, the process by which Hangan finally becomes unable to restrain himself from drawing his sword in spite of his gentleness is delineated in a truly superb way. The dramatic development, in which he is hated by Moronō through bitterness at having his advances rebuffed by Hangan's wife and is gradually driven into a tragic situation, is acceptable to one and all.

The result of all this is Hangan's death, and the parting of husband and wife and master and retainers, and so the harakiri and 'The Forfeit of the Castle' scene, in which Ōboshi Yuranosuke leaves the stage after taking his sad farewell at the castle which has lost its lord for ever, both stir deep emotions as tragic situations.

In the interval after a performance of this play in America, I met Kawabata Yasunari in the foyer. He opened those big eyes of his even wider and said "Kabuki really is tremendous, isn't it." When I asked him what had prompted this remark, he replied "Why, all the people round me were foreigners, but many of them—and not only the ladies—were weeping into their handkerchiefs." I shall never forget the emotion in his voice as he said this. It was neither a lie nor an exaggeration. Having sat among the audience every night and watched their reactions, I knew very well that it was an absolute fact. It was the same not only in New York but in Los Angeles and San Francisco, in Berlin, Paris and London too.

I have been writing about the way pieces were received abroad, but the trends noted there are backed up objectively by the consolidated results of the surveys. If we take as an example the performances in Europe in 1965, the following figures were obtained in answer to the question "Which work did you like best?":

Programme A: *Shunkan* 561, *Musume Dōjō-ji* 142,
              Kuruma-biki 82
Programme B: *Chūshingura* 667, *Kagami-jishi* 217

When performances were given abroad, there were many things to provide important clues to a comparison between east and west, not only in the responses to the performances themselves but also in the procedures at the setting-up stage and at rehearsals. For example, the problem of the *ma* 'interval' or 'timing' typified by the coordination of the tempo of the wooden clappers with the opening and closing of the curtain; differences in theatrical sensibilities implicit in the troubles we had in setting up a temporary hanamichi . . . and so on. I will raise such things later, and here I shall just bring in two interesting comments from reviews of overseas performances which provided me with valuable suggestions for my later research.

One is from a review by Brooks Atkinson, dramatic critic of *The New York Times*. In it he has a sentence which says that the key which distinguishes Japanese plays from those of the west is that, while the latter are based on representation, Japan has a theatre of presentation.

The other, from a drama critic of the *Abend Zeitung* writing about the performances in Munich in 1972, was the comment that the style of Kabuki is that of 'stylized naturalism' (stilisierter Naturalismus).

Both of them are, I think, important keys to the essential nature of traditional Japanese theatre and, hence, of Japanese culture.

What, then, do these things mean? Specific consideration of them will again be left as topics for later chapters.

An Acquisitive 'Snowdrift' Culture

The Difficulty of Comparisons

As clues for considering what I might call Japanese-type things, I have so far brought up the matter of overseas Kabuki performances from the standpoint of my own personal experience and written about a number of concrete examples, from the special nature of a composite drama, the affair of the harakiri debate, and the effectiveness of 'wave-drumming,' to the discerning comments of foreign drama critics. Although they may vary in importance, they all, I believe, lead us on towards our goal.

Particularly at variance with general expectations was the fact that dramatic pieces won a far greater response than the dances which had been expected without question to be well received. Thinking about it carefully afterwards, we can see that this was understandable but, even so, it was a little bit like discovering the New World, being something which was only found and proved by actually going there.

Of still greater importance for the purposes of this book is the fact that these unexpected results from the responses confirmed the existence of an item common to Japan and foreign countries, in the form of the universality of drama. We might even call it the greatest common measure.

Put the opposite way, the confirmation of a common item

makes clear the existence of a diversity of character. Because of this, it is a necessary operation in comparative research which should be carried out before anything else, but often when looking at things Japanese in the past there has surely been a danger of going no further than emphasizing only those things which at first glance *appear* diverse in character and, as a result, of falling into a facile theory of comparison which is lax and at times mistaken.

The existence of the female impersonator, for example, is often brought up as a particular feature of Kabuki without parallel elsewhere in the world. Certainly, it can be said that at the present time it is without parallel in the civilized countries of the west; but Nō and Kyōgen are of course performing arts of the east in which even now female roles are usually played by men, and it was the same in the west before the Renaissance. This means that, if western drama is taken to have a history of 2,500 years since its beginnings in Greece, then it was usual to have female impersonators for eighty per cent of that time.

If, then, we simply have in mind men playing the part of women, it is not correct to say that this is a particular feature of Kabuki alone. After we have recognized the widespread existence of the female impersonator in the world by going back into the past, it is meaningless unless we ask why it is, then, that they disappeared in the west after the Renaissance but continued to exist in Japan, and in what ways do those in Japan differ from those in other countries.

This is only one example, but if we seem unable to confirm what is held in common, we shall really be unable to identify what is different. The first thing is to search out the common items. After that we work outwards from there, sift out what is truly unique to Japan and, at the same time, distinguish also what is found abroad but not in Japan.

Somehow this seems like the mathematical theory of sets,

but it is surely only after carrying out such an analysis and assessment that the question of what is Japanese will be brought into focus.

Well now, that is what we have in mind to do, but when we come down to practicalities, all kinds of troubles arise. I shall just give one or two of them.

The first is that, though we may talk about comparing Japan and the west, it is throughout impossible to set things out against each other by simply dividing them up into east and west like the lists of wrestlers for a Sumō tournament. After all, plays are many and varied, so that even within Japan different types are jumbled up together; and not only is the situation the same in the west but, in the opposite way, there are unexpectedly similar things shared by both.

Consider the following, for instance. So far we have taken Kabuki in particular for our examples, but Kabuki is no more than one particular sphere within Japanese drama. If we compare it with Nō, it should become clear how different things are able to exist within a single country.

Nō is song and dance, performed with masks on a plain-wood stage devoid of curtain or scenery. Kabuki consists of plays which unmasked actors perform on the basis of actions and lines, on a large stage with lavish equipment, a hanamichi, and a revolving inner stage. Nō is solemn and majestic, and thrives in an aristocratic atmosphere of elegant beauty; while Kabuki is lively and low-class, and reeks of common humanity. The audience at Nō appreciate the performance so silently from their 'viewing area' (*kensho*) that they are said to 'reverently observe the Nō'; while at Kabuki they shout out the traditional 'house names' (*yagō*) of their favourite actors as they eat and drink and thoroughly enjoy themselves. . . .

The two could be called complete opposites. This of course comes from the difference that Nō is a performing art refined according to the ideas and tastes of the upper-class warriors who were the rulers in the medieval period, and Kabuki is the theatre of the people, reared by the townsmen who were the ruled in the pre-modern Edo period. Both, however, were produced by people who were equally Japanese, and it is impossible to say that one is Japanese and the other is not, or any such thing.

Since the west is a mixture of territories and races, and its history is long and complex, it is not easy to pick out its particular features and to say that this is western drama. Even so, it is possible to see a common thread running through, for example, the classical Greek theatre, the classical theatre centred on seventeenth-century France, and the modern plays of Ibsen.

The dramatic construction is strict, characterized by events following a single line, in the same place, and completed within the span of a single day and night—a dramaturgy known as the rules of the 'three unities' of time, place and action. But some western drama itself—the works of Shakespeare, for one—is altogether unrestricted by this, and will move about in time and place with bewildering rapidity. There can surely be no need to illustrate this with such plays as *Hamlet* or *Macbeth*.

Furthermore, if we now put Japan and the west on the same plane, we find that in one sense Nō and Greek drama have common ground, and also that Shakespeare and Kabuki are strikingly similar in character. Concrete examples of these will be given later, and here I would only like it to be borne in mind that it is dangerous to proceed on a simple opposing relationship of east and west, not only with reference to drama, and that while we always remain aware of what might be held in common, it is necessary to consider such things from all sides.

The second is the difficulty of discerning what is *truly* specific to Japan.

Let us take again as an example *Musume Dōjō-ji*, the Kabuki dance piece that I called 'Japanese, all too Japanese.' Since this is a standard work of Japanese music and dance produced by

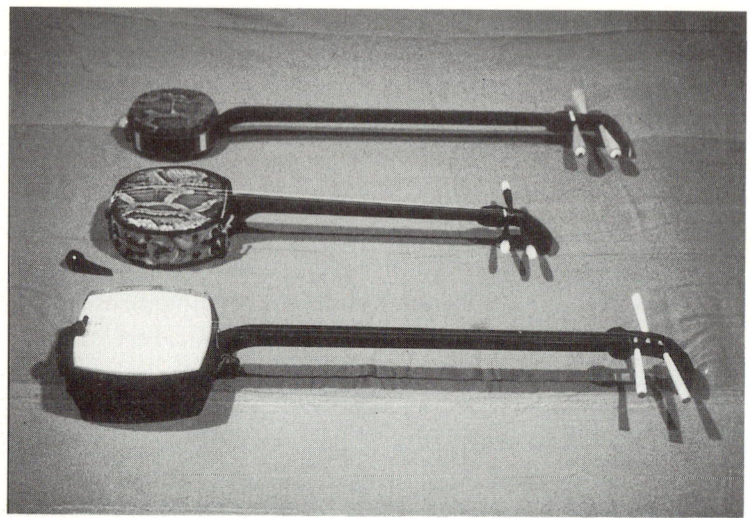

Types of samisen (from the top, Chinese, Okinawan, Japanese).

the ordinary townspeople in the Edo period, it might be thought that it would be more purely Japanese than anything else. If we go into it a step or two, however, all its elements turn out to be originally imported and we lose all track of where the Japanese originality in it began.

First there is the samisen. Its music comes to mind as soon as Japanese music is mentioned—but it was originally an imported instrument which came in through the port of Sakai in Izumi province from Okinawa over 400 years ago, around 1560. The Portuguese brought the matchlock gun to Japan in 1543; the missionary Francis-Xavier brought Christianity in 1549; the method of glass manufacture was introduced in 1570; and it was in this more open period that this instrument came in too.

There being various theories about its origin, it is impossible to be definite, but the generally accepted theory has come to be that it originated in Egypt or Persia, or in the region of Turkey, and that at first it was not a stringed but a percussion instrument. It went from these areas into mainland China where it was remodelled and became a three-stringed instrument covered in snakeskin. It then came to Japan by way of Okinawa.

The Japanese liked its sound, and began to make the instrument their own as the fashion dictated; but since it was difficult in Japan to obtain snakes with skins big enough to cover the body of the instrument, catskin was used instead and it is this type that is the present-day samisen. The name samisen is said to be a corruption of *sansen* (pronounced *sanshin* in Okinawa) 'three strings.' Because the Okinawan name is *jabisen* 'snakeskin strings,' it is popularly supposed that samisen is a variant of this, but *jabisen* seems to be a newer word than *sanshin*.

It is clear, then, that the samisen which is inextricably linked with Japanese sentiment is not in fact an invention of the Japanese. Then what about the singing done to the accompaniment of this samisen, in the nagauta, *tokiwazu, kiyomoto,* and gidayū styles, for example? These too are not of purely Japanese origin.

They can be said to be considerably updated forms of the chanting done to the accompaniment of the *biwa* which had flourished in the preceding period. The biwa is an instrument which first arrived from far away, along the Silk Road or the Fur Road—the Tianshan Northern Road—more to the north. The musical style of the biwa pieces which were narrated to its accompaniment arose from the style of religious chant called *Tendai shōmyō* said to have been brought over from T'ang China by the priest *Jikaku-Daishi* in the middle of the ninth century. Since *shōmyō* is a musical recitation of sutras at Buddhist ceremonies, it is also called *bonbai* 'Sanskrit songs.' The origin was of course Indian, and in Japan it flourished through the Heian and Kamakura periods, that is, from the ninth to about the end of the thirteenth centuries. The biwa music, particularly the *Heike biwa* (also known as *heikyoku*), which gave rise to samisen music is said to have developed from the Buddhist prose tales called *kōshiki* 'lecture ceremonies' forming part of shōmyō. The music of Nō texts (*yōkyoku*) too could not have been brought to completion without the influence of shōmyō music.

The style of the Kabuki dance has taken in all kinds of elements such as various forms of folk dance, popular ceremonies, and aspects of the gay quarters, apart from Furyū which is considered to be a direct precursor. It is therefore extremely difficult to distinguish these one from the other, but since the Nō *Dōjō-ji* is the original on which the Kabuki piece was based and it is therefore at least connected with Nō, we surely cannot ignore a connection with Sarugaku and Dengaku from which Nō came and, hence, with the popular entertainment called Sangaku which came over from the continent in the eighth and ninth centuries.

If we then think that at least the subject-matter, that is, the Dōjō-ji legend, is safe enough, we find that even that cannot be said to be peculiarly Japanese.

Since olden times there has been a traditional hand ball song in Wakayama in Kii province which begins:

> 'Ton-ton, the Dōjō Temple,
>   Up its sixty-two steps we go
>   And there stand the guardian gods'

and ends:

> 'When Kiyohime turns into a snake,
>   Anchin brings down the hanging bell and
>   hides inside.
>   Seven-fold is it wrapped around,
>   Once round and once again.'

Since it even reached the level of a children's song, it can hardly be unknown to anyone—but the earliest mention of this legend is in the collection of Buddhist tales entitled *Dai-Nihonkoku Hokekyō Genki* 'The Great Japan Record of the Wonders of the Lotus Sutra' and compiled in 1040, so it is of course Indian in origin.

To be sure, its original source and the route of its transmission are not definite. Some scholars say that it came from the story of the Buddhist saint Anaritsu in the *Daizōkyō* 'The Great Collection of Sutras,' while others maintain that it concerned Anan, one of the ten great disciples of the Buddha. Recent years have also seen the appearance of theories that the origin was not the sutras but a passage in the collection of Buddhist tales called *Jātaka* 'Past Lives of the Buddha'; that this came into China as the famous *Baishe-chuan* (J: *Hakuja-den*) 'The Story of the White Snake'; and that this became *Dōjō-ji* when it arrived in Japan. In any case, there is no mistaking the fact that the tale came from abroad and is not a story unique to Japan.

How to Prepare Cultural Delicacies from Abroad

The Search for What Is Native

If we just look at *Musume Dōjō-ji*, then, the situation is this: putting it in an extreme way, it can be said to be a medley of imports. It can probably also be said that this hybrid character in which foreign varieties are mixed together is something which runs through not just our theatre but the whole of Japanese culture. It seems to me that we can easily find it too in the basic elements of our daily life.

It goes without saying that this is the result of a great volume of advanced culture pouring into Japan from the north, south and west since she is an island country in the Far East, and there collecting, piling up and mixing together, and then fermenting and maturing. With the Pacific Ocean an impenetrable barrier to the east, this culture inevitably piled up in Japan.

It is my view that the Japanese responsible for setting up the early Yamato court were formed from a nucleus of people from a southern race who came in on the Black Current and who later intermarried with, and were dominated by, a northern race of invaders from south Korea. Leaving aside for now the question of our ethnic origins, however, we can see that the culture of the original Japanese, who spoke the Japanese language and brought with them the technique of rice cultivation, was mixed in a complex way with the cultures of Han

China, Korea and Buddhism which surged in during the sixth and seventh centuries, and with the culture of the southern barbarians, that is, of the west, which came in during the sixteenth and seventeenth centuries. This, then, is what is known as the 'traditional culture' of Japan, which came to fruition by the end of the Edo period in 1868.

Now if Japanese culture or traditional drama is such a snow-drift of mixed and varied elements, which on earth are the 'Japanese' ones among them and how is it best for us to look at them ?

In this land of ours, we Japanese absorbed some things from abroad and discarded others; we changed what we had absorbed to suit our own predisposition; and we arranged and brought together what existed here to create new things. In the last analysis, is there any alternative to saying that it is to these developments that we must look in order to find the things that are 'Japanese' ?

We might call this a kind of cuisine or choice of food in which we prepared foreign material to suit our own taste. Indeed, the same kind of thing can be said about our use of food itself.

Tenpura 'deep-fried sea-food,' for example, is a type of cooking learned from the Portuguese, as can be seen from the original word *tempero*; but it is eaten with a sauce made from a broth of dried bonito with soy sauce and ordinary or sweet rice wine, into which grated giant radish (*daikon*) is mixed, making a uniquely Japanese dish. It is the same with *sukiyaki* 'fried beef and vegetables': the eating of beef came in from the west, but a 'Japanese flavour' was given to it in Japan by cooking it in a sizzling broth based on soy sauce, sweet rice wine and sugar.

Likewise, if *sashimi* 'sliced raw fish' were simply a matter of eating uncooked fish, then it is also to be found in Europe, China and Mexico; but to eat it with Japanese horseradish and soy sauce is what one might call the Japanese style.

If we extract from these three examples just one uniquely Japanese element common to them all, then it must surely be the flavour of Japanese soy sauce. The method of making the flavoured bean paste which forms its base is said to have been learned from China, but both the period and the route of its transmission are no longer known and it can now be said to have a uniquely Japanese flavour.

But I have digressed and will now give just two examples from the performing arts: a pattern of 'transformation' to be seen in dramatic stories, and pictorial beauty in make-up. The material is again from the now familiar *Dōjō-ji*.

First, the story, as we have said before, is thought to have had its source in an Indian tale and to have come into Japan through China. If we try comparing various aspects of it in order to see how it was prepared for consumption in Japan, we notice that a great change took place. The difference is that, in contrast to India and China where a snake changes into a woman and makes advances to a human male, in Japan a human female takes on the form of a snake on account of a jealous malice. This point has also been made by Aoe Shunjirō in his *Nihon Geinō no Genryū* 'The Sources of the Performing Arts of Japan."

In the Indian story, which has much the same content as *Dōjō-ji*, a snake living at the water's edge sees a handsome young man and approaches him in the form of a beautiful woman, but when she is thwarted by the power of the Buddhist law, she departs frustrated in her love, revealing her true nature. The Chinese story in its original form tells of a white snake which changes into a beautiful woman to visit a man out of gratitude for his having saved it, and pledges its love for him. In both cases, a snake falls in love with a human being and changes into human form before approaching him, and although there is an element of pathos about it, the main motif of the story may be said to be rather the strangeness and uncanniness of the ghostly transformation.

Dōjō-ji, though, is just the opposite: the girl Kiyohime declares herself to the handsome priest Anchin and, on being rejected by him, turns into a poisonous serpent, all of ten metres long, as a result of her irrepressible jealousy and hatred. Furthermore, there is the awfulness of her obsession which leads her to burn up the bell and the man she loved. But it is not only a terrible thing in itself. Rather, we should surely see the real theme of the story as being the violence and sadness of the 'karma of passion' of a woman who, although she knew that the man could not fulfil their love because his calling as a disciple of the Buddha required him to observe the Five Precepts, was so incapable of controlling the flames of her evil passion that she changed into a serpent to follow him.

In Nō there is the famous play *Aoi no Ue* 'Lady Aoi' which deals with much the same theme. The story, taken from *Genji Monogatari* 'The Tale of Genji,' is about the wraith of Lady Rokujō, Prince Genji's former lover, who night after night intrudes into the sleeping chamber of Lady Aoi, her successor in his affections, and persecutes her there. When she does so, she wears a snakeskin-patterned robe and a *hannya* mask depicting a creature half-woman, half-serpent. When a woman burns with the karma of passion and the flames of jealousy, she turns into a snake—this is a uniquely Japanese motif.

Eventually the wraith is subdued by the prayers of the saintly priest Yokawa no Kohijiri and driven off in despair. As she leaves with drooping head along the *hashigakari*, the covered passage-way leading to and from the stage, her expression is still frightening but, at the same time, the bitter misery of a woman ashamed of her own ugliness and weeping at the wretchedness of her karma cannot fail to move.

This may perhaps be a reflection of the Japanese woman who 'in the beginning, was the sun' but who, since the time of the male-dominated Yamato court, had been compelled to submit to oppression and maltreatment and to follow a life of gloom and submission. Be that as it may, what can be said is that in the escape from the ghostliness of the Buddhist story and its recreation as a human elegy to what we might call 'the sad history of Japanese womanhood,' lies a purely Japanese motif.

The other thing to be considered here is the aesthetics of the striking type of Kabuki make-up known as *kumadori*, literally 'taking up (= bringing out) the shadows (of the face).' The usual way of presenting *Musume Dōjō-ji* today is for the curtain to close when the beautiful woman has climbed up onto the bell and there struck a dramatic pose (mie). But if it is staged in its complete form, she goes in under the bell as it falls and, when it rises again through the prayers of the priests, she is revealed in the frightening form of an evil serpent.

Inside the bell the actor changes into a snake-patterned costume as in the original Nō play, but since masks are not used in Kabuki, he puts on a special type of make-up called *hannya-guma* 'snake-like kumadori'—the instantly recognizable fearsome expression of a vindictive spirit, typically that of a jealous woman, achieved by painting the face with any number of thick blue lines over a white base.

This evil spirit in serpent form throws aside and kicks over the priests who have gathered at the bell and sets off along the hanamichi. At this, a great voice shouts "Wait, eeee—!" from the curtain at the side of the auditorium, and a wild-looking warrior carrying a thick bamboo staff makes his entry by stamping along it on tall wooden clogs and then pushes the evil figure back onto the stage. This is an example of the *aragoto* 'rough-style' performance called *oshi-modoshi* 'pushing back,' which is one of the classic *Kabuki Jūhachiban* 'Eighteen Kabuki Pieces.' The heroic character has a face painted white with thick red lines on it—a typical type of kumadori symbolizing super-human strength and an upholder of righteousness. Inherent in the way kumadori are designed is an aesthetic sense peculiar to the Japanese.

Japan is not alone in having a style of make-up in which the face is painted in vivid colours in order to show the nature of the stage character, whether it be good or evil, strong or weak, god or devil, king or princess or retainer. The performing arts of such countries as India and China, and also those of Nepal and Bhutan which were introduced to Japan by recent performances, have strange, beautiful and colourful make-up which is very striking.

A make-up which bears particular comparison with the kumadori of Japan is that called *jian-pu* (J: *kenpu/renpu*) used in the Peking Opera, the famous song and dance drama of China. There are even people who say that Kabuki kumadori were imitations of this jian-pu, though this is of course mere speculation. I think instead that, because Kabuki abandoned the masks used previously, kumadori were devised as forms of facial expression in their place from such things as the faces found in Nō masks and the dolls of the puppet theatre, and the angry expressions found in Buddhist sculpture.

Leaving aside discussion of the truth of this, however, the decisive point of difference between the kumadori of Japan and the jian-pu and the like of other countries and peoples is the fact that, in contrast to these types from other regions which are wholly mask-like in that the colours are heavily painted in the same density over the whole face and the change from one colour to another makes a clear-cut line, the Japanese make-up uses a 'shading' technique.

The creation of kumadori is attributed to Ichikawa Danjūrō I (1660-1704), but it seems that what he used in playing the role of Sakata no Kintoki (Kintarō) was not so much kumadori as deep red paint on his face and thick black lines on his eyebrows. *Kuma* means 'shaded part,' and kumadori represent the violent rush of blood and tension of muscles by shadings of red and blue. It was Danjūrō II, the son of the first Danjūrō, who was responsible for this development, and one version has it that it occurred to him to shade off the edges of the red lines while he was gazing fascinated at the petals of a peony flower.

It is probably the artist Yokoyama Taikan who made most use of the shading technique in modern times, and every time I see it in an aragoto role, I feel that it is in this technique shared with Japanese-style painting that the aesthetic sense peculiar to Japan is to be found.

The transformation into serpent form and kumadori in *Musume Dōjō-ji* are only minor examples, but they seem to me to be ones which are comparatively easy to follow. It is not easy, however, to extract things that are truly Japanese from all the complex and varied aspects of the theatre. It is easy enough to develop abstract theories but I, for my part, can only persist in a search for principles among individual facts and demonstrable phenomena.

What has been discussed so far has been by way of introduction. In the next chapter, I plan to begin with the flavour the Japanese give to their treatment of time and space.

Chapter Two

FREEDOM OF TIME
AND SPACE

EMPTY SPACE

Flights of the Imagination

A plain-wood stage, perfectly square, with sides about six metres long. It has nothing more than a roof resting on a pillar at each corner and, to the left of the stage, a kind of gallery—the hashigakari—leading off to a curtain that can be raised from the bottom. There is no front curtain and no stage set. The wooden wall at the back of the stage, known as the 'Mirror Wall,' is painted with a picture of an old pine tree flanked on both sides by bamboo, and three small pine trees are planted alongside the hashigakari. A plain stage, with nothing more. . . .

It is of course a Nō stage.

On occasions, though, when a property is required for a particular piece, this is brought quietly onto the stage: a pine tree in *Hagoromo* 'The Robe of Feathers,' a bell tower in *Mii-dera* 'Mii Temple,' and a boat in *Funa-Benkei* 'Benkei in the Boat,' for example; but such a property will only be a drastically abbreviated 'made-up thing' (*tsukuri-mono*), little more than a framework to suggest the reality. Originally, the general rule was to have nothing on the stage.

The only background is the painted pine tree and bamboo to left and right at the back of the stage, and this never changes whatever the play. The poet and dramatist Paul Claudel, who was the French ambassador in Japan for five years from 1921, was a devotee of Nō and he is reported to have said, "To right

A Nō stage.

and left on fresh butter-coloured wood green bamboo, and on the Mirror Wall at the back of the stage a great pine are painted. Nature is to be found in them and, because of this, nothing more is needed." Certainly, neither the pine nor the bamboo loses its greenness throughout the four seasons, and so they are well suited to make a permanent stage-set. The pine tree in particular is a symbol of youth and long life and, what is more, since ancient times in Japan there seems to have been a belief in it as a sacred tree to which the gods descend. It is possible to think of various reasons like this why it should have been used as the background for performances of Nō, which came into existence as votive entertainments at Shinto shrines and Buddhist temples.

At any rate, the Nō stage might thus be called an almost completely 'empty space.' Overseas performances of Nō are much easier than those of Kabuki in that respect, but it is the texts of the plays which turn this bare stage into a seashore or mountain hideaway, a city thoroughfare or boat. Also, the scene is freely changed within a single play. As the audience follow these changes through their power of imagination in keeping with the text of the play and the movements of the actors, they quite naturally place themselves at the scene and in the situation, and lose themselves in its atmosphere. . . .

An unrestricted use of space, the conception and imagination which create any scene at all by a simple device—is this not one of the main characteristics of traditional Japanese drama?

I will give just one example, the Nō *Takasago* which is often sung by guests at wedding receptions and the like who pride themselves on their Nō singing.

A priest of the Aso Shrine in Kyūshū visits the coast at Takasago in Harima Province—modern Hyōgo Prefecture—on his way to see the sights of the capital.

> '. . . in my travel robe/On my way to the far-off
>   capital,
> On my way to the far-off capital,
> I resolve today to cross the swelling waves of the
>   bay.
> A peaceful passage in the soft spring breeze—
> How many days has it been? Both past and future
> Are lost to me in the white of distant clouds.
> But as I think how far we have come,
> Along the long-awaited coast of Harima
> We come to the bay of Takasago,
> We come to the bay of Takasago.'

We have now arrived with the priest at the beach at Takasago . . . whereupon an aged couple appear there. Following some enquiries from the priest, the old couple tell him that

The Nō *Takasago*: the main actor (*shite*) on the right, and his companion (*tsure*) on the left.

they are the spirits of a pine at Takasago and another at Sumiyoshi in far-distant Settsu Province, that is, in modern Osaka, where they will await him, and then they disappear. The priest hires a boat and sets off for Sumiyoshi. Here follows the part of the text which is often sung:

> 'At Takasago/We raise the sail on this coastal boat,
> We raise the sail on this coastal boat,
> And set out with the moon across the rising tide.
> Over the waves far beyond Awaji island
> We have passed offshore from Naruo,
> And arrive now at the inlet for Sumiyoshi,
> And arrive now at the inlet for Sumiyoshi.'

Having arrived at Sumiyoshi, the priest sees the old man appear in the form of a god, the spirit of the Sumiyoshi pine, who sings and dances for him in celebration. This is the Nō

Takasago. Yet how smooth and quick it was to come to Sumiyoshi from Takasago! As can be seen from a map, to go through the straits between Akashi and the island of Awaji, passing by far-off Naruo, now so near to Kōshien baseball ground, and reach Sumiyoshi in Osaka is a considerable distance even by a direct sea route—eighty or, rather, a hundred kilometres, perhaps. How long must it have taken by boat in olden times?

On an empty stage, the 'journey' is done before the eyes of the audience in the few minutes it takes to sing the above lines. Nowadays, on television or in a film, it would be nothing at all for a narrator to describe it as the picture shows a ship or train racing along, but in Nō and Kyōgen this technique has been used since the far distant past.

In fact, however, is such a treatment of space found only in Japanese drama?

No—if it is simply a matter of seeing various different places on the same empty stage, then in fact it is something which has been done everywhere from olden times. In periods before stage sets were developed, this must rather have been the norm. For instance, in the Greek theatre which flourished 500 years B.C.: the classical plays given in the great open-air theatres which still remain had nothing like stage sets or scenery. The 10,000 and more spectators supposed the stage to be the square before the palace of Thebes in *Oedipus Rex*, or the coast of the Black Sea with towering cliffs in *Prometheus Bound*, and appreciated them as such.

It seems that in the west, however, apart from in very recent times it seldom happened that there was a change of place or a change of scene within the progress of a single play and on the same stage in front of the audience. I wonder whether this is because of westerners' rationalism or their natural liking for realism.

In the previous chapter I wrote that a critic in America said of Kabuki performances there that Japanese drama was 'presentation' and western drama 'representation.' This is another way of saying 'realism,' and the idea behind it is that drama is the faithful representation of aspects of human life. This is shown in its most uncompromising form in the naturalistic realism of the late nineteenth century. It was Emile Zola, famous for such naturalistic novels as *L'Assommoir* 'The Dram-shop' and *Nana*, who set this movement on its way.

In 1873, in the preface to his play *Thérèse Raquin* which he himself adapted from one of his novels, he insisted that future plays should not be classical or romantic, but 'life itself.' The ideal, he said, is for the stage to re-create a slice of life as close to reality as possible: the audience would then study life and people by watching it.

This is the essence of modern realistic drama. It was the Norwegian writer Henrik Ibsen who practised and perfected this in the world of drama. His best-known work, *A Doll's House*, became the forerunner of the modern drama movement in Japan after it was performed here for the first time, in 1911, by Matsui Sumako at the Literature Society (*Bungei Kyōkai*) led by Tsubouchi Shōyō; and Ibsen's stage directions show to what extent it was written in a realistic vein:

> 'A room, comfortably and tastefully, but not expensively furnished. In the back, on the right, a door leads to the hall; on the left another door leads to Helmer's study. Between the two doors a pianoforte. In the front a window. Near the window a round table with arm-chairs and a small sofa. In the right wall, somewhat to the back, a door, and against the same wall, further forward, a porcelain stove; in front of it a couple of arm-chairs and a rocking-chair. Between the stove and the side-door a small table. Engravings on the walls. A what-not with china and bric-a-brac. A small bookcase filled with handsomely bound books. Carpet. A fire in the stove. It is a winter day.'

This set for the living-room in the house of a bank employee named Helmer—a very ordinary office worker who has only just managed to gain promotion to branch manager—is dressed almost exactly like the real thing.

Here his wife Nora, knowing that her husband's feeling for her is not true love but no more than the attachment a child has to a doll, tells him that she is leaving home to find a life for herself as a woman and as a human being. From this the famous drama unfolds; but the scene is the same throughout the long three-act play, never changing. The action, moreover, is over within twenty-four hours, from the evening of Christmas Day until the following night.

One scene to represent reality. Development within a single day. One story complete in itself.—It need hardly be said that this is the most natural, rational method of giving the audience the illusion that what takes place on the stage is real life.

If there are bewildering changes of scene and leaps of time from month to month or even year to year, entertaining though they may be, the illusion, the fantasy of real life, is utterly destroyed. In other words, it may be said that the drama in which the three elements of time, place and action are unified or radically compacted, as it were, is the most representative form of realism in the theatre.

It has already been mentioned in the previous chapter that this unified nature, known as the 'three unities,' is in fact not a modern product but the basic character of a rigorous dramatic structure that has run through the 'classical' theatre since the days of ancient Greece. It is there, of course, that its roots are to be found.

If we take *Oedipus Rex* by Sophocles, regarded as the greatest masterpiece of its kind, we find that the place is before the palace of the king in Thebes, and the time-span is about half a day. The story develops to its conclusion along a single path as the king, led by an oracle of the gods to save his land from disaster by searching for a criminal who has murdered his father and shamefully married his mother, discovers that it is he himself who has done these things and blinds himself by putting out his eyes. Since Greek drama was performed in the open air and had neither sets nor lighting, events happening in the same place on the same day were better suited to maintain the emotional involvement of the audience and to persuade them that the play was the truth and real life.

Because of this, it is natural that Greek drama and the classical drama derived from it, which were based on rationality and realism, should have striven to avoid as far as possible internal changes of scene and so on even though, like Nō, they were performed on a bare stage.

Might it not be said that, although the use of time and space which permits free movement on a Nō stage in company with the text creates a world which is largely irrational and unrealistic in western terms, it amply demonstrates on the other hand the particular Japanese characteristic which accepts without demur free flights of the imagination?

There now remains one other question.

While the dramas of Greece and Ibsen which observed the three unities do not have changes of location, Shakespeare's plays have changes of scene one after the other. Even though the stage used in the Elizabethan period was an 'empty space,' it was extremely fluid. Where did it differ from the Japanese idea of the treatment of space? This is the question.

Certainly, locations change and time moves on again and again in Shakespeare. In conjunction with other points, this means that it has a structure very similar to that of Japanese theatre, especially Kabuki. If we take *Macbeth* as an example, the changes in location are as follows:

'Scotland: a desert heath—a camp near Forres—the same: a heath—Forres: a room in the palace—Inverness: a room in Macbeth's castle—the same: before the castle—the same: a room in the castle—the same: a court within the castle—the same:

without the castle—Forres: a room in the palace—
another room—a park before the palace gates—a
room of state in the palace—a heath—Forres:
within the palace—a cavern—Fife: a room in Mac-
duff's castle—England: before the King's palace—
Dunsinane: within the castle—near Dunsinane—
Dunsinane: a room in the castle—near Birnam
wood—Dunsinane: within the castle—the same:
before the castle—a battlefield.'

The scene on stage thus changes from one place to another
in Scotland and England. The time too, of course, spans quite
a long period. As I mentioned before, this means that it joins
with Spanish drama, for example, to form a separate line in
contrast to the classical. Even in these very free and fluid plays
of Shakespeare, however, each individual scene unfolds realistically in one fixed location. There is no great movement of place
or time within a single scene as there is in *Takasago* where,
in just a few moments, the priest travels from Takasago to
Sumiyoshi. In that sense it is similarly based on the western
spirit of rational realism, thus differing from the irrational and
unrealistic leaps and versatile freedom found in Japan.

Leaving aside for a moment the question of where this very
particular treatment of space sprang from, let us look next at
the situation in Kabuki.

As was stated before, unlike Nō Kabuki has scenery and
sets which are lavish, colourful and large-scale. Kabuki was
born in 1603, and in the very early period it copied the simple
form of the Nō stage. From about 1650 this adopted stage began
a sudden development in which the stage itself was enlarged
and stage sets were continually invented and developed.

By the same token, however, its images must have become
limited and its freedom restricted in comparison with the bare
Nō stage. What happened here to the utilization and versatil-
ity of the imagination?

A Stage with Freedom Transformed

From Building Collapse to Erasing Cloth

My memories of the plays and films I saw as a child may be fragmentary, but at least the parts I remember made a very vivid impression on me in most cases. I have clearly in my mind, for example, a number of pictures of a play with Ennosuke II (the person who played Shunkan in Russia) which I saw at the Kabukiza theatre.

That was in August 1934, when I was nine. I had seen a few plays before that, but it was my first time at Kabuki. It being summer, a lot of chilling ghost stories and light comic scenes had been worked into the programme. The comedy *Izumo Dōchū Hizakurige* 'Travelling To Izumo by Shanks's Mare' with the main characters Yaji and Kita was extremely amusing. What come back to me more clearly than any other scenes are the one where the whole stage appeared to be under the sea by the use of a magic lantern projector and an octopus fastened on to the unclothed Yaji and Kita as they swam around among the seaweed and rocks, and the one where the two of them work themselves into a lather chasing a thief along the stretch of pine trees at the famous beauty spot of Ama-no-hashidate.

In this pine-tree scene the three characters concerned raced across the stage for all they were worth—or, rather, they stayed on the same spot and pretended to run. This was something like the indoor exercise that is often done nowadays, but the backdrop behind them moved steadily from right to left. The illusion is exactly the same as the feeling that one's own train is moving when one on the opposite platform starts off, and in this case it seemed as if the people were moving from left to right. To a child like me, this kind of simple device was a great delight.

When I went into my library just to check and looked up the *Engei Gahō* 'Theatre Pictorial' of the time, my eye was caught by a stage photograph and a passage in 'As I Saw It' (Theatre Notes) to the following effect:

> '. . . Suddenly noticing, the two went off in pursuit, their woebegone faces telling of their consternation.—To lively music, Yaji and Kitahachi chased, and Shinkichi was chased, all along the three kilometres of pines at Ama-no-hashidate. This is a panoramic composition in which the mountains of Tango Province and the great cut-out pine trees in the background slip away behind the three men running along.'

A change of location in full view of the audience—this was the form in which Kabuki produced the same idea of the free treatment of space which we saw on the Nō stage.

As indicated by the description of it as a 'panoramic composition,' this method is based on a very simple idea, but the sense of unquestioningly accepting such a flimsy device and unquestioningly enjoying a world of make-believe and the appeal of transformations transcending the logic behind them, these feelings are indeed, to my mind, an essential element in Japanese theatre.

This idea may have come directly from the puppet plays.

The puppet theatre is of course a fantasy world poles apart from reality. Its most highly developed form is that known as Bunraku, that is, *ningyō jōruri* 'puppet recitations.'

Bunraku's character of fantasy and its free movement and leaps over time and space are probably due in part to its having arisen in the first place from 'narratives' (*katarimono*)—recited narrative poems—unconnected with the narrow limitations of its stage. Kabuki greedily took over from Bunraku not only its plays but also musical elements and its fantastic, non-realistic stage techniques, and then made them its own.

Still today Bunraku often uses the technique found above in the travels of Yaji and Kita for its *michiyuki* 'travel passage' scenes in which two lovers decide to commit suicide together and hurry off to the appointed place. In the case of Chikamatsu's great play *Shinjū Ten no Amijima* 'The Love Suicide at Amijima,' for example, there is a michiyuki for the journey of the prostitute Koharu and her lover Kamiya Jihei from his house at Tenma in Osaka to the Daichō Temple at Amijima. This is a famous passage known as *Nagori no Hashi-zukushi* 'The Sequence of Bridges Seen for the Last Time.' As this name suggests, it is interwoven with the names of bridges along the way the lovers take as the background scenery moves across little by little behind them.

> '. . . Her fragrance would cling to him, but what is to become of it now, as they arrive at the Shijimi River? Looking to the west he sees Tenjin Bridge which he used to cross morning and night, and his thoughts turn to Tenjin himself who, exiled to Tsukushi when he was the Minister Sugawara, was so missed that he was followed to Dazaifu in one leap by his favourite plum tree. Now they are at Plum-field Bridge, and this is followed by Green Bridge just as the old evergreen pine followed the plum, and then by Cherry Bridge, though this tree

could not follow but stayed to yearn and grieve at parting. . . .'

The passage contains a total of eleven names of bridges. At the same time, as may be seen from this extract, there are also worked into the composition such things as the legend of the 'Flying Plum Tree' which tells how, when Sugawara Michizane was exiled to Dazaifu, his long-cherished plum tree missed him so much, it seems, that it flew from the capital to the garden of his place of exile in Kyūshū in a single night.

Thus, it may also perhaps be said that yet another characteristic of Japanese theatre is the skilful use, in describing scenes and emotions, of place-names, local features, legends relating to the area and so on which are thoroughly familiar to those who see and hear the performances.

It will be necessary to talk about the michiyuki suicide passages again in a later chapter as the expression of a different characteristic, but I am here reminded that Earle Ernst, a specialist in Japanese drama and former professor at the University of Hawaii, said at one time in comments he made about Nō that the Japanese have a much stronger attachment to placenames and local features than westerners have.

The change of location within one and the same scene which we have just looked at was achieved by the most simple and elementary method which could even be described as a mere childish trick; but Kabuki has invented more radical methods for using and transforming space. Let us look at a few of these now.

First, some conversion sets such as the *seri-age* 'lifting trap,' *seri-sage* 'lowering trap,' *aorikaeshi* 'backward turn,' *yatai-kuzushi* 'building collapse,' and *hiki-dōgu* 'receding set' which are on a scale large enough to transform the whole stage.

The seri-age is a device for lifting a big square platform built into the stage and called an *ōzeri* 'big trap,' which carries on it a huge set such as a building. Such is its size that, in the

A line-up of the main characters in the Kabuki *Shiranami Gonin Otoko*.

play *Sanmon Gosan no Kiri*, for example, when a stage set representing the upper storey of the gate-house of the Nanzen Temple in Kyoto comes up carrying the great robber Ishikawa Goemon on its roof, from below comes another with the even bigger lower storey and on it Ishikawa's old enemy Mashiba Hisayoshi (that is, the famous historical figure Hashiba—later Toyotomi—Hideyoshi) dressed as a pilgrim priest.

There is a similar scene in the famous *Shiranami Gonin Otoko* 'The Five Robbers' (usually known as *Benten Kozō* after the name of its hero). Near the end of the play the thief Benten Kozō flees onto the roof of the Gokuraku Temple in Kamakura to escape the pursuing constables, but when a crowd of them close in on him even there, he holds them at bay after a great struggle and, as he does so, commits harakiri. This is known as a *tachibara* 'standing harakiri,' and as he plunges the dagger into his stomach the great roof slowly revolves backwards, with Benten still on it. This is the aorikaeshi 'backward turn' of a set.

As he disappears from view and the roof completes a ninety-degree turn, the splendour of the vermilion-painted upper storey of the temple gate is revealed, in front of a distant view of the temple itself and seated there, very much at his ease and looking exactly like Ishikawa Goemon at the Nanzen Temple, is the leader of the five robbers, Nihon Daemon. As the set creaks its way up still more, the lower storey of the temple gate is revealed and the historical figure Aoto Fujitsuna comes on the scene. . . .

The play was written by my great-grandfather Kawatake Mokuami in 1862, in the late Edo period, and although this is a spectacular scene taken over exactly from the Nanzen Temple one, it is novel in the way it was made more complex and colourful by the addition of the aorikaeshi technique.

Being worked by a motor these days, a large mechanism such as this presents no difficulty, but foreigners are struck with admiration at the originality and technique of it when they learn that it was developed in the period before electricity when everything had to be made and worked by hand.

Yataikuzushi is also superb. *Yatai* refers to a building constructed over virtually the whole stage, and this noisily collapses in full view of the audience. Naturally, since the same play is given day after day, this would not be possible if the set were broken up completely, and so it is precisely designed so that, even though it falls apart, it can be immediately re-assembled.

A spectacular example of yataikuzushi is the very original one in the dance play *Masakado* in which a splendid mansion collapses into a ruined heap with a great clatter because of the magic of a witch called Takiyasha-hime, and onto the fallen roof there slowly emerges a huge toad.

Chūshingura has a famous scene which makes effective use of a hiki-dōgu. It is the one known as 'The Forfeit of the Castle' after the suicide of the young lord, which made such a great impression and won such acclaim at its performances abroad.

The lord has committed harakiri because he broke the

ordinance of the Tokugawa administration which said that to show even a few inches of bare blade in the shogun's palace would be regarded as having drawn a sword and would be punishable by disembowelment the very same day, and the end of the transgressor's house. That night the front gate of his residence is tightly closed. His estates have been confiscated and his residence already occupied by an official of the Tokugawa authorities.

At this point his excited young samurai rush in, ready in their impetuosity to die in battle there. It is Ōboshi Yuranosuke who bars their way and, rebuking them for their rashness, sends them back. From then on, it is he alone who holds the stage, with not a word spoken except by the gidayū chanter who describes the scene and his state of mind.

From the folds of his robe he takes out the dagger which his lord used in his suicide and gave to him as a keepsake, and fixedly gazes at it. Here productions often have him lick the blood on its tip, as an affirmation to himself of his resolve to take vengeance. He then detaches the carrying-pole from the lanterns at each end, reverently raises to his head the paper from one of them bearing the Enya family crest and, having folded it up, puts it away into his robe. He then rises to his feet, whereupon a crow caws once or twice, causing this to be known sometimes as the 'Crow Caw' scene. Lost in the turmoil of his thoughts, Yuranosuke leaves the stage, looking back as he goes. As he does so, the set of the castle gate is silently pulled backwards on a slight slant.

The combination of a few steps from Yuranosuke on the stage and the withdrawal of the gate in the background physically and psychologically increase the sense of his moving away from the castle. As he starts onto the hanamichi, the gate moves further back and, within this make-believe world, the audience feels that it too, like Yuranosuke, has moved far away from the building. A few moments later Yuranosuke, choked with

The Kabuki *Ichinotani Futaba Gunki*: the distant-view (*tōmi*) technique in the fight scene.

tears and with drooping head, hurries along the hanamichi and makes his exit.

Among those who were struck with admiration at this 'receding set' of the main gate was Yokoo Tadanori as a young man. Some dozen or so years ago when I was living at Seijō in the Setagaya district of Tokyo, he moved next door and proved to be a very good neighbour. Before long he began to develop an interest in Kabuki, and on one occasion I persuaded him to do the cover illustration for the National Theatre programme for *Utsunoya Tōge* 'Utsunoya Mountain-pass' by Mokuami for which I was then acting as assistant producer.

He is our foremost graphic designer, and his admiration for this 'receding set' method as a thoroughly fresh idea in our modern period overladen with logic made me then come to admire it myself as a concept which had never appeared in the west.

Incidentally, I should just like to add here that there is a means of achieving a similar effect called *tōmi* 'distant view.' In 'The Forfeit of the Castle' scene in *Chūshingura* described above, the upper part of the castle gate which has already moved back falls forward to show its other side and make a new backdrop of a much smaller gate. This is a distant view effect.

Also, in the play about the historically famous battle at Ichinotani, in the scene in which Kumagai Naozane and Taira no Atsumori face each other in single combat, there can be seen a more imaginative type of distant view. It is the 'Hand-to-hand Fight' scene in *Ichinotani Futaba Gunki* 'The Tale of the Two Young Warriors at the Battle of Ichinotani.' It is of course adult actors who play the parts of Kumagai and Atsumori on the main part of the stage, but when the warriors mounted on black and white horses fight upstage in the sea, they are played by boys of five or six dressed in full armour. The idea is that, since the warriors are fighting far away, they should appear smaller. People who look at this with modern, coldly logical mentalities may well call it an utterly infantile trick, but if they were to see it as a piece of theatrical interest in a world of make-believe, they would probably find it an enjoyable scene of immense charm.

This *tōmi* and the like are, I believe, techniques which certainly came from Bunraku. In any case, whether it be Bunraku or Kabuki, it must not be forgotten that both were popular theatres to please and impress the common people of the Edo period and not demanding types of drama produced from some elevated artistic consciousness. The very fact that they belonged to the ordinary people, pure and simple, means that we can discover within them the spirit and sense of beauty of the Japanese as a whole.

One of the things that surprises people, including foreigners, who see Kabuki for the first time is the use of stage assistants known as *kurogo* 'black robes' and *kōken* 'back-watchers.' In *Musume Dōjō-ji* a helper dressed in formal kimono is unobtrusively in attendance throughout. When the main player is dancing and takes off his tall court hat, he takes it away, and when the dancer has a quick change of costume in view of the audience, he helps to remove in a flash the red robe worn over the white one underneath by ripping out from behind the threads holding the top robe together. This quick-change method, known as *hiki-nuki* 'pulling out,' is another example of the fondness for change in Kabuki, and the helper who does it is the kōken.

A kurogo 'black robe,' as the name indicates, is an assistant who is dressed all in black and even has a black cloth hanging over his face. He acts as a prompter by hiding behind a stage property and reading the text in a low voice to put an actor right if he forgets his lines, and he also of course helps like the ordinary kōken. What is interesting is that he clears away during a play anything that might be in the way and stage properties that are no longer needed. He is often to be seen swiftly leaping out to retrieve with great agility a rustic gate, for example, that had been needed earlier when a stage character had to call at someone's house.

It is not only things that he deals with: on occasions he also makes people disappear. For example, the body of someone who has been killed would be in the way if it were left on the stage indefinitely and, in such cases, two kurogo come out with an open length of black cloth carried just above the floor of the stage and use it to hide the body as they take it away. In fact, the actor playing the dead person escapes by crawling along the floor, hidden by the cloth. This is called *keshimaku* 'erasing cloth.' Sometimes a piece of the scarlet cloth on which musicians sit is used instead, but in Kabuki the colour black, as found in both kurogo and the normal keshimaku, signifies non-existence—this is an accepted convention which causes no problem at all for those familiar with Kabuki, but people seeing it for the first time may perhaps think that some of the 'invisible' black-clad warriors known as *ninja* have come on the scene.

This reminds me of a classic *rakugo* 'comic monologue' called *Mōsen Shibai* 'The Magic-cloth Play.'

A young lord who had succeeded to the headship of the house on the death of his father resolved to make himself more cultured and thought that he would first see these 'theatricals' so beloved of the common people. Ignoring the objections of Sandayū, his senior retainer, he summoned some players and had them perform for him. The play was *Utsunoya Tōge*, which showed how a young man, a sad blind masseur called Bunya, was cruelly murdered on the mountain pass one night by someone called Jūbei because he was carrying a large sum of money.

Having watched this with tears in his eyes, the lord ordered the culprit to be seized, whereupon the man's hands and arms were securely tied behind his back. The lord then drew his sword and rushed at him shouting, "You wretch! I'll kill you with my own hands." The ashen-faced leader of the troupe intervened to say to him, "He killed the blind man, to be sure, but it was only a theatrical performance."

"I don't understand—What do you mean by that?"

"How can I explain it? Bunya was killed but he was hidden with a cloth and he's no longer on the stage. He has gone to the dressing room, and is in there worrying about what's happening to Jūbei."

"What? Are you saying that someone who has died
   can be brought back to life by a cloth?"
"Yes, the cloth hid him from view."
"H'mm, is that so. . . . Sandayū, Sandayū."
"You called, my lord?"
"My father was killed at the battle of Ishibashiyama,
   wasn't he?"
"That is so."

"Didn't they have any cloth there then?"

This is the punch-line of the story.

Any play will do for the one in the story so long as it has a body, but I mentioned earlier that the *Utsunoya Tōge* used here was given at the National Theatre when I was an assistant producer. It was a happy task for me, because we had the very best cast, with Nakamura Kanzaburō as Bunya and Matsumoto Kōshirō (Hakuō), who has since died, as Jūbei; and being the first complete play given for quite a while, it had a good reception.

At that time, I called on the rakugo master Kokontei Imasuke, who is now dead too, at Ikenohata in Ueno, and he recited the piece for me in his living-room. With its humanity and glimpses of the popular nature of Kabuki, it is for me a good example of its kind.

Clear away what is no longer needed—this can surely be described as one of the real rules of behaviour of the Japanese people which runs right through their daily life. With the spread of western culture and the rise in living standards at the present time, a western life-style is becoming the norm, and such standard items of furniture and equipment as refrigerators, washing machines, driers, television sets and hi-fi are eating away at the space in our houses.

Until recently, however, we had a thoroughly free and flexible way of life in which one Japanese-style room with *tatami* floor-mats became a living-room when a table was set up, an open space when the table was folded up and put away, a bedroom when mattresses were laid out on the floor, and a sitting-room when the bedding was taken up and replaced by a brazier and cushions—a room where a sunken hearth was installed for warmth in the winter and where anything not needed was cleared away. It was in general quite different from the western feeling for living, which has a dining-room with table and chairs, a drawing-room with a sofa and permanent fireplace, and a bedroom dominated by a bed.

Even now the impression that foreigners have of Japan seems

to be that her houses, her streets, and her social life itself are small-scale and restricted, but it is said that, in the Edo period, there was still less indoor living space per person even though the population was very much smaller.

It may be, therefore, that the sensible use of a single room for a number of purposes by clearing things away arose from the limited space available in Japan and the poverty of her people.

Leaving aside the basic causes, however, it seems to me that this kind of traditional style of living led to the development of the clear-stage principle and Kabuki's freedom and flexibility in its treatment of space as things which, far from being irrational, were perfectly natural.

THE REVOLVING STAGE

An Invention of the Japanese

So far we have looked at various aspects of the very free treatment of space, from the large-scale trap and building collapse to the removal of a body by means of an 'erasing cloth,' which would be absolutely unthinkable in, for example, modern realism subject to the three unities. When it comes down to it, though, the most original and typical things in Kabuki are the revolving stage and the hanamichi. It is these two things that may be said to be Japan's greatest inventions.

So it was that, with the coming of the modern period, while Japan was feverishly engaged in absorbing the modern realism of the west and ignoring or despising her own traditions, the west was studying and even beginning to adopt these original Japanese structures as one means of breaking through the 'modern' impasse in which it already found itself.

First, a word about the revolving stage. We tried it several times abroad and it made a great impression there. During the first visit to America at the beginning of 1960 described in the opening chapter, it was used in *Chūshingura* and *Tsubosaka Reigenki* as well as in *Kagotsurube* (a play from *Yoshiwara Hyakunin-giri* 'A Hundred Killings in the Yoshiwara' by Sano Jirōzaemon), and it was also used in *Shunkan* in the Soviet Union the following year.

The revolving stage in Kabuki is made to turn with one or

two sets for subsequent scenes already assembled on its back part, and although it goes without saying that it serves to speed up a scene change, that is not all. While I believe that the motive for its invention was to shorten the time between acts or scenes, as it was being developed it was discovered that the audience found it more entertaining to have the creaking change of scene done in front of them with the curtain left open, and this then became part of the atmosphere of Kabuki.

One example of this is to be found, once again, in *Chū-shingura*, when there is a change from the scene in the great hall of the castle where the harakiri takes place against a back-drop of silver-coloured sliding doors, to the next one outside the main gate where it is decided to relinquish the castle to the authorities. The same mood of deep sadness runs through both scenes, but it is not easy to describe the contrast between the inside and the outside of the residence and the emotions felt as one's eyes follow the grief of the earlier scene and at the same time, as the stage revolves, see the gradual appearance of the even more desolate night outside. It is completely different from having the curtain abruptly close to cut short the prevailing mood and then, later, making a fresh start with a complete and stationary scene before the castle gate. It gives a natural flow of emotion and mood—what might perhaps now be called physiological satisfaction.

In *Shunkan* the site remains the same but, as curtain-time approaches, the stage is given a half-turn to remove Shunkan's tumble-down hut now that it is no longer needed with the end of the action, and this makes way at the front of the stage for the papier-mache rocky crag which had been positioned upstage in readiness. . . .

The revolving stage, then, is something that is needed without fail in order to provide a real taste of Kabuki, and so it was decided to use it as far as possible in overseas performances too.

We were alarmed to find, however, that the theatres chosen for the first performances in America—even the all-important one in New York—did not have such a stage. For all that this was the City Centre on Broadway, a theatre of standing as the home of the New York City Ballet, it was old and had no revolving stage. Although the name Broadway probably conjures up a picture of modern theatres standing side by side, this is not the case since most of them are old ones built in the middle or later part of the nineteenth century.

We therefore tried everything we knew to find an answer. It turned out to be the extremely primitive method of putting a big round wooden platform onto the normal stage and making it turn from the back of the stage by means of a cable wound round it. We were very concerned about whether or not it would turn with the weight of two heavy buildings on it, but we were surprised how easily this was done by a single big American sceneshifter, even though it doubtless had a good winding mechanism and smooth-running bearings under the platform.

But such a big platform would not fit on a goods wagon. The next performances were to be in Los Angeles and San Francisco, and it had to be transported there by transcontinental railway ahead of the company. Our revolving stage therefore had to be made so that it could be divided up into small triangular sections—eight or sixteen of them, I forget which—like a pizza, then crated and reassembled after arrival. One has to go to all kinds of trouble to show a genuine piece of theatre in foreign parts.

While on the subject of the circular-platform type of revolving stage used in the American performances, I should here like to look at the way revolving stages developed in Japan and the west.

The method used in America—putting a round platform on a stationary level stage and turning it with the sets built on it—was the one employed in Japan too when the revolving stage was invented, and I therefore described it above as 'primitive.' Since it is, so to speak, like an *oka* 'hill' (the raised stage) surmounted by a *bon* 'dish' (in the earliest period there was a four-sided framework underneath, with a lot of rollers round the circumference), it is known as the *okabon* 'hill-dish' type.

It is not known exactly when it was devised, but there is no doubt that it was in the first half of the eighteenth century. A book entitled *Kabuki Kotohajime* 'The Beginnings of Kabuki' records that at the end of the Genroku era (1688-1704) a playwright called Nakamura Denshichi startled his audience by having a revolving stage known at the time as a *bunmawashi*, literally 'compass.'

This early type is of course not to be found in the big modern theatres but, according to my notes, in November 1954 I went with a number of fellow members of the Japanese Drama Association on a study trip to investigate the Kabuki stages in farming villages in Gunma Prefecture, and on that occasion saw for the first time a hill-dish type framework which, though no longer in use, survived on one of the old stages.

Now, many years later, the study of country Kabuki is carried out systematically and many examples have been discovered all over Japan, but among them all the one with the oldest revolving stage in working order is that at Kami Miharada, Akagi-mura in that same prefecture.

It is well equipped: apart from a revolving stage, it has a hanamichi of course, and also a lifting trap and a two-tier structure set up as required on the main stage for such things as dance pieces. It was designated as an Important Cultural Asset by the prefecture in 1960. Its revolving stage is not of the hill-dish type, however, but is set into the stage like those at the present time and has a big trap in its centre. It therefore has no central axle fitted but has instead a kind of hexagonal box underneath, which is turned by six men working together in what is known as the 'Hell' below the stage.

This stage at Miharada is said to have been constructed by a renowned local carpenter called Nagai Chōjirō in 1819, but some sixty years earlier, in 1758, the Osaka Kabuki playwright Namiki Shōzō had perfected a revolving stage of the present-day kind worked from below by fitting a circular section into the normal stage. Later a 'bull's-eye' revolving stage consisting of two concentric circles was produced and electric power came to be used in modern times, but it was Shōzō who established the revolving stage which, as mentioned before, gives Kabuki a unique flavour.

This writer originally worked in the Bunraku puppet theatre, and so he introduced into Kabuki its various illusionary tricks and contrivances and brought about a rapid development of Kabuki stagecraft. I constantly think how effectively Shakespeare would have used the revolving stage if he had known about it.

The west, however, did not have the revolving stage in his day and, in fact, only had it for the first time quite recently. In 1663 a German called Joseph Furttenbach did put forward the idea of having several stages around a revolving auditorium in the middle, but this was never realised.

The first revolving stage outside Japan was employed in the opera *Don Giovanni* by Karl Lautenschläger in Munich in 1896. There is not sufficient evidence to know for sure whether or not there was any influence from Kabuki in this, but its next use by Max Reinhardt in *A Midsummer Night's Dream* in 1905 was clearly adapted from Kabuki: he was given the idea by a friend living in Japan.

As Reinhardt was the famous producer who, in an effort to overthrow modern realism, built a great theatre in Berlin for 5,000 people and dominated his day with fresh non-realistic productions, he had enormous influence and the revolving stage he used spread around the west. The fact that theatres in Europe today generally have revolving stages may be seen as an influence from Kabuki through the medium of Reinhardt.

Thus, although there is no doubt that, on balance, Japan is in debt to the west for what she has received from it, there is conversely quite a bit that she has given to the west. The absence of revolving stages in theatres on Broadway is simply the result of their having been built in the period before Reinhardt.

THE HANAMICHI

A Frustration in Performances Abroad

The hanamichi, even more than the revolving stage, is essential in Kabuki. It goes without saying that this passageway running through the lefthand side of the auditorium is not simply a means of entrance and exit for the actors but an important acting area.

Whether entering or leaving along the hanamichi, the actors unfailingly pause at a point not far from the main stage and there speak their lines or strike a dramatic pose. Since this is seven-tenths of the way along from the curtain at the back of the auditorium and three-tenths back from the stage, it is known as the *shichi-san* '7-3' point. The audience greet a favourite player not so much as a main actor in the play but as the man himself, by shouting out his traditional house name (yagō). He comes to a halt in the most leisurely way, displays himself to the audience to his best advantage, and responds to their greeting by identifying himself in his opening lines. Thanks to the hanamichi, stage and auditorium are brought together to enable the actors and audience to exchange greetings and to react to each other in close proximity.

Nō also has its hashigakari for use by actors making their entrance but, like the main stage, it is clearly separated from the audience by a gravel surround called the *shirasu* 'sand bar.' This is because the Nō stage was originally a sacred place where gods and other supernatural beings would dance, on a different plane from the space where mere humans sat and watched. In Kabuki, however, both stage and auditorium occupy the same human world—and this can be taken as a basic difference from Nō.

There is a story to be told here, about the time towards the end of the nineteenth century when the most popular star of the time, Nakamura Fukusuke (later famous as Utaemon V, the father of the present Utaemon), performed *Musume Dō-jō-ji*. Having emerged onto the hanamichi from the back of the auditorium and paused as usual at the 7-3 point, he took out a paper tissue and gently wiped the sweat from his face to convey the impression that he was having a brief rest after climbing the sixty-two stone steps up to the temple. He then unthinkingly dropped the tissue, and it fell from the hanamichi into the audience—

At that instant, the girls who had been watching from seats as close as possible to the hanamichi, hardly daring to breathe, reached out with one accord to try to catch it and, as they fell over each other, started a great uproar which, it is said, even led to some injuries.

What is more, there was a story going round later that a sharp character had seized on the actor's popularity and made a lot of money by going round selling doubtful-looking balls of paper which he had wrapped and brazenly labelled 'Fuku-suke's Spittle.' True or not, the story shows very well, I feel, the relationship between the Kabuki actor and his audience, the significance of the hanamichi, and the importance of its role.

So important is it that, in plays like *Sukeroku* among the traditional Eighteen Kabuki Pieces, for example, the player makes his entrance onto the hanamichi and after going through various movements at the 7-3 point, opens his umbrella one-handed with a grand gesture and strikes a dramatic pose; and his reputation can be decided according to the fine figure and the grand scale of the character he portrays there. Benkei's final bounding exit by what is known as a *tobi-roppō* 'flying in six directions' is an indispensable highlight in *Kanjinchō*, and the same is true of Yuranosuke's rush to the scene of his lord's harakiri and the love-suicide journey of O-Karu and Kanpei in *Chūshingura*—but without a hanamichi for such moments, the fascination of Kabuki would be lost.

This brings me back at last to performances abroad, and what gave us most trouble there was the temporary installation of this hanamichi. Although there are theatres which have a revolving stage, there is not one with a hanamichi. Such a thing would, after all, have been unthinkable in the west which, since the Renaissance, has been occupied with a quest for rationalism and modernity. Our first big hurdle, therefore, was to convince people of the necessity of a hanamichi.

Certainly, its installation meant a double loss: not only did it cost money but it also took up space that would otherwise have been occupied by seats for the audience. Since the west takes a rational approach and well developed economic views of all things, we often had one built while still arguing with the local people concerned when they told us that it was out of the question and that we should somehow make do without one. Since it meant sacrificing sixty seats in Moscow and no fewer than two hundred in Leningrad, for example, it is understandable that the other side should have dragged their feet over it.

The Odeon Theatre in Paris, used on the first visit to Europe in 1965, was a difficult case. When I arrived in Paris, having gone on ahead on unrelated business, I was asked by someone from the embassy to go and reason with the manager of the theatre. He had said, I was told, that if we claimed a hanamichi was absolutely necessary, he would resign himself to boarding over the gangway through the centre of the auditorium for us to use, and when told that that was no good because in Kabuki it is traditionally on the lefthand side, he countered by asking why it had to be like that—and this the

official had been hard pressed to explain. I therefore went off
to see him and finally won his agreement after pointing out
all kinds of things such as that Yuranosuke's performance as
he made his way to where the harakiri was taking place, to
give just one example, would hardly come over very well if
he spent all his time with his back turned on half the audience,
and that in Japan as elsewhere a central catwalk was only found
in musicals and cheap strip shows.

Briefly, then, what I am pointing out is how unique to Japan
is the hanamichi—and yet, once it was actually built and
rehearsals began, the local people concerned came to understand its significance, their doubts changed to admiration, and
they began to cooperate with us enthusiastically. This meant
that our headache became their own, and we were happy and
relieved to discover that they too were theatre people after all
and had instinctively understood our need.

When performances were given abroad there were many
reviews which touched on the unique quality of the hanamichi,
but I will just give here extracts from one about the performances in London in 1972 which appeared in *The Times*. This
is one of the foremost quality newspapers in the world, and
the writer is the drama critic Irving Wardle.

> '. . . Its conventions pass swiftly from the exotic
> to the directly expressive. One of these is the famous
> *hanamichi* ("flower path") . . . along which
> characters make delayed entries before arriving on
> the scene. Nothing of the kind exists on the Western
> stage. . . .'

He then continues with a review of *Sumidagawa*, which had
been in the programme of the day in question. This piece is
a Kabuki dance version of the Nō play of the same name, and
on this occasion of its first performance overseas, the main
role was taken by Utaemon.

'The advantage of the Japanese design is that these preparations take place in the midst of the audience. Characters are at once very close, and sunk in the private meditation that precedes action. The sight of Utaemon, as a bereaved mother, pausing half way along the bridge and holding out a blossoming branch to a man in the stalls—physically within touching distance, but a thousand miles removed in terms of dramatic reality—epitomizes the relationship.'

This passage frankly describes the writer's shock at a perception of reality and the physical senses which, unimaginable in western tradition, confronts him by transcending in a moment the logic of time and space.

In fact, however, there had been earlier western interest in the hanamichi. The Russian anti-modernist producer Meyerhold is said to have studied the hanamichi and other forms of stage space from 1912 to 1917, and then in 1924, after the Revolution, to have put the idea of the hanamichi into practice in his production of Ostrovsky's play *The Forest*; and Reinhardt, who was responsible for the spread of the revolving stage, is also said to have used the hanamichi in a mime piece he took from *The Arabian Nights*.

Even though the use of the revolving stage has spread, the hanamichi has been looked on as something much more unwestern. Productions using a gangway through the auditorium have been tried in the past, as if someone had remembered it from time to time, but there has not yet been any permanent installation.

It is clear, therefore, that the hanamichi is not to be found anywhere in the west in modern times, but if we look more widely over time and place, can its existence really be said to be limited to Japan alone?

The answer is no. The hanamichi, in the sense of making

a stage entrance from the auditorium, is to be found elsewhere too.

First of all, a majority of oriental performing arts have a hanamichi. For example, the masked dances of India and Nepal, performances of which I was invited to see in the spring of 1981 in the third Exchange of Asian Performing Arts sponsored by the Japan Foundation.

These were originally performed in the areas concerned on level ground outdoors surrounded on all sides by spectators, like Japanese folk entertainments. The players mostly represent gods or demons and enter from the dressing rooms by making their way through the audience. In other words, they enter from a hanamichi, and before reaching the 'stage' they violently shake their bodies and shout—and one is not unmindful here of the wild aragoto style in Kabuki.

In the west, the theatres as such do not have a hanamichi, but it is to be seen on occasions outdoors. A long time ago now, I saw an open-air religious play in front of Notre Dame Cathedral in Paris. It was a very impressive sight as Jesus, gasping under the weight of the cross he was made to bear, entered in a great procession of soldiers mounted on real horses and officials and troops on foot as they all threaded their way through the specially built stands. It was, of course, a modern production staged for the tourists, but religious plays in medieval Europe were originally given outdoors and there were presumably occasions when they too used just such a hanamichi.

Wherein, then, lies the uniqueness of the hanamichi in Kabuki?—It seems to me that it is to be found in two points: that it made a great advance by being not only a means of entry and exit but also 'acting space'; and that it evolved from the primitive level of being for the use of gods and spirits to being a place for ordinary mortals.

In the west, from the Renaissance onwards the hanamichi suffered a complete decline in the face of the demands of logic

An Edo-period Kabuki theatre still existing in Kagawa Prefecture.

and realism. In the countries of the east, apart from Japan, it has remained within its folk entertainment function of providing access to the stage for divine spirits. Kabuki alone boasts its own special hanamichi. It is likely that the sense of taste and beauty applied to their hanamichi by the Japanese is to be seen in the fact that, although the starting point may have been the same, far from abandoning the hanamichi, they raised it into something of their very own. It is itself a problem to say what this sense is, but before coming on to that I should like to say a brief word here about the establishment and development of the hanamichi.

There are various views about its origin—for example, that it was a variant of the hashigakari in Nō; that it is seen as a development of the aisle (*michi*) through the centre which allowed a representative of the audience to approach the stage to present a gift (*hana*); or that it is the same as the entrance for divine spirits found in folk entertainments—and one cannot come to any definite decision.

Let us leave aside any discussion of that here, then, and note

that the middle of the seventeenth century saw the beginning
of the boardwalk through the centre of the auditorium which
is seen as the original form of the hanamichi; that in the early
years of the eighteenth century this began to be in frequent
use as a performing area; and that before long this moved to
the lefthand side as one faced the stage. Towards the end of
the century the same thing happened with the boardwalk on
the righthand side which, with the increasing size of the
theatres, had been introduced as an aisle for the use of audience
and ushers, and for theatre employees bringing in cushions,
tea and food. This came to be called the *kari-hanamichi*
'temporary hanamichi,' and the one on the left the *hon-
hanamichi* 'main hanamichi.' The two were linked by a boardwalk at the back. . . .

At the present time, both the National Theatre and the
Kabukiza have only a main hanamichi, with a temporary one
being set up only when it is absolutely necessary. Until the great
earthquake of 1923, however, the Kabukiza auditorium was
filled with small square cushioned enclosures as in the present
Sumo stadium in Tokyo, and both hanamichi were permanently installed.

In passing, I will just mention the *suppon*, literally 'turtle.'
This is a small rectangle cut out of the hanamichi at the 7-3
point and made into a lift. As it momentarily goes down and
then comes up again once the player making his entrance has
taken his place on it, it is said that it was given such a name
because it resembles a turtle stretching up its head. Be that as
it may, the important thing is that this suppon is used particularly for the entries and exits of supernatural characters.

Examples of these are the fox which appears in the form
of the warrior Satō Tadanobu in *Yoshitsune Senbonzakura*
'Yoshitsune and the Thousand Cherry Trees,' and Takiyasha-
hime in *Masakado* who uses the witchcraft of a toad. In *Sendai Hagi*, a great rat is seen stealing a precious scroll by a
samurai called Arajishi Dannosuke, and when he strikes it on

the head with an iron-ribbed fan, it escapes down into the suppon. Before long, a strange white smoke comes up from there and this is followed by the appearance on the lift of the villainous ninja Nitsuki Danjō who, dressed in grey and making mystic signs with his fingers, carries the scroll in his mouth and a wound on his forehead. . . .

Thus, the suppon is used for supernatural characters such as apparitions, ghosts and ninja, and the hanamichi more particularly for the entries and exits of ordinary human beings. The same holds good for turbulent, aragoto-type heroes for, no matter how much superhuman power they may possess or how much they may be revered and feared by ordinary people as wild god-like beings, they still remain *human*.

Gods and evil spirits have to be satisfied with the small suppon, for the main stage is above all a space reserved for the activities of earthly beings. This, it may be said, is typical of Kabuki in its role as a theatre of the people and a 'hymn to humanity.'

What kind of functions, then, does the hanamichi have in practice, and what kind of characteristics of the Japanese people does it reflect ?

A Sense of Presence from Two Hanamichi

A Subtle World of Identity and Dissociation

As a case which best displays these characteristics, let us look at a play which uses two hanamichi.

The long play *Imoseyama Onna Teikin* 'An Example of Noble Womanhood' has a third act known as *Yama no Dan* 'The Hills' or *Yoshinogawa* 'Yoshino River.' The two main actors enter by two hanamichi, left and right: onto the main hanamichi, on the left, comes Sadaka, a widow from the Dazai house; and onto the one on the right, the senior magistrate Kiyosumi.

On the stage the audience sees the residence of the magistrate on the Se-yama hill to the right, facing that of Sadaka on a similar hill, Imo-yama, to the left, and between the two the flow of the clear waters of the broad Yoshino River—a perfectly symmetrical stage in all its splendour. Here unfolds the tragedy of the son and daughter (Koganosuke and Hinadori) of two houses which, through generations of ill will, have confronted each other like the hills on each side of the river and which are finally reconciled when the tragic love of the young couple leads them to die together and to seek their union in the next world.

As everyone will realise, this tragic situation is exactly that of Shakespeare's *Romeo and Juliet*. Since this was written some

A Kabuki dance scene using two *hanamichi*.

180 years earlier than the Kabuki play, there is a theory that the story of Shakespeare's play was brought in by the westerners who used the island of Dejima at Nagasaki. The possibility of course exists but, without any definite proof as yet, I will simply mention the theory here for its own sake and restrict myself to a discussion of acting space.

The important thing in the present case is that the two hanamichi are *assumed* to be the two banks of the Yoshino River. When the two characters come out and stop to face each other at the 7-3 points, there is a fixed movement in which Sadaka on the wider main hanamichi takes a step forward: the feeling behind this is that she instinctively moves closer to the water's edge so that, in her exchanges with the magistrate, her voice will carry that little bit more easily across the wide expanse of water.

In other words, the central part of the auditorium is, as it were, the river and, as a result, the audience vividly experience the direct physical sensation of being in the middle of the river and, hence, of the drama which is taking place across it.

With the existence of the hanamichi enlarging the acting area and bringing it out into the auditorium, the whole theatre becomes the very site on which the drama unfolds. From this comes what might be called a 'sense of presence'—something not to be found in western theatrical tradition.

This enlargement of the acting area and the sense of personal presence are further strengthened by the boardwalk linking the two hanamichi at the back of the theatre. An example of this is in the first act of the domestic drama *Kirare Yosa* 'Yosa Put to the Sword' (the full name of which is *Yowa Nasake Ukina no Yokogushi*). In the scene where O-Tomi and Yosaburō fall in love on the beach at Kisarazu in Chiba Prefecture, Yosaburō and a manservant leave the stage by the temporary hanamichi, pass through the audience along the boardwalk at the back, and go down the main hanamichi to return to the stage proper.

While they are making this circuit of the auditorium, they chat away casually to each other, and as the temporary hanamichi and the boardwalk are only sixty centimetres wide (a third of the width of the main hanamichi), this is greatly enjoyed by the audience. The actors too are relaxed, and since they are supposed to be walking along the seashore among people searching for shellfish at low tide, they will raise a laugh by looking around at the audience and ad-libbing to each other about the crowd that has turned out there. This is the kind of thing that gives the light domestic dramas their appeal.

Nevertheless, even though good relations and rapport with the audience may be heightened in this way, a line will be drawn at a certain level so that there will always be a clear distinction between audience and actor. I feel that this is an extremely important element in the theatre, and it will be considered again later.

Now while the actors make their way round the auditorium, on the stage itself sliding sets of the background and buildings are changed to show their progress. It can be said that such free and flexible treatment of space has never existed in mainstream western drama.

An extension and enlargement of dramatic space come from the hanamichi and boardwalk, and an artless imagination and sense of presence accept that the entire theatre is a river with its banks or the seashore. These ideas sink into the minds of the audience, and from the world of make-believe that is created by their assumptions comes a kind of discerning freedom.

These aspects have also existed as basic principles of the treatment of space in Nō which, being solemn and succinct, may appear at first sight to be the complete opposite of Kabuki. It may also be said that these aspects of Kabuki are no more than extensions and embodiments of those in Nō. Can we not find here a uniquely Japanese conception?

In the passage in which mention was made of a line always being drawn between actor and audience, we have seen already that the two are brought into the closest possible proximity and relationship by the hanamichi and boardwalk. This means that Kabuki audiences can indulge themselves as fans to such an extent that, if they are really carried away, the result can be much like a victorious Sumo wrestler being slapped on the back as he makes his exit or some favourite actor of the popular theatre being bustled by his female fans. The earlier story about Utaemon dropping a tissue from the hanamichi may be seen as a case in point.

In recent years certainly, it has been rare for Kabuki audiences to show such unbridled enthusiasm, perhaps because they see themselves more generally as coming "to appreciate a traditional art," but it has been mentioned already that it was originally Kabuki's place to be such a theatre of the people.

A relationship, friendliness, rapport; and a feeling on the part of the audience that they too are sharing the same time and the same dramatic space. These may certainly be said to create an *identity* between audience and stage, arising from the sense of presence that is felt. Paradoxical as it may seem, however, and in spite of such a physical and spatial proximity brought about by the hanamichi, there is on the other hand a clear realisation that the audience and the stage are inescapably distinct and that it is all make-believe. That is to say, the hanamichi serves to create identity and, at the same time, *separation* or *dissociation*.

For example, when a favourite actor appears on the hanamichi, voices will call out not the name of the character he is playing but his house name and conventional greetings. These are a form of acclamation, but if the people concerned were psychologically wholly immersed in the play and had had their emotions taken over by it, they would scarcely be able to shout out what they do.

Also, on the other side of the hanamichi can be seen row after row of faces of other members of the audience just like themselves. Naturally, any illusion of identity will then be shattered, since they are not characters in the drama. This is why the hanamichi and the like would be out of the question in western realistic drama, which has as its ideal a thorough-going identity, illusion and immersion.

On the other hand, there has been someone in the west who preached and practised what he called *Verfremdungseffekt* 'distancing effect.' This was Berthold Brecht, famous for his *Threepenny Opera*, *Mother Courage and her Children*, and *The Caucasian Chalk Circle*.

He believed that, through an excessive concentration on the stage, the concept of identification in modern realism became so besotted with mood that it lost its ability to judge content and had no part to play in the development of a socialist world. He therefore devised a technique whereby, if the audience were about to lose themselves in a piece, he would interrupt their slide into identity by suddenly dousing them with cold water, as it were, by using a revolving stage, music, or scenes with something unexpected. He made a close study of Chinese and

Japanese plays and adopted a good deal from them, and I imagine that he may well have gained a hint for his distancing effect from the non-realistic techniques of Kabuki.

Even in the case of realistic western drama, however, there is no telling what might happen if identification went too far and the line between reality and make-believe really disappeared.

Or, rather, even in the Japanese theatre which is almost entirely built on make-believe alone, if by some chance the clear realisation that it is make-believe, if this basic premise of the theatre were no longer to apply, a calamity would be sure to happen. The truth is that, in both Japan and the west, cases have arisen in which a villain in a play has been killed by being taken for a villain in real life.

I would, though, like to leave this subject for a later chapter, as an example of the problems which lie at the root of ideas about solidity and emptiness, truth and lies, reality and make-believe.

Chapter Three

PLASTIC BEAUTY AND A SENSE OF SOUND

THE PLEASURES OF SIGHT AND SOUND

In Search of Stylized Beauty

Tsuki mo oboro ni
  shirauo no
Kagari mo kasumu
  haru no sora
Tsumetee kaze mo
  horoyoi ni
Kokoromochi-yoku
  uka uka to
Ukare-garasu no
  tada ichi-wa

Negura e keeru
  kawabata de
Sao no shizuku ka
  nurete de awa
Omoigake-naku
  te ni iru hyakuryō . . .

Under a hazy moon, even
the flicker of fish
Is dimmed against the sky
of early spring.
The wind is cold but,
mellow with wine,
I am idly making my way
along the river bank,
Back to my nest like a
lone crow in the
moonlight,
When in my hands, wet
from the punting pole,
Like bubbles from the
water
I suddenly find a hundred
pieces of silver . . .

These are very well-known lines, in an obvious metre of seven and five syllables. It is a famous passage from the character O-Jō Kichisa in the Sumidagawa river-bank scene from *Sannin Kichisa* 'Three Robbers Called Kichisa,' a typical picaresque play by Mokuami.

It is the northern side of Ryōgoku Bridge in Edo, at dead of night. A misty moon hangs in the sky, and in front is the clear flow of the Sumida River. Standing with one foot resting on a stake in the river and dressed in a long-sleeved kimono with a dappled scarlet under-robe peeping enticingly from the hem is the elaborately coiffured figure of a young woman, beautiful even in that light—or so it seems, but this is O-Jō Kichisa, a strange robber who appears dressed like a woman in the guise of the tragic girl Yaoya O-Shichi, the heroine of the play of that name. It may well be said that it is due to this delightful figure of O-Jō and the attraction of the excellent text that the long seven-act *Sannin Kichisa* has always been counted among the most popular of Kabuki plays.

Striking figure and melodious text—these are the two elements which Japanese theatre prizes above all others. In Kabuki there is the saying "First, performance; second, voice; third, looks." Sometimes it takes the form "First, voice; second, performance; third, looks," but either way there is agreement that the actor's performance and voice take precedence over whether or not he is handsome. This is so not only in Kabuki but in Nō too: at the beginning of his *Kadensho* 'Writings on the Transmission of the Flower,' Zeami (1363-1443) says:

'Only one who avoids coarseness in his speech and
is attractive in his appearance can be called an
accomplished master;'

and in the following text he repeatedly states that the voice and appearance are the most basic constituents of the 'Flower' (*hana*), his symbol for the essence of beauty in Nō.

The sense of beauty through eyes and ears, sight and sound—these are treated as the first consideration, not only for actors and other stage performers but for the entire stage and the theatre as a whole. We saw in the previous chapter a way of dealing with time and space which is so easy, free and fluid that at times it could even be called expedient. This is no mere expediency or passing fancy, however, but is governed by the fundamental principle that, even though the beauty of sight and sound may be heightened, it must never be spoiled.

As we shall see below, this beauty of sight and sound is not the beauty of nature and reality as such, but a beauty given an extra dimension by selecting its elements from nature and reality according to an individual aesthetic sense and then re-creating it by restricting, exceeding, or accentuating particular aspects. We shall call this "stylized beauty" and the process of re-creation "stylization."

The method and extent of stylization are of course not fixed. They differ considerably in Nō and Kabuki, and within Kabuki itself dance pieces and ordinary plays, historical plays and domestic dramas, the macho type of acting known as aragoto 'roughness' and the soft and graceful one known as *wagoto* 'gentleness,' have each their own particular style. Music, though, forms part not only of dances pieces, naturally enough, but even of ordinary plays too, and this can be said to be a feature peculiar to Japan.

It is not the case, for example, in the west. Greek drama in its earliest period had music derived from the circular dancing and chorus singing in honour of Dionysius (Bacchus), the god of wine, and at its height was recited drama with music and chorus; and medieval religious drama was probably produced to music with due solemnity. As time passed from the Renaissance onwards, however, a complete division developed into spoken drama, music-based opera, and ballet which exists for the dance. Among these, a peak was reached by spoken drama in modern times with the realism of Ibsen.

As we have seen already, his ideal was the 're-creation' of reality and he therefore shunned anything excessive or illogical. In that sense, Japanese theatre was still in an undivided state, and one reason for this was probably that the Japanese are more concerned with the five senses and their direct physiological links than they are with logic or reason. Apart from obvious examples involving sight or sound, they produced the tea ceremony in the field of taste and the game of incense judging in the field of smell. The fact that, in such cases, they developed a fixed and formal approach known as a "Way" (*dō*) is another characteristic of Japan, and we shall consider this later.

In the case of the sense of touch, however, it is not clear to me what form it took. It seems to me that the Japanese are very sensitive to the feel of things, and it can be said that for them sculpture is not only something to look at but, albeit indirectly after completion, something to touch as well. The proof of this is to be found in the bronze and stone statues polished smooth by stroking hands.

It may be said, though, that an emphasis on sight and sound exists not only in Japan but also in the other countries of East Asia and in those to the south. True enough, folk entertainments outside Japan also have music and dance—physical movement and rhythm.

This brings back to me a vivid impression from a film I saw on a dim screen set up in the playground of my primary school in Shibuya one night during the summer holidays. It was a dynamic scene of a line of women of the aboriginal Yami tribe on a small island called Kōtōsho just east of the southern tip of Taiwan. On the beach there they performed a frenzied dance in which they threw their bodies violently backwards and forwards with their hair flying in disarray. After that I dreamed time and again of the South Seas where towering waves come crashing in. . . .

What makes the case of Japan different from the generality of the countries of East Asia, however, is surely the fact that, *in spite of* the establishment of drama of a literary nature in the western sense at least from the time of Chikamatsu Monzaemon in the Genroku era, there was no loss of formal beauty. I say this not from any particularly partial viewpoint but simply as a fact; and because of this I feel that the nature of form in the case of Japan probably arises not from what might be described as following in others' footsteps but, more deeply, from her individuality as a nation.

Let us look, then, into various ways in which this beauty of style is revealed.

DRAMATIC POSES IN PICTORIAL SCENES

Form in Introduction, Development and Climax

In our everyday speech there are a surprisingly large number of words which come from the theatre. A handsome man, for example, is called a *nimaime* 'second liner,' and an empty-headed laughing-stock a *sanmaime* 'third liner.' This is because old Kabuki programmes used to list handsome young male leads in second place, and comics in third. Then there are other such terms as *sutezerifu* (literally 'parting line') 'sharp parting remark/threat'; *kuromaku* ('black curtain') 'wirepuller, manipulator'; *ōzume* 'final scene, conclusion'; *makugire* 'fall of the curtain, final scene'. . . .

Another of these terms is mie 'dramatic pose.' In Kabuki this means a performing technique by which an actor strikes a certain pose at main points in the action and holds it for several seconds. It can be taken as something similar to what is known as a tableau in the west, though this seems in most cases to be held for somewhat longer. In the west, however, although there are instances of the whole company suddenly standing motionless just before the final curtain, for example, these are wholly exceptional and there is never any posing at numerous fixed points within a play. Even this kind of final tableau I have only ever seen at the very end of Gogol's *The Inspector General*.

The *Kuruma-biki* 'Pulling the Carriage' scene in the Kabuki *Sugawara Denju Te-narai Kagami*.

The Peking Opera uses many dramatic poses during a performance, but even these are poses which take a direct line across a break in the action when it suddenly stops and then equally suddenly starts again. This is unlike the Japanese mie in which, as a climax is reached, a moving figure comes into a 'perfect set' by means of smooth lines, thus giving it the softness of a curve. There is surely at work here the same aesthetic sense as that in the shading of the kumadori make-up which we saw as a Japanese characteristic in the opening chapter.

The mie naturally takes many forms according to the direction and extent of the stylization. The oldest and most typical is the 'Genroku mie,' named after the Genroku era, and the classic form of this is to be seen among the Eighteen Kabuki Pieces of the Ichikawa Danjūrō house in such roles as that of the hero in *Shibaraku* 'Wait!' and of Umeōmaru in *Kuruma-biki*. If we take the former as an example, the hero, wearing a multi-striped scarlet kumadori make-up, cries out 'Wait! Wait!' as he comes from the hanamichi onto the stage and there in front of the line of villains strikes a mie pose on a grand scale: he stamps his left foot down diagonally in front of him, lowers his body by bending his right leg now drawn back behind him, grips the scabbard of his sword with his left hand as he twists it over ready to be drawn, and stretches his right hand high up behind him. This stance, with the right hand stretching out towards infinity, seems to have about it the grandeur of the boundless universe.

The fixed form, as he strikes this pose, is for him to 'glare' by opening his eyes wide and then crossing them. Why should he do this? My own personal idea is that it was possibly a device for making it appear that he is glaring at each and every person in every corner of the theatre.

According to the spirit worship which existed in pre-modern Japan, it was thought that diligent worship of the wild gods who would otherwise bear a grudge would turn them into protective deities to subdue evil spirits. Such a hero as the main character in *Shibaraku* was also an object of worship for ordinary people, being regarded as the incarnation of one of these wild gods. There is a close link between this and the fact that Danjūrō's belief in the Buddhist divinity Fudō, worshipped at the great temple at Narita, led to 'Naritaya' becoming his professional 'house name.'

All the audience, then, hoped for this god in human form to glare at them and drive away evil spirits and the devils of disease. It would normally be impossible for a single actor to do this for hundreds and hundreds of people but, if he crossed his eyes, it was possible for everyone to imagine that, like the dragon credited to the famous wood-carver Hidari Jingorō, he was looking straight at them even though there was no focus to his gaze. Was this not perhaps the idea behind the 'glare'?

But to return to the subject of the mie itself, there are innumerable kinds, including the one in which the actor looks up sharply at the bell in *Musume Dōjō-ji*, which was mentioned several times in the opening chapter; and even in domestic dramas such as *Sannin Kichisa* and *Benten Kozō* which are very realistic in Kabuki, a climax is usually signified by a mie and a memorable line.

Because of this, as was mentioned earlier, the Kabuki actor sets particular store by his appearance, that is, his form and style when he moves or gestures. Onoe Kikugorō V, who stood with Danjūrō IX as one of the two greatest players of the Meiji period (1868-1912), was so concerned about this that he is said to have insisted that even the most minor property brought onto the stage for a scene of his should be put in exactly the same position every time, never an inch out of place. Hailing from Edo, Kikugorō was typically short-tempered, and the story goes that once, when he was angry, he went to hit his wife O-Sato. Demanding to know what he thought he was doing, she jumped back to avoid him, whereupon Kikugorō stood looking at her with his hand still in the air and, completely forgetting their quarrel, said to her, "O-Sato, that wasn't a very graceful movement."

The word mie is certainly not used in either Nō or Kyōgen, but they have fixed forms which are handed down even more strictly and artistic traditions which are very firmly established. Since such artistic traditions are a main feature of the Japanese theatre—or, more broadly, Japanese culture—I shall consider these further in the final chapter.

I shall continue to take my examples mainly from Kabuki, but formative beauty may be said to go beyond the individual to the stage as a whole.

The scene on stage must be attractive as a picture—that is, as a pictorial scene—at any given moment. In particular, the one at the final curtain remains in the minds of the audience, and so every effort is made at this point.

Let us again take *Musume Dōjō-ji* as an example: The shirabyōshi Hanago, young and attractive, climbs up onto the bell and there strikes a dramatic pose to make a colourful and beautiful pictorial scene at the final curtain. When the piece is given in full, however, she goes into the bell to change both make-up and costume, and then reappears wearing snake-like make-up and scale-patterned robes as a vengeful spirit in serpent form. At this point the hero, with scarlet kumadori and carrying a green bamboo stave, appears on the hanamichi. After a violent clash, both strike dramatic poses: he an aragoto-type one a little to the left of centre stage, and the spirit while standing on the bell brandishing a short staff in her hand.

The curtain closes on these mie, but as it does so the crowd of would-be captors who had previously come on to the stage and fought with the spirit clasp each other round the waist, form a line across the stage and gradually sink down one after the other until the last one remains standing in order to support the figure in front of him, in such a way that they appear to be perfectly joined to the evil spirit on the bell. Since they are all wearing scale-patterned robes, the line they form looks for all the world like the body and tail of a serpent, and gives to the pictorial scene an echo of the form of the serpent, the incarnation of Kiyohime, as it clings to the bell which is now the focus of its malice.

Such echoes are one of the devices which the audience can enjoy by making the kind of 'assumption' we touched on earlier. A similar example is the scene in which the famous Soga brothers are taken to the residence of their father's enemy Kudō Suketsune in order to establish his identity, and there see him for themselves. This *Soga no Taimen* 'The Soga Brothers' Confrontation' scene is traditionally played at New Year as an auspicious play.

As its finale, a general dramatic pose is taken, with Kudō on a dais on the right of the stage, standing with his left arm stretched out to show the wide hanging sleeve of his kimono, and, to the left but a little right of centre stage, a group in the shape of a mountain, with the elder brother Jūrō on the

Dramatic poses (*mie*) in the Kabuki *Soga no Taimen*.

right, Asaina on the left, and between them the younger
brother, the hot-headed Gorō, who has had to be restrained
by the other two.

In this piece Kudō is presented as a thoroughly worthy
character who is prepared to be killed by the brothers seeking
revenge for their father's murder when his official duties as
organiser of a forthcoming great hunt around Mt. Fuji are over.
It being a pleasing play in that due revenge will be taken and
all the main characters are to be admired, the hanging sleeve
of Kudo symbolizes the open wing of a crane, regarded as a
very auspicious bird, and the three-man group on the left
symbolizes Mt. Fuji.

Pictorial-scene mie are an essential element in Kabuki even
without such echoes or symbols and even when they do not
occur as final scenes, and what strikes me as interesting about
them is that they are hardly ever symmetrical. Whether or not
there is a character in centre stage, the point of balance of the
whole thing is generally slightly to the right and a shape is

created which has its base on the stage and 'the feeling of an unequal-sided triangle.'

For me this basic shape brings to mind that used in Ikebana, which was established in the Edo period after it began as floral offerings to the gods and buddhas and passed through such stages as the rich *tatebana* style reflecting the culture of the Momoyama era (1568-1600) and the plainer tea-ceremony style which looked to nature itself for its inspiration. There are countless schools of Ikebana, but the basis of them all is the unequal-sided triangle made by the arrangement of the three main branches—variously named, according to the school— which derives from the three-deity form of the early floral offerings.

I do not know whether there is any direct connection between Kabuki and the aesthetics of Ikebana, but I feel that it is not forcing things too far to consider that these two arts which came to fruition in the same period had something in common. Also, one cannot help feeling even more strongly that there is a concept common to Ikebana and Kabuki, and by extension to Japanese culture as a whole, on hearing that these three elements in Ikebana correspond to *ten-chi-jin* 'heaven, earth and man' or *jo-ha-kyū* 'introduction, development and climax.'

This jo-ha-kyū is, in the performing arts, a structural theory found in Gagaku, the music which was handed down at court in the Nara and Heian periods (710-1185) as it still is today in the Music Department of the Imperial Household Ministry. It did not remain, however, as a concept current among the ancient nobility, but flowed down into the mainstream of the performing arts in Japan. First of all, in the medieval period (1185-1573), it was adopted as a principle of development in Nō, which had reached its full form as a samurai entertainment, and it even came to be recorded in Zeami's *Kadensho* of 1400:

'Since introduction, development and climax are to

be found in all things, Nō is no exception. They
should be decided according to the nature of the
play.'

Furthermore, this concept of a three-stage jo-ha-kyū development was adopted early in the Edo period into the popular
entertainments of the puppet theatre and Kabuki, where it
produced the basic structures of five-act historical plays and
three-act domestic dramas.

Looked at like this, I cannot help thinking it more natural
on balance to feel that the mie and structural form of the
pictorial scene in Kabuki have some similarity to form in
Ikebana.—At least, I consider that one aspect of the aesthetic
sensibility peculiar to Japan is to be found in this area.

When, at this point, I happened to look up the article on
Ikebana in Heibonsha's *Dai Hyakka-jiten* 'Great Encyclopedia'
which was published as long ago as 1932, I found the following
opening passage:

> 'Ikebana is a method of flower arrangement which
> has long been traditional in Japan. It is a technique
> which seeks to show the ideal perfection of natural
> beauty by taking flowers and plants to arrange in
> a container, and displaying them there to reveal a
> form produced in nature. This does not mean a form
> exactly as it occurs in nature, but one which lies
> within the truth without being true and in a
> falsehood without being false. It is there that a form
> in Ikebana is put together, with a distinctive skill
> that exists only in Japan.'

This seems to me to be a definition which is brief and to
the point, and its mentions of 'the ideal perfection of natural
beauty' and the subtle area between reality and unreality tie
up with matters we shall touch on in due course: the rela-

tionship between the theatre and nature, and what is known as Chikamatsu's 'Reality and Unreality Membrane' on the essential nature of the arts. The whole thrust of the argument is indeed no different from the essential nature of 'stylized beauty' which I discussed at the beginning of this chapter.

The left-right symmetry is broken not only in flower arranging and dramatic poses but by the very stage itself in both Nō and Kabuki for, in contrast to the symmetry of the stage in the west, they have on the left the hashigakari and hanamichi respectively. It is true, though, that the whole scene preserves a delicate balance, in the case of Kabuki, for example, by locating a dramatic pose slightly to the right as opposed to the hanamichi on the left.

At least the stage used for the ancient court dances known as Bugaku is symmetrical, but this is surely because they were by and large adopted intact from the Asian continent without any Japanese influence and because, as a court entertainment, it had to fit into the symmetrical court system of the Heian period (794-1185) with its Divisions of the Left and of the Right. The result was that concepts inherent in the Japanese people had no opportunity to take effect.

In the Heian period, apart from such things as the invention of phonetic writing, Japanese-language poems and diary literature, pretty well the whole of Japan's culture consisted of imports or imitations of the advanced cultures of the continent. It seems that it was only after that period that native Japanese traits appeared in recognizable form.

Be that as it may, if we take the case of gardens, in the west a majority of them are built symmetrically as at the Palace of Versailles and Schoenbrunn Palace whereas, in Japan, even a pond of a symmetrical round or square design did not exist before modern times in the famous gardens of Kyoto or in any other such place.

Where, then, does this characteristic of asymmetry come from? This is not known for certain, but one view is that it is in imitation of nature: plants in Japan bend before nature because of the strong winds found near the coast and on the mountainsides, and this makes the branches grow out one way to form an irregular shape. This is said to have been the model, and it is further said that the dense and symmetrical flower arrangements of the west are the result not of any particular difference in aesthetic concepts but because they copy the trees and plants there which grow straight upwards.

If this is accepted, it looks as if the asymmetrical character of Ikebana and of various elements in the theatre has its roots in the last analysis in the natural features of Japan—but I wonder whether it is really such a neat fit. We shall have to consider this relationship with nature in a later chapter.

Colour and Elegant Vitality

Kabuki Make-up and Nō Masks

It goes without saying that colour has an important place in the creation of form or the formal aspects of space. Nō masks and costumes glisten and shine in their splendour, and yet give a feeling of good taste and dignity. Kyōgen costumes are fresh and lively, with the cheerfulness to be seen in the dragonflies or snails which are sometimes painted right across the back of formal robes. In Kabuki the backgrounds and costumes have bright rich tones in many colours. The skill with which these many colours are harmonized must surely be unparalleled elsewhere in the world.

Since it does not seem necessary to demonstrate in general terms all the various points about colour harmony in Kabuki, I shall just give here a few random thoughts on the subject.

The brilliant artist Kishida Ryūsei, who died in 1930, before he was forty, wrote a well known essay called *Kyūgeki Biron* 'On Beauty in Kabuki.' He is famous for his series of works called *Reiko-zō* 'Portraits of Reiko' which depict his beloved daughter, but after studying western painting in France and returning to Japan, he took a fresh look at its traditional beauty. Then, at the very end of his life, he achieved with Indian-ink painting the free and flowing heights in expressing the "elegant vitality" which he saw as the essence of Japanese painting. He says in his piece on drama,

'What I find very interesting too is the very frequent use made of "red" among the colours found in Kabuki. A deep red is used for all kinds of things, such as aragoto roles of course, red faces in historical plays, and the dais (*yamadai*) for musicians and singers in dance pieces. And this is not only on the stage: red cloth is spread along the upper and lower galleries facing the two hanamichi, and red lanterns are hung there too.'

This refers to the old pre-war Kabukiza which, though it already provided seats for the main body of the audience, still had more gallery 'floor-cushion' accommodation along the sides than the present Kabukiza, with much of the old theatre atmosphere. What, then, of this colour red, and what does it signify in Kabuki? Ryūsei goes on to discuss these questions.

'This colour of red was originally something primitive, with no possible touch of refinement. It is immature, with a good measure of barbaric flavour about it. It is heretical, in some cases bringing to mind blood and fearsome devils. While it is a rich colour, it is never elegant but has instead a common rustic flavour. Yet Kabuki has gone beyond this and used it as the means to create before discerning eyes a strangely beautiful world which is both rough and fragrant. . . .'

Ryūsei's argument in the essay as a whole can be summarized as saying that Kabuki has created a sphere of 'beauty' not to be found in any other genre by bringing together things that are grotesque, erotic, evil, vulgar, ignorant and so on—things that are contrary to the idea of beauty as it is generally understood.

This beauty he can be said to have sought, like the artist

he was, by taking a thorough look at form and colour. He distinguished it from the beauty of Nō, the tea ceremony and Greek art by referring to it by such terms as "the beauty of forbidden passion," "the beauty of the world of desires" and "the beauty of the floating world." These names of his become understandable when one thinks of how he went to the Gion geisha quarter in Kyoto in his last years and there, surrounded by Japanese emotions, passed his days in dissipation, not to say self-destruction. Among these expressions that he created, however, perhaps the most universal and yet the most inspired one is "common beauty."

His idea of a common beauty has greatly helped those who, from pre-war days, have supported the cause of a stylized beauty in Kabuki. It thus has some historical significance too, but I will put that aside here and look only at this 'red' that he gave as one element in his common beauty. This colour of red is of course found in Nō too, in such things as the wide divided skirts worn by the main actors in *Shōjō* 'The Elf' and *Aoi no Ue*, and the brocade top-robes of dancers in young-woman roles; but on the whole there are few such cases compared to the more frequent use of quiet sober colours. There is no doubt too that Kabuki has a greater variety of colours than Nō, that they are vivid and strongly contrasted, and that the proportion of red is greater.

But this red which is so widely used is not, even in Kabuki, the fresh crimson shade found among western paints, but a soft quiet tone which has in it a touch of dark or Chinese red. This is still more true of other colours which, though they may be bright and full, are 'middle tones,' with a feeling of sobriety somewhere in their richness. It is much like coloured theatre prints where the older ones are in sober, quiet, middle tones, in contrast to the gaudy primary red and blue colours which resulted from the wide use of chemical painting materials from the Meiji period onwards.

This colour sense is perhaps innately Japanese. It too may

originally hark back to nature. When I first went to America twenty-five years ago to do some research on comparative drama, we made a stop at Wake Island on the way to Hawaii. It was no more than a refuelling stop in those days of propeller aircraft, but I was struck at the time by how dark was the green and how startlingly bright was the red of the unfamiliar trees and flowers on this tropical island. On the white ground lay solid colours quite unlike the shades of the cherry and plum here in Japan, and the slides I took of them with my still cherished Nikon F2 are preserved even now in my first slide case, for all that their colours are somewhat faded.

Someone told me a similar story which I believe was in connection with the first performances overseas after the war, those mentioned in the opening chapter as having been given in China by the former Ennosuke (En-ō). The design plans for the sets were sent from Japan, and the sets were prepared at the other end, but I understand that, when these were seen, there was consternation because they had been made in the wrong colours with absolutely primary reds and blues. Since this can happen in China and Korea, so near to Japan, it would be even worse in such places as India or Africa, with everything in solid reds, blues and yellows as striking as the pictures children make with coloured paper.

In contrast, European countries for the most part work on a basis of darker, heavier and more sombre colours than does Japan. There can be little doubt that this difference is closely connected with the brightness, the intensity of the sunlight, the composition of the atmosphere, and the colour tones of the natural environment in which people spend their lives.

In the high-latitude countries of Europe, the sunlight is weak, the nights long, dark leaden skies the rule, and conifer forests make seas of dark green. In such places anything that is too bright or too solid in colour stands out too much to be fitting. If we accept that human beings never lose their defensive instincts, it is natural that they should tend towards deeper darker colours. Children's fairy-tale plays and new avant-garde drama apart, virtually none of the many plays and operas I have seen in Europe has been staged with costumes and sets which had any primary or strikingly bright colour about them.

Japan has a warm, damp climate and is situated in the temperate zone far north of the tropics and much further south than countries in the upper part of Europe. It has prided itself since mythological times on being 'The Rich Reed-plain Land of Fresh Rice Ears' but, in return, the high rainfall means that there is no escape from the damage of typhoons generated in the tropics. It has places which, while they may not suffer from the impenetrable density of a London fog, seem always to have mists trailing over them and to be softly and faintly obscured as if seen through thin gauze. A mist is often painted in the forefront and background of folding screens and woodblock prints, and this expresses very well for me the natural character of the country.

I plan to consider nature again later, but the middle colour tones shown so uncompromisingly in the theatre and in woodblock prints may well have become established in the light of experience as being most in harmony with this kind of natural environment. Similarly with Nō: since it was originally an entertainment given for the deities in the precincts of shrines and temples, strident primary colours would not have suited the background of dense groves of moss-green cryptomerias.

I felt this very keenly in the summer of 1963, when I went to seek out some old Nō masks in the mountain village of Tenkawa-mura in the Yoshino area of Nara Prefecture. We were on location for an investigative series called 'The Pearl Box' for Mainichi Television. Thirty ancient Nō masks and one Kyōgen mask had been preserved in the Tenkawa Shrine in the village, and the most precious of them all was an old-man mask called Akobujō which Zeami's son Jūrō Motomasa (d. 1432)—the author of the play *Sumidagawa*—had used and donated to the shrine when he performed *Tōsen* 'The Chinese Ship' there.

Following the death in 1408 of their greatest patron, the shogun Ashikaga Yoshimitsu, the two players were gradually shunned and oppressed by the shogunate and were deprived too of their official positions. As a result, Motomasa left his father to go to Ise and sadly died alone there two years later at the age of thirty-nine. It is sometimes said that he was murdered on suspicion of being a spy for the Southern Court faction opposed by the Ashikaga in the dynastic dispute of the time. It does indeed seem that he relied on the power of the Southern Court when he took the road from the capital to Ise through this village of Tenkawa in the old province of Yamato.

At any rate, after he had performed there, he departed leaving behind the mask that still survives; but the stage on which this tragic Nō master played has only corner pillars and a roof. There is no back-wall, and behind it stands a dense grove of Yoshino cryptomeria trees. Since Motomasa's performance was a solemn and majestic one for the gods and was given in such an awesome, dark and lonely place, there could of course have been no place in it for costumes in cheap and gaudy colours or masks like brightly coloured children's pictures such as might be seen in the Peking Opera or Indian dancing. What are known as 'women's masks' in Nō are regarded as classic pieces in the field of Japanese aesthetics, and it is an atmosphere like this, so full of dew and dampness, that truly brings to life their subtle 'middle expression' which, by the merest change of angle, can move between joy and sorrow.

In the opening chapter I raised as one aspect of an innate Japanese sense of beauty this indeterminate, indistinct, mist-covered feeling which may perhaps be thought of as deriving from the natural conditions of the country; and it seems to me that this shares common ground with the feeling behind the 'shading' (*hokashi*) of kumadori which was mentioned in conjunction with the mie in this chapter.

Although the story that the idea of shading came from the petals of the peony may be apocryphal, there is no doubt that in the first half of the eighteenth century Danjūrō II created

Kabuki *Kumadori* make-up (Umeō-maru in *Kuruma-biki*).

a shaded type of kumadori decisively different from the make-up used by other races which has distinct lines between one colour and another and a lack of differentiation within a single colour that give it the look of a sticky-paper picture.

A similar example can be seen in the method of dyeing known as *Bingata*. A certain amount of shading is used even in Okinawa, its place of origin, but the colours have the clarity and brightness of primary colours. Although it does happen that they are used like that in Japan too, they stand out so vividly that in most cases they are given a more muted tone by the addition of Indian ink and a much more effective use of shading. This tendency is even more marked in Yūzen dyeing, regarded as a purely Japanese method, which is clearly characterized by the technique it too knows as bokashi 'shading' or kumadori. It seems unlikely to be a coincidence that this Yūzen dyeing was established in the period 1688-1735 which also saw the birth of Kabuki kumadori.

Kumadori, with its bold and forceful shading over a white ground which is not blotted out as it is in an oil painting, is also in the spirit of Japanese painting with its emphasis on empty space and its 'elegant vitality'—the feeling of tastefulness which is yet full of life.

This attitude to empty space is to be seen, for example, in the display of art objects. Japanese generally prefer to position a piece of art only after consideration of its relationship with the surrounding space and its balance with other items, as is done with the arrangement of the various players in a picture-scene mie. Westerners, however, are usually content, so long as they can appreciate each item individually, to fill up the space available by setting the exhibits out in rows without such considerations.

One point more, about the symbolism of colour.

In the west, in the extempore mime theatre popular among the ordinary citizens in ancient Rome, the colour of the costume showed the category of the stage performer, that is, the character being played: for example, white for an old man, purple for a young man, grey for dependants, and yellow for a prostitute. The parts were categorized, and within the company the players had more or less specialised roles.

In China, villains paint their faces white, while heroes use red or brown. Kabuki too in its formative period came to have general broad categories of colour according to the different roles: white, in contrast to China, for a young leading man as a hero; red for a villain—called an *akattsura* 'red face'— bent on violence, and so on. In kumadori too red lines, for example, symbolize a man who is good and brave, and indigo an utterly evil man who has treason in mind.

In Nō it is the eyes that are interesting. The mask of a woman of this world has black pupils with small square holes in them, with the whites of the eyes naturally left white. In the case of supernatural beings such as gods, devils and vengeful spirits, however, the whites of the eyes or the surrounds of the pupils are painted gold. Devil gods also have the holes in the pupils rounded. When these eyes shine gold on a dimly lit stage, they do indeed give a feeling of supernatural power.

I once talked about this when I was asked to give a lecture on 'Characteristics of Traditional Japanese Beauty as Seen in Nō Masks and Kabuki Make-up' at an international dermatological conference. It seemed to go down very well with the foreign participants, and I understand that at the evening receptions and on the sightseeing buses 'golden eyes' became quite a catch phrase.

It is said that 'The eyes speak as much as the mouth,' and it may be that the subtleties expressed by the eyes are one of the distinctive features of Japan.

A Seven-five Metre and the Great Drum

A Culture of 'Intervals'

Whether it be Nō, Kabuki or Bunraku, musical elements occupy a very important place.

Nō has a musical accompaniment from four instruments: flute, small hand-drum (*kotsuzumi*) held on the shoulder, large hand-drum (*ōkawa*) held on the hip, and a still larger stick-drum (*taiko*). Kabuki has samisen music and that from the various instruments played in the *geza*, a space on the left of the stage closed off by a screen. Bunraku has the gidayū style of chanting, to the accompaniment of a bigger and heavier type of samisen known as a *futozao* 'thick neck.'

In spite of the fact that Kyōgen is played on the same stage as Nō and that, traditionally, the two are performed alternately, it is in all respects the opposite of Nō—masks are not usually worn, its themes are comic, its language is close to everyday speech, and it does not as a rule have musical accompaniment—and it has fewer musical elements than the other forms. Nevertheless, the language it uses has a distinctive intonation and since, in addition, every piece has a place where a song and dance are performed, music is similarly indispensable to it.

This is rather like Kabuki which, at a climactic point, will use a dramatic pose and drop into a metre of seven and five syllables even in its extremely realistic domestic dramas. This metre, far from belonging to Kabuki alone, could be said to represent an innate Japanese sensitivity arising, perhaps, from the particular nature of the Japanese language itself.

I have heard somewhere the view that the ratio of seven to five makes this metre sound attractive because it approximates to the golden section. Also, in his *Nihongo Bunpō* 'Japanese Grammar,' Inoue Hisashi introduces results of psychological tests which indicate that twelve syllables of Japanese are the maximum that can be spoken in one breath, and he offers what seem to me plausible explanations of seven-five or five-seven: a connection with the fixed five-syllable epithets used in ancient poetry and the fact that, since most basic vocabulary in Japanese consists of two syllables, common combinations of two or three words and a one-syllable grammatical particle naturally produce five or seven syllables.

Whatever its origin, however, the seven-five metre has come down in traditional types of poetry from the time of the eighth-century *Manyōshū* 'Collection of Ten Thousand Leaves' anthology, through linked-verse forms to puppet-theatre texts and Kabuki, and in modern times from songs of political satire beginning in the latter part of the last century, through the wildly successful 'Katyusha's Song' from Matsui Sumako in the stage version of Tolstoy's *Resurrection*, to the present day where it still lives on in popular songs. . . .

It is true that there are people who lament the fact that modern songs may be losing the seven-five metre, but that itself is simply because this rhythm is something essentially Japanese. It is not surprising, then, that together with poetic plays on words it causes more difficulty in translating than anything else. I myself had some small experience of this. When I made my first study trip overseas in 1957, to the Harvard-Yenching Institute headed at the time by Professor Edwin Reischaeur, I was immediately asked by a radio station to give a talk on the characteristics of Japanese, for a series called 'Living with Languages.' I brought up the subject of the seven-five metre only to find that, as it was an English-language broadcast, I had to struggle for a whole evening to translate the passage 'Under a hazy moon. . . .' along the Sumidagawa riverbank from *Sannin Kichisa* quoted earlier, to set beside poems such as the one beginning 'Dawn light over the eastern moors. . . .' and the haiku 'Ah, an old pond.'

Not only monologues in seven-five metre but Kabuki lines generally have a samisen musical accompaniment known as *aikata*. So standard is this that when there is no samisen at all, an actor at a rehearsal will make a point of warning that he is having to do it solo. There are also occasions, for particularly emotional passages and the like, when a type of fiddle is used.

This accompaniment comes from the geza, which is shut off from the rest of the stage by black-painted bamboo blinds and filled with all kinds of musical instruments—from the samisen, fiddle, flute, the *ōdaiko* 'great drum,' various kinds of smaller drums, gongs, temple bells, fire bells . . . down to the hollow wooden temple drum.

In Gagaku music (also called Bugaku when accompanied by dance), which was brought over from the continent well over a thousand years ago and established without change as a court entertainment, regular use is made of sixteen different types of musical instrument, covering wind, string and percussion. In medieval Nō, these were radically reduced to only four, but when Kabuki arose in the early seventeenth century as part of the popular culture, it produced many and varied kinds of instrumental music including those familiar to the ordinary people in their daily lives.

Combinations of such varied instruments and singing to samisen accompaniment reveal by their musical colouring the mood of a play, the feelings of its characters, and so on: country type for a rustic scene, festival style for a popular local festival, a drinking song to convey the atmosphere of the Yoshiwara gay quarters, or an accompaniment from the fiddle for a lament. Various types of this *kuromisu ongaku* 'black-blind music,' as it is called, were scored and published under the title *Kabuki Ongaku Shūsei* 'Compendium of Kabuki Music' by Kineya Eizaemon, who died in 1982 at the age of eighty-eight, but he used to say that there would be 2,000 kinds if the unpuded ones were included.

I have written in a previous section about formalism on the visual side, but what about the other side of the same coin, the sound aspect? Let us consider this by taking as an example the ōdaiko, the biggest of all the instruments in the geza and the one which plays a central role.

In the opening chapter I told how the opening of the curtain in the performance of *Shunkan* in the Soviet Union was met with warm applause. It was mentioned then that this was no doubt due to the combined effect of the ocean scene, so like a woodblock print, and the sound of the waves—from the ōdaiko—so recognizably true to life.

The wave sounds from the ōdaiko are produced by slender oak sticks nearly a metre in length beating on the drum—'don, don, don, don . . .'—gradually faster and faster and more and more loudly until, at the end, come two beats in quick succession—'don-don.' The earlier part represents waves rolling in towards the shore rising higher as they come closer, and the final 'don-don' depicts in sound their crashing against the cliffs.

Modern realistic drama often uses 'gravel waves,' for example, in *Shibahama* and the coastal scene at Atami in *Konjiki Yasha* 'The Slave of Gold': gravel is spread thinly in a big rectangular wicker container, held between the hands and tipped repeatedly to and fro to produce a sound like waves on a beach. This is also much used as a seashore sound effect in radio drama, but classical Kabuki does not use sound effects like these gravel waves which seek to copy nature as closely as possible, but employs instead sounds which 'feel similar' through the use of true musical instruments.

What made an even greater impression at the Russian performances of *Shunkan* was the scene on the hanamichi in the last act. The boat finally sets off, leaving Shunkan alone on the island. At the lines:

'Resigned though he is,
His feelings are those of any other man . . . '
from the gidayū chanter, Shunkan starts onto the hanamichi as he follows the boat. At this, the audience burst into applause, mistakenly assuming that this was the end. But wait—the play goes on. From the direction of the curtain at the far end of the hanamichi comes the rustle of 'wave cloth.' A blue cloth dyed with the white crests of waves is being pulled along with cords by stagehands behind the stage. At the same time, the sounds of the rising tide from the ōdaiko begin to echo more and more loudly.

At this, the audience held their breath and strained their eyes to follow the movement of the cloth. As it moved towards the stage—towards the shore, that is—Shunkan was gradually driven back by the oncoming waves. The audience, however, were now all but oblivious of such things as the characters in the play, so enthralled were they by the representation of the rising sea by a combination of sight and sound in this scene, and so intrigued were they by a uniquely Japanese mode of presentation. Their reactions were exactly the same as those at the first performances in Europe later on, when Shunkan was played by Kanzaburō.

To return to the ōdaiko itself, there are said to be as many as forty different ways of beating the drum.

Its basic sound is for use in festival music, or in battlefield scenes and the like. When its 'dodon' is overlaid with the echoing 'jan-jan-jaran' of the gong—a combination known as 'donjan' or 'donjaran'—it signifies a long-range attack or hand to hand fighting on a battlefield.

This drum can also signify many natural phenomena apart from the sound of waves: rain, wind, thunder, a gale blowing down a dark valley deep in the mountains, running and splashing water. . . . The snow sound is interesting. In nature snow falls soundlessly, but its steady fall is expressed by the ōdaiko. This drum sound is produced by using rather thick and short 'snow sticks,' which are tipped with balls of cotton to give, with a gentle touch, a low, soft sound. At the same time, from a long open-weave basket suspended from the flies above the stage, white paper snow comes fluttering down. Nowadays the paper is cut into squares by machine, but the real thing is 'triangles of snow.' There is even a piece of writing with that title, and it seems to me that kinetically, too, the triangular shape is better suited to flutter and dance like snow.

When things come to this level, there is no way that sound effects can cope. A 'presentation' that goes beyond the bounds of re-presented reality—that may be said to be the advance made by the ōdaiko in its function of creating atmosphere.

The creation of atmosphere or mood—as a classic example of this, we might take the case of ghostly manifestations like that of the tormented wife O-Iwa whose death by poisoning is depicted in *Yotsuya Kaidan* 'A Ghostly Tale from Yotsuya.' When the ghost makes its entrance, nowadays the lighting is simply turned down a little , but in earlier times it was necessary to rely on candles and natural light—as a rule the theatres operated during the daytime—and so the man responsible would make it darker by quietly closing some of the windows and skylights. At this point, from the geza comes the low, soft, fast sound of the ōdaiko.

The play-book annotates this as 'doro-doro' or 'faint doro-doro,' though 'doro-doro' actually represents a sound like distant thunder. Added to this is the unearthly, rising notes of the flute, represented as 'hyū-hyū' and called *netori* 'pitch setting.' Then again, the samisen sometimes comes in here too, and so this combination is called *yūrei sanjū* 'ghost trio.' Just as the ghost eventually makes its appearance, there comes the loud beat of the ōdaiko—doron doron don don don—known as 'big doro.'

I do not know how it is now, but when I was a child our comic books always used the phrase 'hyū doro doro' when a ghost or spirit appeared. This was of course derived from the Kabuki 'ghost trio.'

This is not a representation of reality but a stylized presentation which nevertheless gives a convincing impression of something that is real and natural. The ōdaiko follows the principles of Ikebana that we looked at earlier, and may be said to be a good example in the field of sound for proving the validity of the foreign critics' 'theatre of presentation' and 'stylized naturalism' mentioned in the opening chapter.

When I talk about stylization in Japan or abroad to the few people familiar with traditional Japanese drama, I always reproduce these 'sound effects' of the ōdaiko as I do so, by using my fists and knuckles on the desk.

Wooden clappers (*hyōshigi*) are one of the things peculiar to Kabuki. It is simply a matter of banging together two sticks of white oak, but one side of each is carved so that it has a convex shape. These two sides are banged together, and the accepted view is that the best sound is only produced if they are cut back to back from the same piece of wood.

These clappers are used for signals at the start and end of a performance, though the closing ones are regarded as being especially difficult because of the variety of different beats required. For example, when the actor in the main role gives some sign by saying a particular line and banging down his sword or opening his fan with a snap, the clappers are struck once with a loud 'choon.' A further line will lead to a picture-scene dramatic pose, whereupon the beats go 'chon chon . . .' and the curtain closes. If it is an historical piece full of ceremony in which the main character is a nobleman or warrior, however, there is at first a loud slow 'choon choon chon chon' beat that gradually becomes faster; but in an informal domestic drama, the beats are in contrast short and quick, becoming gradually slower.

What is critical in all this is the *ma* 'interval,' hence, 'timing.' It could well be referred to instead as 'breath' or 'breathing,' but this matter of the interval is regarded as so very important, whether it be in Nō, Kabuki or Bunraku, that a progressive research group called The Traditional Performing Arts Society which has continued since the war carried out a study of the subject over several years.

At the time of the first performances in the United States, one of the things that did not go well with American staff no matter what we did was the opening and closing of the curtain. Kabuki does not use a drop curtain, but a 'pull curtain' opening from left to right. The opening has to be done with a gradually increasing 'touch of speed' in time with the rhythm of the clappers, but at rehearsals it was done time and time again at the same speed, either too slowly or too quickly. In the end, it was decided that this depended on a uniquely Japanese awareness, and at each performance a Japanese assistant took charge of it.

This increasing touch of speed involved in the opening of the curtain is not easy to achieve, probably because it is something physiological, acquired not by reason but by personal experience. The clapper effect known as *tsuke* is very similar. When there are dramatic poses or fights in aragoto scenes, a black-robed stage assistant sitting in the front righthand corner of the stage will beat a violent rat-tat-tat on a thick wooden block with two clapper-like sticks at fixed points in the performance. This is the *tsukeuchi* 'beating,' and its function is to give added emphasis to the stylized nature of the performance by using this extra sound. If the timing is off, the sound itself will sound ludicrously off-beat.

In Kabuki the clappers and the beating, in Nō the sound of the drums and the calls of the drummers—like the 'cloth-tearing cries' in sword fighting, these are all delicate, split-second interval markers which, so to speak, cut up time and space.

Through such a meticulous sense of timing, plastic beauty and a sensibility to sound use the medium of drama to portray a world of formal beauty in space and time—this is what gives Japanese theatre its special flavour. Content and literary quality are all very well, but first and foremost it is beauty of form which delights the physical senses.

As we saw at the beginning of this chapter, in the west the modern period brought with it a complete division of a comprehensive theatre into three lines concentrating on drama, music, and the dance or other plastic forms—whereupon a figure emerged to advocate the creation of a 'comprehensive performing art' as a harmonious whole by reuniting these same three elements. This was Richard Wagner (1813-83), immortalized by such works as *Tannhauser*, *Tristan and Isolde*, *Lohengrin*, and *The Mastersingers*. His proposal having been for a synthesis of the above three elements (sometimes called the 'Three Ts Principle' since he referred to them as Tichtkunst, Tonkunst and Tanzkunst respectively), Japanese theatre can be said to correspond in form to this comprehensive performing art of his, albeit with some variations in balance among the elements depending on type.

It can also perhaps be said that it was this 'comprehensiveness' and the 'physical sensation of formal beauty' which attracted the west to Japanese things in modern times, for it had long been without them and was already aware of the impasse it had reached with its modernism while, conversely, Japan was gradually forgetting the existence of its own traditional arts in her efforts to learn the realism of the west.

In this connection, I am reminded that in recent years the term 'total theatre' has been much in vogue. Everyone has his own idea of what it means and it seems to be awash with high-sounding theory and sociological interpretation, but I feel that what it comes down to is a contemporary search for a comprehensive theatre with roots going back to Wagner—in other words, a search for a Japanese-style theatrical form.

Chapter Four

EMOTIONS AND LAMENTATION

Partings and Tears

The Drama of Separation and Ephemeral Life

So far we have been searching for purely Japanese conceptions as we examined forms of presentation in Nō, Kabuki and the like: the free and fluid treatment of time and space; stylized aesthetics which gives pleasure to both eyes and ears, by sight and sound, at the same time; pictorial scenes; asymmetry; introduction, development and climax; middle-tone colour; seven-five metre; intervals and timing; and then, to bring it all together, the artistic boundaries of 'presentation' instead of representation. . . .

What, then, is traditional Japanese theatre seeking to put before the audience by means of these unique forms, and what is the audience looking for in the plays?

Plays being undeniably an end in themselves, the aim of giving anything or gaining anything through them is surely only secondary. I should say, though, that plays having this aim do of course exist. Medieval religious plays in the west, for example, had the particular purpose of propagating and reinforcing Christian teaching. In Japan too the Shinpa theatre which began in 1888 was a means of encouraging the spread of the movement for democratic rights, and the proletarian drama movement of the 1910s and 1920s was clearly in the service of the political movement aiming at social revolution.

What we are going to consider here, however, is not the various 'messages' that were the aim of such propaganda plays but, more purely, what aspects of humanity do Japanese plays treat as their most important material.

If the answer is that, since it is a matter of the content of plays, it will be 'dramatic material,' that could be an end to it; but there are surely all kinds of dramatic material. One can see it in Greek drama, for example, as being the struggle between man and a mighty destiny beyond the power of man or god, and in the modern drama of Ibsen as being the struggle between the individual or the self and conventional society. In each case, though, they were plays which take issue, logically and verbally, with the 'dramatic dissension' itself.

There are, of course, dramatic dissensions in Japanese plays too. Some people put forward the view that there is no drama as such in Japan, but this is nonsense as we have seen already from such plays as *Shunkan* and *Chūshingura*. The question is a quite separate one, however, when we come down to asking whether or not following through the dramatic development is itself the whole of the content, or the main feature of the content, presented on the stage.

In other words, when the Japanese watch a play, can they achieve satisfaction or at least an emotional catharsis by following the dramatic development in a logical way?

To start from my conclusion, it is my feeling that generally in the case of Japan, at least in the case of her traditional theatre, satisfaction is gained through the faculties of sight and sound, and through the enjoyment of the 'emotions' and 'lingering feelings' arising from the process and results of the dramatic development—but why should this be so?

In this chapter, therefore, I shall consider how these emotions and lingering feelings, in fact the emotional nature of the Japanese generally, are shown in plays and where they come from. What then looms particularly large in this is the emotion of grief, especially the feeling of sadness at parting.

This is not only true of plays. The most honest evidence of such inclinations is to be found in media forms close to everyday life such as popular songs and television drama. I have beside me a song-book belonging to my young daughter and entitled *1,001 Melodies from the World of Song*, and it is surprising how many of them have words like 'tearful,' 'parting,' 'journey,' and 'sadness' just in their titles. Since this is the case even at the seemingly hard-bitten present day when rock and the samba are in fashion, it is only reasonable to suppose that tears and partings must have appeared still more frequently before the war when the mood was expressed by the tango and blues. It has often been said too that even our bright songs sound sad to foreigners. I think perhaps the start of these melancholy songs was *Katyusha's Song*, which was such a big hit from 1913 onwards. This is the song mentioned earlier, from Shimamura Hōgetsu's stage version of Tolstoy's novel *Resurrection*, in which Matsui Sumako took the lead.

'How wretched am I, your Katyusha!
Parting is such pain—
Before the snowflakes melt,
Let us at least pray together, ra-ra,
To the gods above'

The composer, Nakayama Shinpei, is said to have had great trouble because Sumako was tone deaf. It is rather ironic, but he apparently put in the meaningless interjection 'ra-ra' because he could not do anything else for her at that point, only to find that it caught on and brought the song enormous popularity. This would probably never have happened if it had been written for a singer with professional training but, instead, it had been composed for an actress who had no grounding or aptitude in music and this produced a popular song that could be sung by anyone.

As can be seen from the above lines, it is a song about the sadness of parting. Even the audiences of ordinary people who knew nothing of Tolstoy the author were moved to sentimental tears by this melancholy song from Sumako in the role of Katyusha, in the scene where she leaves her lover and is sent off through the snow to Siberia for a murder she did not commit. The extent of the play's popularity can be judged from the fact that no fewer than 444 performances are on record as having taken place in all parts of Japan and, further afield, in Taiwan, Korea, Dalian and Vladivostok.

Then too, the sales of records of the song put out by the Orient Co. are said to have reached 20,000, a level without precedent at the time. In my opinion, this *Katyusha* song marked the change from the songs of street entertainers which began as vehicles for ideas about democratic rights to the period of ordinary popular songs as at present. Having been born after the Great Kantō Earthquake of 1923, I do not personally know that period, but when my mother was well into her eighties she told me nostalgically that it was a favourite song for her when she was in her mid-teens and that it was to be heard everywhere in even the most out of the way places.

Not only current songs but also the most widely popular films and TV dramas—this is not said wholly in a bad sense—generally have a theme of separation, in the form of either a simple parting, a reunion after a sad parting, or a situation in which it is impossible to meet. What are called 'mother pieces,' represented by *Mabuta no Haha* 'Long-lost Mother' and *Ganpeki no Haha* 'Quayside Mother,' are one such type, and this kind of separation within a family is particularly common.

These feelings of grief at separation, which have continued from *Katyusha* to the present day, are directly connected with the puppet theatre and Kabuki of the immediately preceding Edo period and, if earlier roots are sought, it is probably possible to go right back to the time of the eighth-century *Manyōshū*. I intend to look at this again when we consider the michiyuki 'travel passage' (usually in the sense of a 'lovers' suicide trip') which seems to me to show this particular feature best, but there can be no doubt that the Japanese are a race that enjoys grief, sorrow and melancholy.

This kind of mood is of course not limited to Japan. If we take songs, for instance, such things as the French chanson, Spanish flamenco, and the love song of an Arab I once heard on a dhow on the Nile as dusk fell, all show that sorrowful songs are to be found throughout the world. The countries of southern Europe, including France, are particularly susceptible to moods and fantasies. For example, the French films *Pépé le Moko* and *La Paquebot "Tenacity,"* directed by Julien Duvivier, are numbered among the great films of the past and became famous for their closing scenes of parting in an atmosphere of indefinable emptiness and sorrow.

To go back a little further, there are the Romantic plays of the nineteenth century, especially the later works known as melodramas and well made plays—'well made' in the sense of keeping the audience on the edge of their seats and moving them to tears. A good example of this is the masterpiece *Camille*, by the younger Dumas.

This story has been made even more famous by Verdi's *La Traviata* and, as everyone knows, is about a prostitute whose very devotion to a young nobleman leads her to sacrifice her love for him by giving him up. The last scene is a sentimental one of reunion and parting when the man, having learned why she broke with him, rushes back and finds her on her death-bed suffering from a lung disease aggravated by grief.

This is certainly to the taste of the Japanese, so much so that in fact it was adapted for modern Japanese drama and staged by the Shinpa theatre as early as the Meiji period, and the dramatic story was used in many fine plays such as *Zangiku Monogatari* 'The Story of the Lingering Chrysanthemum.'

Incidentally, apropos of the melodramatic nature of films mentioned earlier, the new medium of films can be said to have inherited this characteristic from the later Romantic theatre represented by this same *Camille*. This is not an original view of my own, but was a thoroughly sound one, in my opinion, put forward by Nicholas Vardac in his excellent book *Stage to Screen*.

When television came along, it was taken over again by TV drama, and this has brought melodrama into our living rooms. Now that this has happened, however, and the west has the same kind of theatre too, it may give rise to doubts about whether the undoubted Japanese liking for a mood of sadness can any longer be called a particularly Japanese trait.

It is certainly not something that exists only in Japan. Love, sadness at parting, and suffering are virtually instinctive emotions between relatives, married couples and lovers. It is only natural, therefore, that they should be involved as common factors, but when I venture to present them here as a particularly Japanese trait, it is because I feel something very singular in this dominance of the emotions—the tendency to give the biggest part to the feelings and aftermath of sorrow, grief and so on—being found in *all kinds* of plays.

Kyōgen at least may be said to be an exception, but I think this is because these plays developed as 'interlude comedies' performed between one Nō play and another. As Nō is a very emotionally charged song and dance form, they doubtless took the contrasting form of comic, rather cynical and unemotional sketches in order to refresh and restore the spirits of the audience. Nō and Kyōgen supplement each other by reciprocal forms and methods, to create between them a complete human world.

Melodrama certainly exists in the west. In one period it was the representative type of theatre and it has been kept alive among the ordinary people ever since. But the mainstream of western drama is the line in which audiences gain satisfaction not so much through the emotions as from following the kind of dramatic development mentioned above through the exercise of reason until a logical conclusion is reached. For example, after nineteenth-century western drama gave up melodrama to the world of films, it saw the blossoming of virtually the opposite type of bloodless plays which, as if they were 'laboratories of human life,' required their audiences to use their reason to consider what human existence is all about—that is, Ibsen's plays about social problems. It is in fact this type that has been the mainstream since the drama of ancient Greece.

In Japan a popular literary drama was firmly established by Chikamatsu Monzaemon (d.1724), but even this has as its first consideration scenes which made an even greater appeal to the emotions. To put it the other way round, we could say that complicated drama in Japan will not engage the sympathy of the audience unless it has parts which appeal to the emotions.

This is not unconnected with the particular trait noted in the previous chapter, by which the mainstream of drama in Japan aims primarily at form through musicality and plastic beauty, as opposed to that in the west where the drama is verbal. Melodrama itself arose from 'plays accompanied by music,' as can be seen from this originally Greek word, a combination of *melos* 'music' and *drama*.

Westerners generally are good at the verbal expression of reasoned argument and logical exposition, and will pursue a discussion through to the bitter end. The Japanese, though, tend to become more understanding at some suitable point in a discussion and to bring it to an end by creating the right atmosphere with some inconclusive comment. This difference may be said to be reflected in their theatre too.

Let us, then, take the questions of what is meant in the west by 'drama' and where the distinctive features of Japanese theatre are to be found, and examine them in a concrete way by looking at how plays are put together and how the high points of sight and sound are created.

Scenes of Grief

Emotions and the Principles of Plot

I have already had occasion to say something about the structure of western drama, in the course of which I wrote that the essence of drama lies in the struggle and the dissensions between man and his fate, or the individual and society. It is worth adding in this connection that the Chinese character for *geki* 'drama' also originally contained the idea of 'dissension.' It is made up of three elements, with the meanings of 'tiger,' 'wild boar' and 'knife,' to signify a situation in which two fierce and well matched creatures like a tiger and wild boar bare their knife-like fangs and claws and, as the saying "Two heroes will not stand side by side" goes, fight to the death of one or the other of them. In other words, it signified 'dissension' or 'strife.'

It therefore came to mean 'violent, fierce,' as in such words as *gekiyaku* 'violent poison, powerful drug.' The original and classic example of this drama of violent strife is the Greek tragedy *Oedipus Rex* which was mentioned before, and in Aristotle's *Poetics*, the famous treatise on tragedy in which he discusses this as a model work, he has the following lines:

'A tragedy is an imitation of a serious action which,
   having due magnitude, is complete in itself. . . .'

In these lines, he states succinctly that, since drama is performed before an audience, it should not be unduly long but brought to a conclusion within a suitable span; its purpose is a representation of human life; and the material treated is one coherent action. He defines the meaning of 'completeness' by saying 'A complete thing is one that has a beginning, a middle and an end.'

Although playwrights such as Shakespeare and Lope de Vega in Spain's Golden Age ignored or criticized the very forms required by the three unities, the essence of their work lies in such things as a unified type of drama with a beginning, a middle and an end; and in scenes which, numerous though they may be, are each based on a represented realism and move ahead unswervingly by means of a reasoned development of a confrontation fought with words. There is thus nothing to choose between them and the classicism running down from Greek drama to Ibsen and beyond.

In contrast, although Japanese theatre also undoubtedly sets great store by dramatic development as we have seen from the examples of *Shunkan* and *Chūshingura*, its prime concern is nevertheless high points of sight and sound. This characteristic belongs not to Japan alone but to the east as a whole. An indication of this can be seen in the use in this context of the character *gi* 'playfulness, sport' in China and over a long period in Japan too. Until about the middle of the nineteenth century it was used in Japan to mean 'a play'; hence, *gijō* literally 'play place' was used for 'theatre' before it was replaced by the modern word *gekijō*, literally 'drama place.' The use of the character *geki* 'drama' in such compound words as *engeki* 'drama, the theatre' began in the Meiji period after the introduction of the western concept of drama.

Japanese theatre provides rich enjoyment for the eyes and ears by means of high points of sight and sound in each scene, and it appeals to the hearts of the audience not so much through reason as the emotions.

To take Nō first, its plays are, as it were, one-act pieces which have neither curtain nor sets. Instead, they have at their heart not dramatic development in itself but the mood of *yūgen* 'elegant beauty' expressed by song and dance.

Naturally, within Nō there are works rich in dramatic elements which are therefore distinguished by the term *geki Nō* 'dramatic Nō.' A typical example of this kind is *Ataka*, the origin of the Kabuki play *Kanjinchō*. one of the Eighteen Kabuki Pieces: a clear dramatic confrontation develops on the stage between the official at the barrier who tries to stop Yoshitsune and his party from passing and Benkei, the senior retainer, who tries to force a way through after reading out the subscription list which is claimed to be the reason for their journey.

This type of play is, however, exceptional in Nō, and the dramatic element itself can be regarded as secondary even in virtually all the plays within the category of dramatic Nō. One example is *Aoi no Ue*, which was mentioned before. The struggle between the wraith of Lady Rokujō and the priest is certainly a dramatic element, but its development and conclusion are not the main consideration in this Nō. The aim is the expression, through song and dance, of a 'feeling' or 'mood,' in this case of female jealousy or the karma of passion. Still more clearly is this the aim of yūgen-style spirit (*mugen*) works like *Hagoromo*, *Matsukaze* and *Izutsu* 'The Well Frame,' which are regarded as examples of the most representative type of Nō.

The idea of introduction, development and climax (jo-ha-kyū) as a rule of development in Nō was introduced in the previous chapter. This three-stage development is very like Aristotle's 'beginning, middle and end.'

On a broad view, it can probably be said to be a concept common to all things. A human life has youth, middle age and old age. A day has morning, noon and night. Even a written thesis will hardly be in good order unless it is complete with introduction, main text and conclusion. There is nothing that does not have a beginning, a middle and an end. Aristotle is surely not alone in regarding these three parts as a necessity for a drama which mirrors human life.

What is important in this, however, is that in contrast to the western drama concept of beginning, middle and end as three stages in the logical development of a verbal drama, Zeami's introduction, development and climax in Nō is a concept about the progression of song and dance.

If we look for something comparable in the west, we should probably turn instead to opera or songs, with their introductory section or overture, main section or movement, and finale. In his *Kadensho*, Zeami explained his teaching by saying that the introduction should be done 'smoothly and easily,' the development should consist of 'good Nō, performed in an accomplished style,' and the climax should be 'at a fast tempo, displaying every possible skill.'

Since the idea of introduction, development and climax came originally from a musical theory in Gagaku, it is only natural that in Nō too it should be a principle of structural arrangement which has as its criteria such things as the tempo of music and dance and the level of intricacy of their techniques. Zeami applied his ideas on this not only to the structure of a single play but, on a larger scale, to the arrangement of a whole day's programme. For this, five plays with one from each of the five types known as god, man, woman, madness and devil, are considered ideal, and Zeami saw the arrangement as consisting of one play for the introduction, three plays for the development (one each for the same three jo-ha-kyū divisions within the development section), and one for the climax.

In the seventeenth century this concept of introduction, development and climax spread from *jōruri* 'musical recitation for the puppet theatre' to Kabuki. In its earliest period the recitation was descriptive poetry in even-numbered six or twelve sections in keeping with the *Heike Monogatari* 'Tales of the Heike' on which it was based, but it came to be arranged into five sections as its content became more dramatic. One cannot help thinking that there was at work here the five-play structure in Nō and the idea of introduction, development and climax which lay behind it. The final result was five sections for historical plays and three for domestic dramas. Within the five sections of historical plays a sorrowful scene so beloved of the Japanese was clearly positioned in the key third section.

This five-section pattern was formulated by Takemoto Gidayū (1651-1715), the founder of gidayū music (a type of jōruri) which is the samisen music used in Bunraku. In the preface to his anthology entitled *Jōkyō Yonen Gidayū Danmono-shū* 'The 1687 Collection of Selected Gidayū Passages' he stated that a jōruri piece should be in five sections covering five situations: love, bloodshed, grief, travel passage, and dialogue. Thereafter, jōruri texts were generally made in accordance with this principle of development.

The origin of most incidents, now as in times past, is the complications of love between man and woman. That brings about a violent quarrel, that is, a scene of bloodshed. This leads, say, to the death of a relative and the grief of parting from someone in this life. Inevitably, there is then a travel passage during the unavoidable flight or suicide journey. Finally, however, questions and answers having revealed the truth of the matter, evil is brought down and right triumphs, to the relief and satisfaction of all.

This means, then, that grief is placed as an indispensable element within a drama and, what is more, at the peak of its development. Such a dramatic structure has surely never existed in any other country. Here is to be seen, I feel, the particular Japanese feature of putting the emotions first.

It should be pointed out, however, that in adopting the spirit of jo-ha-kyū from Nō, this five-section sequence was defined in auditory terms as narrative and music, rather than as drama itself. The first section, for example, is said to be 'recited very clearly, as if unravelling a tangled thread,' and the second 'with a complete change, but not in too melancholy a way.' What, then, of the third section? This is what Gidayū has to say:

> 'On the Third Section— . . . The third section is the heart of the piece. . . . The grief is to be conveyed in the recitation without neglecting reality but with the piece as a whole in the forefront of your mind.'

The importance attached to capturing the emotions of the audience is clear, and even this short passage makes it obvious too that the third section was the core of the whole thing. At any rate, each section has its own particular mood, there is variety, and the sequence is carefully worked out. It is on these things that Japanese theatre has focussed with the utmost care, rather than anything like a reasoned story line.

Because of this, although the text of *Chūshingura*, for example, was specifically written as if the events took place in the Muromachi period (1336-1573) in order to escape the attention of the authorities, the main scenes such as the lord's harakiri, that of his young retainer Kanpei, the Ichiriki teahouse at Gion in Kyoto, and the final attack, are all unmistakably set in the contemporary world of the first few years of the eighteenth century when the vendetta in fact occurred. Similarly, *Sugawara Denju Te-narai Kagami* has Michizane as its main character and is therefore a tale of the Heian period, but its main scene, *Terakoya* 'The Village School,' has the manners, customs and emotions of the Edo period when it was written.

Such plays treat as secondary the logic and realism of such things as consistency in the period setting and compatibility in its customs, dress and social environment, and they are created on the basis of each aspect of a play having its own existence. This is markedly different from plays like those of Shakespeare, which have a coherence about them even when

they too have a large number of scenes and extend over a considerable length of time.

Kabuki is more visual than the puppet theatre, and is therefore more extreme in its tendency to cater to the seeing eye
and to base itself on its themes. The *Kezairoku* 'A Record of
Playful Treasures' of 1801, said to be the work of the Kabuki
playwright Namiki Shōzō II and thought to have been written by referring to such things as the concepts of jo-ha-kyū
in Nō and the five-section structure of puppet drama, states
that a play is created by bringing together the 'warp' and the
'weft.'

The 'warp' means the world of, say, the *Taikōki* 'The Life
of Toyotomi Hideyoshi' (one of the greatest figures in Japanese
history, who died in 1598) or the *Taiheiki* 'Chronicles of the
Great Peace' (which covers the period 1318-1368); and the 'weft'
refers to subjects such as the famous robber Ishikawa Goemon, the tragic love of O-Karu and Kanpei, or Sukeroku's visits
to the Yoshiwara pleasure quarters. The combination of a subject concerning the visits there of Sukeroku, an eighteenth-
century Edo townsman, and the twelfth-century world of the
revenge of the Soga brothers is hugely popular even today as
Sukeroku, one of the Eighteen Kabuki Pieces. It led to a ridic-
ulous plot in which Sukeroku is said to be in fact the younger
Soga brother, but audiences were similarly quite undisturbed
by such illogicality. After all, dramatic development as such
was not the object of the piece.

What, then, is the content of this 'sorrow' which is positioned at the heart of a play, and where does it come from?
Let us look at these questions a little more closely.

Family Drama

The Dramatic Content of Kumagai Jinya
'Kumagai's Camp'

The most classic scenes of sorrow which appear in the puppet drama and Kabuki are those on the theme of the separation of parent and child. One example is the play *Sugawara Denju Te-narai Kagami*. With *Chūshingura* and *Yoshitsune Senbonzakura*, it ranks as one of the three finest works in the repertoire, and the *Terakoya* section in it is particularly renowned.

This contains a 'parting from a severed head,' when Matsuomaru confronts the head of his own child whom he has sacrificed in order to save the son of his lord. There are, however, two other types of parting in the play: a 'parting in life' when Sugawara Michizane takes a silent farewell of his daughter Princess Kariya as he goes on his way to exile in Kyūshū; and a 'parting in death' when, to atone for a crime against his master, Sakuramaru commits harakiri in front of his father.

This play is the combined work of Takeda Izumo II, Namiki Senryū, and Miyoshi Shōraku, and they are said to have written it by each taking one of these stories about the separation of parent and child.

It is only natural that the stronger the bonds between such close relatives, the greater the sorrow at parting and the sympathy it causes. The popularity of plays about the separation of parent and child can be said to derive from the strength of family ties among the Japanese of the time, but such relationships seem to remain surprisingly close even today.

It was not so long ago that I was surprised at some figures relating to this. The results of the *Comparative International Survey on Life and Perceptions among Old People* carried out by the Prime Minister's Office in January 1981 and published on the front page of the *Asahi* newspaper on 15 September, showed that the elderly in Japan belonged more to the 'family oriented' type than those in Europe or America.

The survey covered five countries: Japan, America, Britain, France, and Thailand. In answers about relationships with children and grandchildren, 59% in Japan said that they would like to live with them permanently. There was the same proportion in Thailand, but in the west the figures were only 7% in America, 6% in Britain, and 12% in France. In America and France, the highest figures were for meeting now and then to have a meal and talk together, with 66% and 82% respectively. In Britain, 40% voted for this 'now and then,' while for 44% it was enough just to have a chat occasionally.

Taken in conjunction with other questions, the results show that old people in Japan are unsociable, relying heavily as they do on married sons and, in particular, on daughters and daughters-in-law. Even so, the size of the gap with the west was surprising. Although Japan is, by common consent, the most modernized country in East Asia, this is simply a matter of industrial and economic power. If the modern aim is 'the autonomy and independence of the individual,' there can be no denying that there is nothing modern at all in the hearts and minds of her people.

There are questions about social welfare and all kinds of other problems; there may also be things to be said for and against in each case; and the Prime Minister's Office survey was itself said to be for the purpose of future policy. But, broadly speaking, the cause in the last analysis is surely the weakness in the modern period of a Japan which had to over-take the modern *civilization* of the west without ever having, as the west had, an industrial revolution followed by a civil revolution which modernized personal freedom among the ordinary people.

In other words, there was no self-produced *Doll's House* to follow *Camille*. Leaving aside what may happen in the future, the continued existence of the mood expressed by Katyusha's song and the retention of melodrama are surely due to the continued but unrecognized vitality of a Japanese-style sorrow, a sadness at partings, which took shape in the pre-modern Edo period.

Returning to our main theme, I would now like to take up the dramatization of the historically famous battle of Ichino-tani, as the most classic example of a play constructed around the situation of a parting of parent and child.

The original story is the true one of the celebrated fight on horseback between Kumagai Naozane and Taira no Atsumori.

> 'Having lost the battle of Ichinotani,
> How sad the young Taira noble, struck down there.
> In the cold dawn, carried by the wind on Suma
>   beach,
> Is this what was heard—his Green-leaf Flute?'

This is *Aoba no Fue* 'The Green-leaf Flute,' with words by Ōwada Tateki, which was designated as the 'elementary-school song' in 1906. It is a well-known song, very familiar to me as one who was a child in the late 1920s and 1930s.

When the Taira forces were escaping to sea in boats, following their crushing defeat by Minamoto Yoshitsune, one horseman fell behind, the young warrior Atsumori. As he urged his white charger into the sea, he was called back by Kumagai Naozane, one of the Minamoto commanders, and after they had fought together, his head was cut off. . . .

The *Heike Monogatari* is a great epic poem, full of tragedy, which depicts the downfall of the Taira clan, and among its various stories this section on 'The Death of Atsumori,' dealing as it does with the death in battle of a handsome boy about to blossom into manhood, is notable for the depth of its pathos and sense of the impermanence of human life.

Kabuki presents the battle on horseback in the sea, and it was mentioned in an earlier chapter how, when it does so, it uses children in an ingenious 'distant view' technique to make the combatants appear smaller and further away. What I would like to raise here, however, concerns Kumagai's initial hesitation and reluctance to kill Atsumori.

According to the original work, Kumagai did hesitate, but seeing that he and Atsumori were surrounded at a distance by his own forces, he thought that, even if he were to let the boy escape, he would only be killed by someone else. Resolving, therefore, that it would be better for Atsumori to die by his hand and for himself to spend the rest of his life praying for the repose of his soul, he then killed him 'weeping and weeping again.' He learns later that the boy was the son of Tsunemori (and the grandson of Kiyomori), and his flute is also discovered. Kumagai was so deeply moved by Atsumori's gentleness and charm, it is said, that life's impermanence was brought home to him still more and this confirmed him in his resolve to enter into the Buddhist life. . . .

Why, then, did Kumagai hesitate to kill Atsumori, and how is this dealt with in the play? These are the questions to be looked at here.

Two reasons are given in the original story in the *Heike Monogatari*.

The first is that Atsumori was 'fifteen or sixteen years old,' was 'lightly made-up, with elegantly blackened teeth' and 'truly fair of face.' The blackening of teeth began as a personal adornment among women of the nobility in the Heian period, but from about the end of the eleventh century it came to be done by the men of that class too. Kumagai therefore realised at a glance that Atsumori was a high-born noble, and was further struck by his good looks and air of refinement which extended even to a light makeup.

It is clear that Kumagai himself was no mere rough soldier either, but a person who understood beauty and elegance. Even on the field of battle he was mindful of such things as flowers and beauty in general—something that could be described, perhaps, as an expression of the spirit of Japan. This is also linked to the way he had been moved by the haunting sound of the flute that could be heard coming from the enemy camp the previous night, and to his actions in blaming himself for killing the owner of the flute, Atsumori, and in giving up his life as a soldier for the priesthood.

The second reason given is that he was overcome by fatherly love. He himself had a son, Kojirō, of the same age, who had been slightly wounded when he was hit in the left elbow by an arrow at the height of the battle the previous day. It was not a critical injury but, as his father, Naozane had been extremely anxious. All this is set out in detail in the chapter immediately before 'The Death of Atsumori.' When Kumagai, then, looked down at Atsumori as he was about to strike off his head, he saw that the boy 'is the same age as my son Kojirō,' and expressed his feelings of deep sympathy in the words, 'When I think how tormented I was when Kojirō suffered just a slight wound, what grief will the father of this lord feel when he hears that he has been killed?'

How, then, was this true story scripted for the stage? Understandably enough, it would be likely to reflect the particular nature of the period and of the class of audience whose support brought the play into being, and although the medieval Nō on the one hand and the later puppet theatre and Kabuki on the other are alike in putting the emphasis on atmosphere, the way they treat the material is completely different. This is what I meant when I was discussing in the opening chapter what is inherently Japanese and said that, although these forms are all parts of Japanese drama as a whole, they are in a certain sense completely different from each other.

The Nō play *Atsumori* boldly ignores the second of these reasons and concentrates on the charm, elegance and refinement of the first. When Kumagai, now a Buddhist priest with the name Rensei Hōshi, comes to the old battlefield of Ichinotani and chants prayers there, the beautiful sound of a flute is heard and a young rushcutter appears. When Kumagai asks about the flute, the young man replies that it was he who had been playing it and then vanishes after revealing himself to be the ghost of Atsumori who had been killed there. Later the spirit appears in the imposing form of Atsumori in former days, sings and dances to a passage telling of his sufferings in the Hell of Warriors, and finally achieves salvation through the intervention and prayers of Kumagai. . . .

It is a fine piece in which the wickedness and futility of war, the transience of human life, and the view of the impermanence of all things which permeated the medieval period together form a sad theme, but it contains only the refinement associated with the flute and the elegance of yūgen, and does not take up anything of the blood and family ties—the bonds between parent and child—which are so hard to sever.

Even in Nō there are of course various plays such as *Sumidagawa* and *Yoroboshi* 'The Infirm Priest' which have as their theme the separation of parent and child; but they depict simply and straightforwardly within an atmosphere of elegant beauty a single emotion, namely, the feelings of parent and child after they have become separated from each other. They are not constructed to show that the two were forced to part for some particular reason, because of duty to a lord, for example, or an obligation owed to someone.

When it comes to the puppet theatre and Kabuki, however, this same story about 'The Death of Atsumori' becomes a completely different kind of play. There are many similar works,

The Kabuki *Sonezaki Shinjū*.

The Kabuki dance p
Musume Dōjō-ji.

The Kabuki *Yanone*.

The Bunraku play *Imoseyama Onna Teikin*.

The Bugaku dance *Ryōō*.

The Kyōgen *Tsuri-gitsune*.

The Nō *Takasago*.

An Edo-period *Nara e-hon* illustration
of O-Kuni Kabuki.

The Kabuki
Yoshitsune Senbonzakura.

The Bunraku play
Yoshitsune Senbonzakura.

The Bunraku play *Dannoura Kabuto Gunki*.

The Kubuki *Kanjinchō*.

The Kabuki *Sugawara Denju Te-narai Kagami*.

The Kabuki *Kuwanaya Tokuzō Irifune Monogatari*.

e Kabuki *Kuruwa Bunshō*.

The Nō *Okina*.

but the finest and greatest of them is the complicated five-act jōruri piece called *Ichinotani Futaba Gunki*, and the highlight of it is the third act, the scene at 'Kumagai's Camp,' which follows the second act showing 'The Fight at Suma Bay.'

This third act was written in 1751 by Namiki Sōsuke and it proved to be the last work of the man who was also the main author of *Chūshingura, Sugawara Denju Te-narai Kagami* and *Yoshitsune Senbonzakura*. It was around that time that the puppet theatre, that is, Bunraku, reached its height, for from then on it fell into a decline as it gradually lost its strength to Kabuki and became a static classic form. Being the work it was, though, this 'Kumagai's Camp' was a tour de force in every respect. Even in modern times, it has been performed successively by such figures as the late Nakamura Kichiemon, Matsumoto Hakuō (Kōshirō VIII) who died in 1982, and Onoe Shōroku.

What, then, is the greatest dramatic fiction in this work?

It is that the person Kumagai killed at Ichinotani was in fact not Atsumori but his own son Kojirō. In the fight scene the audience are not aware of this, and it is only in the following camp scene that this fact and the reason for it are revealed. Apart from anything else, it may be said to be splendid drama of reasoned thought.

What compelled him to substitute his own son and to kill him instead? Behind this question stand the supreme figures of the general Yoshitsune as his lord and, over and above him, the emperor. Beside these, the bonds of parental love are just too insignificant.

On the occasion of the battle, Yoshitsune had issued strict orders that anyone of imperial blood was not to be killed, even if he was on the side of the enemy, and that, if an unavoidable situation arose, a member of one's own family was to be sacrificed instead. It was Kumagai's misfortune to have captured Atsumori. It is established in the play that Atsumori is the natural son of the retired emperor Go-Shirakawa and, in

Kumagai's Camp scene in the Kabuki *Ichinotani Futaba Gunki*.

view of his master's orders, Kumagai has no alternative but
to save Atsumori's life by secretly substituting Kojirō for him
and then to cut off the head of his own son.

Some doubt may be felt about the force of such an order,
but in the Edo period when this play was written the criterion
of the absolute power of a feudal lord was rigidly imposed from
above, and so tragic dilemmas arising from this pressure and
ordinary human instinct were no mere figments of the imagination.

At the time, master and retainer were regarded as being
bound together in three existences, husband and wife in two,
and parent and child in one. The three existences were in the
past, the present and the future. Essentially, this view saw
man's existences, in which the blood bond should have been
the strongest, as having a bond between parent and child in
'this world' alone, and the bond established in this world by
man and wife as continuing into the next; but the bond between master and servant, which was no more than a simple

employment relationship, was the firmest of all, being immutable throughout the three existences.

Although it stands reason on its head, this doctrine was intended to strengthen and maintain the feudal system of Tokugawa military rule. In the play Kumagai wears the helmet and armour of a commander in the wars between the Taira and the Minamoto, but as the hero of the drama he is in fact a man of the times under Tokugawa rule who suffers from the contradictory clash between the feudal order and the natural emotions of an individual human being.

With his killing of his own son in place of Atsumori, Kumagai's tragedy may be said to be over. Of late the scene has become known as a leading example of the grief of a 'mother piece,' as we shall see if we go straight on and follow through the camp scene.

Unaware of what has happened, Kumagai's wife Sagami comes to the camp in her anxiety about her son. When she does so, who should arrive there seeking refuge from her pursuers but Fuji no Kata, the mother of Atsumori. Sixteen years earlier, when Sagami had been in the service of the retired emperor and had been condemned to death for a liaison with a warrior called Satake Jirō, she had been saved by this same Fuji no Kata. Both were pregnant at the time, and the children later born to them were Atsumori and Kojirō. (This is the source of the term *futaba*, literally 'two young shoots,' used in the title of the play *Ichinotani Futaba Gunki* 'The Tale of Two Young Warriors at the Battle of Ichinotani.')

The two ladies are happy to see each other again, but when Fuji no Kata learns that Satake Jirō is now called Kumagai Naozane, she presses Sagami to help her take her revenge on him for the death of her son. For Sagami, it is of course her husband's life that is at stake, and yet she cannot defy the order of a mistress to whom she owed so much in the past. Thus, she too is torn by internal conflict, between her duty as a retainer and as a wife; but when Kumagai returns from the battlefield in due course and shows the severed head to Yoshitsune, the two mothers discover for the first time the truth of what has happened. In that instant, their situations are completely reversed, bringing grief to Sagami and sympathy from Fuji no Kata.

This is an out-and-out mother's tragedy which does not appear in the Nō play and even in the original source. What this camp scene in Kabuki does is to put this within the still larger setting of the tragedy of the father, Naozane.

Before long he discards his armour and helmet for the black robe, shaven head and sedge hat of a priest, and with the words 'No longer do I have any emotions or hopes, for I am on my way to the land of Amida Buddha. . . . Oh, sixteen years are an age gone by—a dream, just a dream . . .,' he sets out on a pilgrimage round all the provinces in the land, 'shedding tears like falling dewdrops' according to the puppet text. The words on his lips are supposed to be for the repose of the soul of Atsumori, but it goes without saying that he has become a priest because of the son who died at his own hands. . . .

The Bunraku and Kabuki audiences did not belong to the warrior classes but were ordinary townsmen and farmers. During the Edo period, however, from about the end of the seventeenth century onwards, feudal morality began to permeate the world of the merchants too, through the dealings and political influence which the richest of them had with the military. For them too the master-servant system was absolute, and within the family the 'duty' demanded from daughters-in-law and adopted sons-in-law came to take precedence even over blood ties. Naturally enough, this gave rise to all kinds of difficulties and tragedies far more depressing than had been the case in the medieval period.

The people of Edo who had to live day after day in this fashion were able to see a reflection of themselves in the make-believe that the historical hero Kumagai was after all an ordi-

nary father like themselves, and they were also able to purge
themselves of their pent-up emotions by the tears of sympathy
they shed at the sorrowful scene of the mothers in the third act.

In his *Poetics*, Aristotle described such purging by the term
'catharsis,' which he mentions in his famous definition of
tragedy in Chapter 6:

> 'Tragedy contains incidents arousing pity and fear,
> by which to accomplish a catharsis of such emo-
> tions.'

The word catharsis was originally a term used in pathology.
The Greeks thought that the human body consisted of four
kinds of fluid and that an excessive increase in any one of them
would bring on illness. The illness would therefore be cured
if the balance were restored by expelling this excess body fluid
by some means. This expelling or purging action was called
catharsis. Even today the word is used through a Latin deriv-
ative in such terms as nasal catarrh, intestinal catarrh and
catarrhal pneumonia.

Aristotle applied this word to mental health, and thought
that it was similarly efficacious to expel harmful 'emotions.'
The mainstream of Greek and other western drama, however,
arouses these emotions by pursuing dramatic confrontation
through verbal argument, whereas in Japan this is done by
appealing to the eyes and ears of the audience through the
emotions themselves.

In the medieval period people were surrounded in their daily
lives by a sense of impermanence but gained purification and
release from it by indulging themselves to the full in the sense
of impermanence presented in Nō within a framework of
elegant beauty. The Japanese of the Edo period sought to
dispel the daily gloom that came from their impaired personal
relationships and to gain emotional stability by weeping at the
plays about sorrow within their feudal society.

Thus, in the Edo period the emotionalism of the Japanese established a pattern of melancholy drama about the grief and lamentation at parting from a close member of the family. I wonder whether this again could possibly be produced by the damp and gloomy climatic conditions found in Japan?

Even nowadays in the 1980s, this emotionalism continues to exist within a pre-modern Japanese 'family orientation,' as is clear from the data in the Prime Minister's Office survey. It could be said, for example, that the popularity of Chekhov in modern Japan has been due above all else to the atmosphere of his works. Even *The Cherry Orchard* he meant as a 'comedy' critical of members of the old landowner class who were unaware of their own fate and lacked any personal identity. In Japan, however, it was accepted as an elegy to something that was collapsing, similar in nature to the *Heike Monogatari*, and as a sad piece which was bidding farewell to the better life of former days. Chekhov's poetic sensibility and delicacy of touch suit the Japanese better than the masculine dramas of Ibsen.

There is just one thing I should like to add here, concerning an unexpected experience when I was lecturing on Japanese drama as a Visiting Professor at the Drama Research Institute in the University of Vienna.

Embassies abroad have introductory films on Nō and Kabuki, but since these are far from adequate for students specialising in drama, with the cooperation of the Japan Foundation and the Ministry of Foreign Affairs it was decided that I should take with me some excellent films of performances, most of them in black and white with, of course, no foreign-language commentary or anything like that. Among them was the 'Kumagai's Camp' piece, in which the main role was taken by the late Kichiemon.

It was a long show lasting nearly two hours, but what impressed me most at the time was the comment of a French girl student who, with tears in her eyes, said "The love between parents and child was just beautiful. You can't see that kind of powerful family love in the west any more."

It seems to me that this love of essentially good people within the same family is made all the more emphatic and attractive by being set in a tragedy of the feudal period. When this is accompanied by a full measure of formal beauty as an appeal to the senses of sight and sound, it must surely have heightened the heartfelt honest emotions of the kind of modern westerners who created *Camille* and *Pépé le Moko*. In that case, it seems to me as I recall the reactions overseas to *Shunkan* and *Chūshingura*, that even the fixed patterns of 'grief' peculiar to Japan have within them the possibility of breaking through the barriers of melodrama and becoming human drama instead.

TRAVEL PASSAGES

Lingering Emotion and Feelings on a Journey

Another thing which exists nowhere except in Japan is the michiyuki 'travel passage.'

It was the chanter Takemoto Gidayū who created the michiyuki phase in the fourth act of a play, to follow the 'grief' of the third. This grieving scene is by any standard very harrowing and poignant and so, although the following travel passage is expressive of sorrow, it must be in an altogether lighter and fresher mood. It is, as it were, a world of 'lingering emotion' (*yojō*) which further romanticizes and beautifies the tragedy of the third act. This is why Gidayū said,

> 'It should be recited so that there are no long intervals.
> It is something to recite gently, to the accompaniment of the samisen.'

He also wrote, 'In the michiyuki, the melodious element is the first consideration.' The term 'melodious element' here means dance-like movements done to music—the presentation of a dance-style description of the passing scene. This could be described as the thing which best displays the peculiarly Japanese feature of giving precedence to emotional atmosphere and the senses of sight and sound.

The word michiyuki probably makes most people think of

a young couple's suicide journey, and this has certainly become the most classic form of it. This form began in 1703—the year after the revenge attack by the forty-seven loyal retainers from Akō on which *Chūshingura* is based—when Chikamatsu Monzaemon wrote the puppet play *Sonezaki Shinjū* for the chanter Gidayū.

Having lost all hope of being together in this world because of insuperable problems of feudal obligations and money, the soy merchant Tokubei and the prostitute O-Hatsu commit suicide together, putting all their trust in the teaching that man and woman can be united in two existences. They hurry along at night to the wood around the Tenjin Shrine at Sonezaki which they have decided on as their place of death:

'Farewell to this world,
   And to this night.
As we go to meet death together,
   We are for all the world
Like this frost on the path
   Leading to the grave
That fades away a little more
   With each step we take.
How sad for us,
   This dream of dreams!
We count the ringing of the bell
   To mark the dawn,
And of the seven we await
   Six have now sounded.
The one remaining
   Will, in this life,
Be the last echo of a bell
   We shall ever hear,
An echo that will take us
   Into the next world and peace at last.'

This is a renowned passage which is said to have excited the admiration of even the presumably strait-laced Confucianist Ogyū Sorai.

Chikamatsu was encouraged by the success of this work, and he produced suicide pieces one after the other. There are ten such plays altogether, including the famous *Shinjū Ten no Amijima*, which was even made into a film directed by Shinoda Masahiro and starring Iwashita Shima.

What is more, all these plays have fine michiyuki passages. The poetic emotion of these laments was made still more beautiful by the plaintive but captivating tones of gidayū chanting—with devastating results, for there was a sudden increase in love suicides by young couples. It was a terrible situation in which the cathartic effect of the theatre went beyond all bounds and can only be described as just too effective.

This fact gives some indication of the harshness of life under the system of feudal morality, and it is also proof of how susceptible Japanese are to atmosphere. For the people concerned, suicide offered their greatest chance of happiness, and it was the authorities who became alarmed, with the result that, in 1723, they issued an unprecedented edict banning the composition of suicide plays. This was the year after Chikamatsu wrote his last such play, *Shinjū Yoi-gōshin* 'Suicide on Holy Night.' In the west, suicide is regarded as a sin according to Christian doctrine, but I have never heard of any play involving suicide being banned by law.

At any rate, the michiyuki—and not, of course, simply the suicide michiyuki—is something peculiarly Japanese. In fact, michiyuki which on balance are not suicide trips, such as those of O-Karu and Kanpei in *Chūshingura* and of Shizuka Gozen and Kitsune Tadanobu in *Yoshitsune Senbonzakura*, are very much more numerous.

The michiyuki is, too, not limited to the puppet drama and Kabuki, but is also found in Nō and Kyōgen. The text from *Takasago*, which was given in Chapter 2 as an example of spatial movement, was a michiyuki passage. Broadly speaking, the term michiyuki refers literally to going along a path or on a journey, and is used to indicate any appearance of this which occurs in the performing arts or literature.

Given such a broad definition, then, can the michiyuki really be said to exist nowhere but in Japan?

A long time ago now, I once asked Frank Hoff, a Toronto University professor who was doing research into the performing arts of the east, particularly Japan, whether or not the michiyuki was to be found in the west too. He was a lively young scholar who said that he had gone into his chosen field on hearing a lecture of mine on Japanese drama given at Harvard University when I was studying in America in 1957. After much investigation and thought on his part, he discovered just one case of a western michiyuki.

That occurs in Aeschylus's tragedy *Agamemnon* (458 B.C.), when the queen Clytemnestra tells how one after the other signal fires passed the news of victory back to the palace at Argos from far-off Troy where the campaign was taking place.

> 'From Ida to Hermes point in Lemnos the news was passed. . . . From the Euripus stream far away came the beacon light and gave the signal to the sentinels on Messapios. They, kindling a heap of withered heather, lit up their answering blaze and sped the message on. . . .'

This description goes on at some length. Later, I myself found a similar passage in the same author's *Prometheus Bound*.

There are, however, basic difference from the michiyuki as found in Japan. One is that the two passages in question are no more than sequences naming places and geographical features which elicit no reflection of the mental images of the persons concerned. Another is that their form is wholly that of relating things from the past instead of, as in the Japanese case, unfolding something that lies before one's gaze and is part of the immediate present. I shall touch on this again later.

At any rate, this is perhaps about as much as can be found in existing western drama, but various other examples can be cited if a search is made throughout history.

First, the account of the ordeals of Dionysus in ancient Greece. Probably because he was a foreign heathen god, he was persecuted and killed everywhere he went as he travelled round teaching how to cultivate the grape and make wine; but miraculously, it is said, he came back to life each time and continued his journeys. In time the chorus recital of this story and the circular dance accompanying it created tragedy, but this motif of an 'odyssey' in foreign lands full of hardships is an important element which is to be found in Japan too.

Book V of the *Manyōshū*, for example, has the following envoy appended to a longer poem written in 902. It expresses grief over the death of a small child called Furuhi.

> 'So young was he
> That he can hardly know the way.
> Oh, messenger from the nether world,
> I make you this offering
> That you may bear him up and carry him there.'

This poem, included in the selection from the *Manyōshū* which we used in my high-school days, was the first to use the word 'michiyuki.' It expresses poignantly and simply the emotions of love and grief for the dead child and, at the same time, reveals to the reader the helplessness, fear, pain, and uncertainty of a solitary journey to a far-off unknown land.

I am reminded here of the end of the Kabuki piece *Tera-koya*. Matsuōmaru and his wife have sacrificed their son Kojirō out of loyalty, and at the point where they send his body off to be cremated, there are some famous lines in 7-5 metre known as *Iroha Okuri* 'The Writing-lesson Farewell.'

'He journeys now to the other world,
And at the temple school there
His teachers will be Amida, Shakamuni,
And Jizō the guardian god of children.
In the sand on the river bank beside their temple
This little one will learn to write,
Now that so sadly
His life has fallen like a leaf,
With no way to hold it back.
Who will there be tomorrow night
To comfort him to sleep?
Faced with this grief,
Such are the thoughts of his parents. . . .'

This passage could indeed be regarded as a second coming of the above poem from the *Manyōshū*.

Briefly, then, the motif of the hardships of travelling to distant parts has an existence common to both east and west, whether it be in the ordeals of Dionysus or the poem in the *Manyōshū*. What is more, even if we look at the performing arts alone, the michiyuki is to be found everywhere, at least in very simple forms.

Greek comedy, for example, arose in the first place from processional songs and, as in medieval religious drama in the west, it took the form of a slow procession of carts on which the various scenes were set up, exactly like the procession of floats found in religious festivals in Japan. This was the origin of the pageant, and there is no doubt that when Christ appeared in Jerusalem or was led to Golgotha, for example, these were in a broad sense michiyuki.

Gigaku, which came to Japan from the Asian continent in 612 during the reign of the empress Suiko, was so essentially a type of processional entertainment that it was also called *gyōdō-e* 'procession ceremony.' Also, even today, such things as the *Nijūgo-bosatsu Raigō-e* 'Ceremony of the Coming of the Twenty-five Bodhisattvas' at the Senyō-ji at Higashiyama in Kyoto and the *Ki-raigō* 'The Coming of the Devils' which is carried out at the Bon Festival at the Kōsai-ji in Chiba Prefecture can be said to be the same kind of processional entertainment as the above cases in the west. Examples at this level can also be found in abundance in various countries in the east.

What is important, however, is that their later development, their historical transitions, were quite different in Japan and these other countries. In the countries of the east, even the forms that still exist have not gone beyond the level of simple processional entertainment mentioned above, that is, spatial movement in the open air. In the west, the michiyuki has completely disappeared since the Renaissance. Japan alone has gone on steadily developing the michiyuki in two streams, one in literature running through traditional short poems and descriptive and lyric poetry from the *Manyōshū* onwards, and the other in stage presentations of the performing arts coming down from post-Gigaku Bugaku, Sarugaku and Dengaku to Nō, the puppet theatre and Kabuki.

It will be immediately noticed that this difference is markedly similar to the case of the hanamichi which was discussed in Chapter 2. It is also interesting that the word *michi* 'way, road' is part of both the terms in question. It seems to me that this cannot be dismissed as mere chance and that it has some connection with a more general 'travel culture' in Japan. But let us leave that aside for the moment and note that in the west the hanamichi was likewise expelled from the covered theatre from the Renaissance onwards, in this case because of the spirit of rationality, that is, the realism required by 'representation.'

It might be said that the michiyuki declined in the west for much the same reasons. First and foremost, there is the irrational and unnatural situation of a person making a journey within the limited confines of a stage. The feeling against this was so strong that even in the early *Agamemnon* drama all that was permitted was a verbal description of things that had happened in the past, and this feeling was still stronger after the Renaissance.

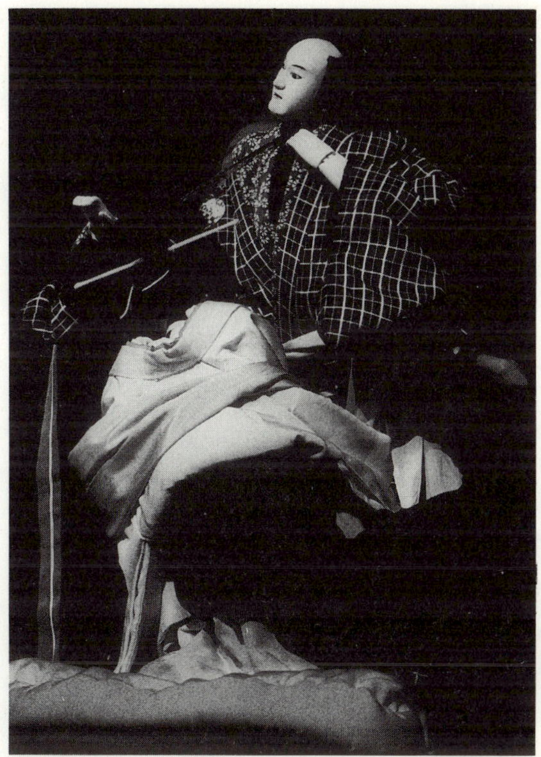

The Bunraku play *Sonezaki Shinjū*: the travel-passage (*michiyuki*) scene en route to Sonezaki.

I cannot help feeling that another important reason is that it is almost impossible to include dramatic complications within the michiyuki itself. The michiyuki in *Sonezaki Shinjū*, for example, simply consists of a couple who have already decided on suicide as a result of dramatic difficulties doing the same thing with a single purpose in mind. Such a michiyuki could not exist in the west, where the main characteristic of drama is to unfold before the eyes of the audience the difficulties surrounding a confrontation between two irreconcilables. Japan in contrast raised the michiyuki in a comparatively unmodified way into a world of formal beauty consisting of scenic descrip-

The suicide scene in the Tenjin wood in the Kabuki
Sonezaki Shinjū.

tion and lyricism. It was firmly established as an independent entity by the confluence of the two streams mentioned just now, the descriptive and lyric literary one since the time of the *Manyōshū* and the one of the performing arts that followed Gigaku. These two streams came together in Takemoto Gidayū's placing of the michiyuki in the middle of a five-act development, and in the love-suicide michiyuki introduced by Chikamatsu in his *Sonezaki Shinjū.*

A descriptive and lyric aspect devoid of any dramatic development—this can be described as a form which had its independent existence as a scene within a play emphasized by the nature of song and recitation as they followed their productive path through the performing arts of Japan.

The michiyuki is not restricted to love-suicide journeys nor to the dramatic aspects of a play. Some examples of it depicted the enjoyment of a pleasure outing, and there are others which delighted their audiences by what was at times a pretty blatant eroticism. Such elements must have been desirable to bring about a change of mood after a particularly oppressive scene.

In Act 8 of *Chūshingura*, for example, there is a colourful michiyuki involving Tonase and her daughter Konami. The scene is known as *Michiyuki Tabiji no Yomeiri* 'The Bridal Journey' since Konami is on her way to Yuranosuke's house to marry his son, and the following are the kind of lines to be found in an earthy passage from a tipsy servant who appears.

> 'If these are willing women
> From Yoshida or Akasaka,
> Give me the girl of seventeen with the fancy hair-do.
> If love's first sweet kisses
> Lead on to what I want,
> I'll make a pilgrimage to Kiyomizu Temple,
> Purify myself under the Otowa Fall there
> And worship like that every day.
> That's the way it will be.
> "May the purple goose find its way in through the
>   opening !"
> To the beat of a festival drum. . . .'

The line in quotation marks is said to have been an invocation from women—of whatever kind—yearning for love's fulfilment, and since the 'goose' and the 'opening' refer to what distinguishes male and female, the meaning is clear enough.

Then too, *Sonezaki Shinjū* has first of all a michiyuki in the tranquil atmosphere of a pleasure outing which is known as 'The Pilgrimage Round the Temples of Kannon.' Some see this as signifying prayers for the repose of the dead, but the fact remains that it has throughout a brightness of mood which is in contrast to the later suicide michiyuki. This means that these two kinds of michiyuki, light and dark, were already established within a single play in Chikamatsu's day, and as time went on these two forms themselves diversified, and on occasions intertwined, to create the all-important sphere of a michiyuki found only in Japan.

It is true, though, that it was the translation into sight and sound of the mood of loneliness, hardship and sorrow found in the age-old 'wanderings in strange parts' that became the main attraction of the michiyuki. But what has happened to this in the modern period, after the literature and theatre of the west were brought in, and the puppet theatre and Kabuki came to be referred to as classical or traditional theatre, when a gulf began to open up between them and the life of the times? And did they not head for extinction in the face of western-style logic and realism, much as happened in the west after the Renaissance?

Certainly, it might be said that, on stage, the michiyuki is restricted to Nō, Bunraku and Kabuki; but is the spirit of the michiyuki not flourishing in a different medium now, in popular songs and other performing arts enjoyed by ordinary people? Such a thing comes to mind in view of, for example, these later lines from 'Katyusha's Song' which was quoted at the beginning of this chapter:

> 'May the snow fall all night long,
> And tomorrow over hill and moor, ra-ra,
> Let it hide the road I am to take.'

> 'Far across the open plain, with dragging steps
> I shall set off all alone, ra-ra,
> When I begin my journey tomorrow;'

and these from 'A Wanderer's Song' used in a stage version

of Tolstoy's *The Living Corpse* which Matsui Sumako made into another hit by her performance:

> 'Shall I go on or shall I go back, beneath the lights
>   of the night sky?
> This Russia, with limitless lands to the north,
> Sees the sunset glow in the west and pale morning
>   in the east.'

The same mood was maintained in later times too, in items ranging from *Tabi no Yokaze*, 'A Night Breeze while Travelling Afar,' which swept the country as the theme song from the film *Aizome Katsura* 'The Love-dyed Wig,' and travel pieces such as *Sakatayama Shinjū* 'The Love Suicide at Mt. Sakata' and *Tabigasa Dōchū* 'Journeying with a Traveller's Sedge Hat,' to *Tsugaru Kaikyō Fuyu-geshiki* 'Winter Scene at the Tsugaru Straits.'

The most important feature of the Japanese michiyuki established by Chikamatsu, however, was its profound and unbreakable relationship with the land, particularly with nature. To take *Sonezaki Shinjū* as an example yet again, we saw that it compared the brief moments of life left to the lovers who 'go to meet death together' to 'frost on the path that fades away a little more with each step.' Just after this come the following lines:

> 'How heartless the departed clouds,
> And heartless too the water,
> For on its surface is the clear reflection
> Of the Plough, and of the Milky Way
> Which separates the Herdsman and
>   the Weaving Maid,
> Fated to meet just once a year
> Across the bridge of ravens' wings.
> We must now pledge our love on Umeda bridge

> For, having crossed it, until the end of time
> We too will be but loving stars. . . .'

Such a passage creates a romantic world, beautiful and grand, in which the emotions and fate of the main characters are conveyed through the medium of celestial spheres in the universe. At this level it is a uniquely Japanese realm completely unlike any other. I can well understand that Donald Keene, a scholar of Japanese literature and an esteemed friend of mine, should have said that 'The michiyuki is probably one of the most Japanese things in Japanese literature'; and that the French literature specialist Jacqueline Pigeot was so captivated by it that she has made it a subject of research.

This strong concern for nature, this spirit seeking harmony with nature to be seen in the michiyuki, make up another important characteristic which has its roots in the land and climate of Japan. In the next chapter, therefore, I propose to make a slight change of direction and to look at the Japanese view of nature.

Having said that, I realise that this present chapter is the third of the five central chapters which, with the introductory and concluding ones, make up this book. As it happens, then, I have been talking about grief in what exactly corresponds to 'Act 3' of a five-act jōruri text. It therefore seems to me to be a good thing to make a complete change from this rather oppressive mood by observing the natural beauty with which Japan has been blessed.

CHAPTER FIVE

NATURE'S EMBRACE

THE FLAVOUR OF THE FIRST BONITO OF THE SEASON

The Theatre and a Sense of Season

It goes without saying that racial character and behaviour are closely involved with nature, climate and other features of the land, but not long ago I heard an unusual view about this on the radio from a German lady living in Japan. When she talks with Japanese people, she said, there are continual interjections and they are so restless and unsettled that she wondered whether this was perhaps because, with the bewildering changes of season in Japan, they were under continual pressure to store away and unpack again different changes of clothes throughout the year.

At first I dismissed it as just an idea from someone with rather peculiar views but, on reflection, I cannot help feeling that there might be some truth in it. After all, most western countries have a long winter and just a short summer, with virtually no spring or autumn. Certainly, there can hardly be a country where the four seasons come round as regularly in equal periods of three months each and cause so much work for the housewife with changes of clothing and bedding as they do in Japan.

On the other hand, there is also a comparable variety and richness in the seasonal changes to be found in nature. Traditionally, the Japanese have not so much opposed these natural phenomena or complained about the trouble the changes cause as judged them on their merits and accepted them. By so doing, they have enriched their lives. At least they can be said to have made efforts in that direction and to have achieved due success.

This can be seen, for one thing, in the high frequency of sentiments about the seasons, seasonal words, seasonal topics and the like in poetry of all kinds, from the traditional thirty-one syllable *waka* produced by nobles for competitions in the ancient court period to the even shorter seventeen-syllable haiku beloved by each and every commoner in the Edo period. An example of the latter, celebrating the delights of early summer, goes:

> 'For the eyes, the green of leaves,
>   Together with the sound of the cuckoo
>   And the taste of early bonito.'

This is a famous composition by the haiku poet Yamaguchi Sodō (1642-1716) who lived in the early Edo period, and it seems to me that it does indeed merit its fame for the vividness with which it expresses in such a short poem the joy felt at the changing of the seasons and, at the same time, its inclusion of the elements of sight, sound and not just taste but even the Japanese love of 'first fruits.'

Being a down to earth person, I would not only follow the old saying in choosing dumplings before flowers but, being also rather fond of blundering about in the kitchen myself, would similarly prefer early bonito to trees or birds. It may be that the reason I like *Kamiyui Shinza* 'Shinza the Hairdresser,' one of Mokuami's numerous domestic plays, as much as his more famous ones such as *Sannin Kichisa* and *Utsunoya Tōge* is because an early bonito figures so prominently in the play.

The scene is Shinza's house, just beside the river in the working-class Fukagawa district of Edo. As soon as the cur-

Cutting up the first bonito of the season in the Kabuki *Kamiyui Shinza*.

tain opens, a ringing voice can be heard from the back of the auditorium calling out 'Bonito, bonito !' The cry comes from the fishmonger Shinkichi, and with him on the hanamichi is Shinza, on his way home from the public bathhouse with a wet towel in his hand.

'How much the fish, Shinkichi ?'
'A whole one ?'
'Don't treat me like a nobody, just because I go round
    doing hair !'

Without a shop of his own, Shinza ekes out a bare existence by visiting his clients to dress their hair, carrying with him the things he needs. He owes money everywhere, to say nothing of being behind with his rent; and yet, when he hears the new season's fish being sold, he just cannot resist buying one. . . . The scene depicts in a lively way the attitudes and the sense of life of ordinary people in a poor quarter of Edo, and with it the bravado of the typical Edo character who prides himself on never keeping his money overnight.

In passing, we might just look at the price Shinza paid for his bonito. After a small reduction, he bought it for three-quarters of a *ryō*. If we calculate this on the basis of the price of rice in order to see what this corresponds to in modern yen, it works out as follows. In 1865, the price of rice in Edo was 1 ryō for just over 51 kilos. With the standard price of rice at ¥400 a kilo in 1982, 1 ryō would have been the equivalent of ¥20,400 and Shinza's bonito would have cost him ¥15,300.

That was a very steep price, a great deal more than it would cost nowadays. What is more, Shinza generously gave him two half-ryō coins and said that he did not want any change, which means that he splashed out with a tip of some ¥5,000.

Of course, the unwillingness in this quarter of town to keep money overnight no doubt came originally from the casual day-workers who just lived for the moment, and must appear the height of folly to anyone from the west of Japan where they pride themselves on being thrifty and saving money. Such regional differences within Japan itself are undeniable, but as far as Edo is concerned, whatever the reason may be, the dashing sense of style which is the pride of the typical inhabitant there is closely linked to such open-handedness, generosity, verve and bravado—all of which surely amounts to the idea that now is the time that matters, while things are new and fresh. It is, in other words, the same feeling as comes from the freshly caught fish which appear twice a day in the market on the river bank there, whether or not they are the first bonito of the season.

Fish are eaten while they are fresh. They are not left until the next day for, in the morning, some new fish will turn up. It is a dietary regime which makes it unnecessary to store the protein or, to make no bones about it, makes it possible to throw away the leftovers. What it comes to, in other words, is that the way one lives and one's views of life, values and what looks attractive are governed by the riches of a land blessed by the warm currents of the sea.

This is what is suggested inadvertently by the early-bonito scene in the Kabuki play *Kamiyui Shinza*. It is a little picture of life which has no apparent connection with the main story, but it seems to me that it is this kind of thing that brings out the true flavour of domestic plays and gives enjoyment in a purely Japanese way not found in western drama.

The beauty, pleasure and, too, the impermanence of ever changing nature. These things are reflected in the Japanese way of life in all kinds of forms and they colour the theatre and other arts. The michiyuki discussed at the end of the previous chapter had in it a Japanese consciousness of beauty not found in any other country in that its song weaves the fate and mental state of a couple on their way to die together into the natural features and surroundings along their path.

So too the drumming on the ōdaiko mentioned in Chapter 3 which, in its different ways, is used to represent rain, storms, waves, snow, thunder and so on. This drumming unerringly conveys the individual features of the myriad aspects of nature by methods it has made into an art of its own.

Reflecting as they do the tastes of the common people, Bunraku and Kabuki express these aspects of nature in a fairly graphic way, but even in Nō and Kyōgen where forms are much more condensed and abridged there is the same close involvement with nature and natural features. In *Yuya* it is cherry blossom in Kyoto in spring, in the third month of the year, and in *Momiji-gari* 'The Maple-viewing' it is the autumn leaves on Mt. Togakushi in the ninth month. Indeed, there are many plays which introduce not only this kind of seasonal atmosphere but plants, animals, natural phenomena and the like. These appear in their own right as the 'spirit' of the thing in question—much like a dryad, nymph or salamander in the west—and play the main role in the piece. To give just the names of some plays of this type, plants or trees appear in *Oi-matsu* 'The Aged Pine,' *Ume* 'Plum Blossom,' *Kakitsubata* 'Irises,' *Saigyō-zakura* 'Saigyō and the Cherry Blossom,' *Bashō* 'The Plantain Tree,' *Fuji* 'Wisteria,' and *Yugyō Yanagi* 'Yugyō and the Willow'; animals in *Kochō* 'The Butterfly,' *Sagi* 'The Heron,' *Shakkyō* 'The Stone Bridge' which features a lion, *Shōjō* 'The Elf,' and *Tsuru* 'The Crane'; natural phenomena in *Yuki* 'Snow,' and so on.

If the scope is widened to include plays in which nature does not provide the main role on the stage but is an important theme beyond being mere background, the list is almost endless: *Ugetsu* 'The Moon and Rain,' *Ochiba* (the name of the main character but literally 'The Fallen Leaf,') *Ominameshi* 'Patrinia Flowers,' *Take no Yuki* 'Snow on the Bamboo,' *Tokusa* 'Scouring-rushes,' *Hajitomi* 'The Wicket Gate,' *Fuji-san* 'Mt. Fuji', *Matsumushi* 'The Cricket'. . . .

Can there be any other country which takes nature and natural features into its stage arts in this way?

This kind of attachment and attention to nature is clearly shown in the aesthetic consciousness of Zeami, renowned as the creator of Nō. Among numerous examples of this are his statement in the preface to the *Kadensho*, one of his essays on his art, that since poetry 'is an elegant pursuit concerned with the life-prolonging [beauties of nature such as the] wind and moon, it should of course be followed,' and another in Part 2 *Monomane Jōjō* 'Items on Mimicry' that 'The various aspects of persons of rank and their words and actions with regard to [nature in the form of] flowers, birds, wind and moon should be imitated as closely as possible.'

Zeami's feeling of reverent love for nature is shown even more, however, by his use of the term *hana* 'flower' to signify ultimate beauty in Nō. This feeling is clear from the title of the work itself, for *Kadensho* means 'Writings on the Transmission of the Flower' (*ka* is a variant reading of the character for *hana*), and it is evident too in the last part of the essay, in Part 7 *Besshi Kuden* 'Appendix on Innermost Secrets,' where he says:

> 'Now since a flower on any of the myriad trees and plants blooms only at its particular time during the four seasons, it is prized because it is fresh and new when its time comes again. So it is with Nō, for when people feel that something in it is fresh and new, they will at the same time feel that it is enjoyable. The Flower, the enjoyment, and the novelty are all three part of the same feeling.'

With the present development of hothouse cultivation, the enjoyment of seasonal changes has been sadly devalued, but hitherto in Japan it was in the course of the seasonal changes that flowers came. By these changes a cycle of the four seasons turned on the passing nature of a 'death' in which flowers would unfailingly wither and fall, and on a belief in the advent of a new year which would unfailingly bring a time when the buds would swell again.

These changes in nature are something absolute, beyond the reach of man. Yet it is understandable that they should shape everything about the Japanese people who live continuously in their midst, from the manner of their daily life to their view of human existence. The blooming and withering of a flower came to symbolize human life and it reinforces the Buddhist concept that 'All things are transient, and what flourishes will unfailingly decline.' The temperate and fertile land of Japan and the belief in the coming of a new year even gave its people the opportunity to enjoy this 'fading of a flower' as a form of *fūryū* 'artistic refinement,' with aspects of it known by such terms as *wabi* 'quiet taste,' *sabi* 'tasteful simplicity,' and *horobi no utsukushisa* 'the beauty of decline.'

Such is Japan. Thus, Zeami goes on to say:

> 'What flower remains, without falling? It is because it falls that a time comes for it to bloom and become new again. So it is with Nō, where it must be understood before all else that the Flower comes from its not being unchanging.'

Leaving until the next chapter a consideration of the attitude which prizes the flower, that is to say, beauty above all else, I will here go on to say that nature does of course constantly play a part also in Kyōgen, which is performed on the same stage as Nō. I will give just one example of Kyōgen plays that always impress me with their power of observation and presentation, namely, the major piece called *Kirokuda* 'Six Loads of Firewood.'

On the orders of his master, a character called Tarō-kaja is on a mountain road deep in snow driving a dozen oxen, six laden with charcoal and six with firewood, when he comes across a tea-shop on the pass. Of course, it being Kyōgen, neither oxen nor the tea-house appear on the stage. They have to be revealed by actions and words alone, and this is therefore regarded as a particularly difficult piece. The tea-shop owner and Tarō-kaja then both look up at the sky and say to each other,

> "There'll be another fall. There'll be another fall, you know. The way it is, it will turn pitch black and down it will come."

Snow, which one would expect to be called white, they call black—but if one looks up at the daytime sky when there is about to be a heavy fall of snow, the sunlight is in fact blocked out and what would normally be a white sky certainly appears to be black. At such a time the snow is undoubtedly black.

A markedly true and accurately expressed observation of nature, this, and one which escapes the general view. When I explained this point while I was showing a colour film of a performance in which the late Nomura Manzō took the leading role, the students were sufficiently impressed to express their admiration.

An inseparable link with the seasons does not stop at individual plays but extends to the way performances are organized and programmes chosen throughout the year. In Kabuki in particular, closely linked as it was to the lives of the ordinary people, productions would be staged according to the season of the year, in step with popular annual events. These were known as the *Shibai Nenjū Gyōji* 'Annual Theatrical Events.'

The beginning of the theatrical year was the eleventh month according to the old lunar calendar, on which the references to months in the following passage will be based. (Since the year under this system could begin anywhere between three and seven weeks later than it would under the western Gregorian calendar, the eleventh month would begin somewhere between about 20 November and 20 December.) In pre-modern times, unlike today, the actors were attached to the various theatres on one-year contracts. When it was decided at the beginning of the eleventh month that, say, the troupe led by Danjūrō and Kikugorō would go to the Nakamuraza, and that led by Mitsugorō and Utaemon to the Ichimuraza, they would belong there until the following tenth month. This meant that the various troupes for the coming year had to be introduced to their audiences. That is, the members would show themselves to an audience by lining up and asking for their kind patronage in the year ahead. This was literally what is still known as the *kaomise* 'face showing.'

In choosing the programme for this occasion, therefore, the hope was to show to best advantage the special character of the troupe as a whole and to make it colourful enough to display the wide range of players and roles. For example, a theatre where Danjūrō was appearing would stage *Shibaraku*, the play mentioned in Chapter 3 when mie and kumadori were being discussed. This was because everything—from the fact that it was an aragoto piece in which Danjūrō specialized and was auspicious in showing the heroic defeat of evil and the triumph of good, to its many and varied stage characters such as a young male lead, villains, female roles, and comic players—exactly suited the purpose of a kaomise.

Before long, it is New Year. Among the plays for this first month, known as *hatsuharu kyōgen* 'early spring plays,' would be 'Soga pieces' based on the vendetta of the Soga brothers. These were especially popular in Edo, where there was a widespread belief in Hakone Gongen, a deification of the younger brother Gorō, and the plays were, in any case, suitably auspicious for the festive season.

The third month was the cherry-blossom season, bringing with it plays like *Sukeroku Yukari no Edo-zakura* 'Sukeroku and Edo Cherry Blossom' (usually known simply as *Sukeroku*), with the flowering trees in full bloom in the main street of the Yoshiwara gay quarter and the tangled love of Sukeroku, the embodiment of dash and pride, and the prostitute Agemaki.

From the fifth to the seventh month was summer, with its heat and high humidity. Since it was an unsuitable time of year for theatrical performances, the main actors rested, and the theatres closed for repairs and renovation. On occasions, minor actors and early efforts by young playwrights could be seen cheaply, and at times these productions opened the door to worldly success. For instance, the great author Tsuruya Nanboku, who is best known for his play *Yotsuya Kaidan*, achieved fame with his play *Tenjiku Tokubei* 'Tokubei's Return from

India' which he wrote for performance at the Kawarazakiza in the seventh month of 1804.

The ninth month, usually October in our modern calendar, meant that autumn had come, and this was the season when the theatres settled down to showing tragedies about the conflict between duty and love, weighty dramas like *Terakoya* and *Chūshingura*; or, since they were the last performances of the theatrical year, there might be plays about separation from a child such as *Shigenoi Ko-wakare* 'Shigenoi Parts from her Child' and *Kuzunoha* 'Princess Kuzunoha,' given as *o-nagori kyōgen* 'farewell plays.'

These are the annual events in Kabuki. In the period before central heating and air conditioning, it was necessary to work out programmes to accord with the seasonal changes. There is even a work which gives Kabuki playwrights directions on this point. This is the *Kezairoku*. The author's name, given as Nyūgatei Ganyū, is considered to be a nom de plume of the playwright Namiki Shōzō II, and the following are some short extracts from the chapter entitled 'On Seasonal Differences in People's Feelings.'

> 'Since winter is the time when people's feelings slide into gloom and, being shut up inside against the cold, no one wants to go out, care should be taken to hire new actors and, for the kaomise, to decorate the outside of the theatre attractively, stir people's interest by putting big lanterns and piles of supporters' gifts there, and generally to concentrate on making everything bright.
>
> Spring is a time when people's only thoughts are to go out somewhere, and so the new plays are the heart of the year's performances and of the greatest importance for the writers. Since it is the season for cherry-blossom viewing, it is vital to ensure that popular interest is not lost.
>
> Since summer is the season when people find their

enthusiasms evaporating as they suffer in the heat, it is difficult to maintain their interest during a play, particularly with large numbers of people. It is best to keep scenes short, and to use a few pieces which will be watched with bated breath. It is advisable to decide on very realistic dramas of low society and pieces in which water can be used.

Autumn is the season when people's feelings quieten and they are at peace with themselves, and so the construction of a play should concentrate on everyday things, often with a logically sorrowful situation for example, in such a way as to capture people's interest and keep them tense with excitement.'

Theatre in the west is similar, in that summer virtually means festivals in cool locations and the main theatrical season is the winter; but can there have been a country other than Japan that has, for the theatre alone, shown such concern and gone to such lengths over the heat and cold of the climate and their effect on individuals?

Thus, in Japan, nature and natural features had an inseparable coexistence with both human life and the theatre which, it might even be said, could not have survived without being in harmony with nature and its seasons.

What is more, this attachment to nature was so strong that simply to appreciate and enjoy it and to seek to harmonize life with it was not enough. It led the Japanese people to the creation of thoroughly natural-looking things—a 'man-made nature' which aimed at a natural beauty greater than that of nature itself—even in places where nature was not to be found.

Manufactured Natural Beauty

Normality and Fabrication

In the early part of July 1981 the First European Kabuki Conference was held in Vienna. There were very academic research papers and discussions by a gathering of some forty people from fifteen countries. Being one of the promoters of the conference, I was asked to participate as a member from Japan and took on the responsibility of giving the opening keynote speech. Lasting three days, it was a serious-minded and fruitful conference.

Leaving aside here its contents and results, however, one of the things about it that remain in my memory is the great number of Bonsai that were used to decorate the conference hall. This was a room with glittering chandeliers in the Alte Hofburg, which is well known as the departure point for the horse-drawn carriages for tourists which are one of the sights of Vienna. It was a room I had used each time during my appointment as a Visiting Professor in Vienna, but it was decorated with Bonsai when the Kabuki conference took place there. A Japanese atmosphere in Europe. . . .

They had not, however, been brought by any Japanese, but put on display there by a Bonsai expert from Vienna, who proudly told us the ages of the maples, pine-trees and so on.

There has been a marked burst of interest in the culture of the Edo period and of Japan recently, as shown by both the Kabuki conference and the Great Edo Exhibition held in

London in the autumn of the same year. Universities in various countries are also vying with each other to establish centres of Japanese studies. Why is this? It may be that the feeling behind it is that, in order to learn the secrets of what can be called Japan's extraordinary modernisation and economic development, it is necessary to grasp the totality of Edo society which gave birth to the modern period and the culture and psychological framework of the Japanese people.

Looked at in this way, the appearance of the Bonsai at the Kabuki conference may be thought to be due to this same underlying feeling. Being small and allusive, one could perhaps say that Bonsai are especially suitable as an *Introduction to Japan* for foreigners.

Small trees and plants in small pots are made into desired shapes by 'the hand of man,' which entails the use of scissors, wire and other implements, the intensive study of soil, and loving devotion in training and scrutinising their shapes over many years. They are nursed and trained to conform to beauty as seen by someone who creates, according to his own will, not an artificial tree or flower but a living piece of nature itself.

What is the point of this? It is surely to attempt to give the appearance of a grand old tree which guards a history from times long past and, when rocks and sand are arranged to suggest the seashore or a dark valley deep in the mountains, to manifest the greatness of nature or the universe in all its limitless time and space, all in one small tree. Using for its materials natural objects themselves, it creates an ideal image of natural beauty as man would have it, by transcending his love and respect for nature itself.—It might perhaps be called 'unnatural nature' or 'nature and the elevation of artifice' but it is, in any case, a uniquely Japanese concept.

The development of potted plants into Bonsai does not, it is true, seem to be all that old. I say 'seem' because, in fact, I am a complete amateur on the subject. A lack of time and money have something to do with it, but since I generally prefer to leave even a garden tree in its natural form as far as possible rather than make it into something too different, I have no inclination to grow or collect Bonsai. Of course, if someone gives me one, I still express my admiration and keep it to adorn the place for a time, but since I am at a loss when it comes to looking after it, it starts to grow in all the wrong places and ends up by being banished to a corner of the garden.

Now I have read somewhere or other that apparently until the Edo period natural plants with interesting shapes would simply be potted just as they were, brought into the house or put outside in the garden and enjoyed in that way. This brings us to the well known story of *Hachi no Ki* 'The Potted Trees,' which is found in both Nō and Kabuki. It tells how, when an itinerant priest—in reality the retired regent Hōjō Tokiyori— was travelling through a snow-covered province in central Japan, an old samurai called Sano no Genzaemon Tsuneyo unhesitatingly cut down his three cherished plum, pine and cherry trees he had in pots in order to burn them and warm his visitor.

This incident belongs to about the middle of the thirteenth century and so the practice of enjoying potted plants (*hachiue*) seems to be quite old. The combination of characters now read as 'Bonsai' are said to date from 1818, but since they were still read there as 'hachiue,' the word is thought to have referred to simple natural cultivation unchanged in essence since the time of *Hachi no Ki*.

The start of a sudden development from this to the present type of Bonsai is said to have swept in on the tide of feeling after the Sino-Japanese war of 1894-95 when, partly as a reaction to the Europeanism of the 1890s characterised by the official international club called the Rokumeikan 'The Deer-cry Pavilion,' there was a swing towards nationalism and a resurgence of taste for things Japanese.

We have digressed a little, but what I cannot help feeling all the more keenly now, having learned that Bonsai is, if any-

The garden of the Shoenbrunn Palace, Vienna.

thing, a new artistic form of the modern period, is that the attachment of the Japanese to nature is perhaps a karma-like charge of mind. If one accepts that in this modern, present-day world they feel obliged to create nature in these miniaturized forms and to 'preserve' it around them by placing them in their living rooms or entrance halls, then this is itself karma.

Or perhaps this mini-nature has developed because the destruction of nature has made such advances and a western-style 'anti-nature' indoor way of life started to be introduced in modern times. If that is so, it surely makes it all the more a visitation of karma.

The urge to create a mini-nature as revealed in modern times in the form known as Bonsai may be said to be the same conceptual impulse that is common to all kinds of things, from *bonkei* 'tray landscapes,' *bonseki* 'miniature rock landscapes,' *hako-niwa* 'miniature gardens,' and *kare-sansui* 'dry mountain-water landscapes' in which only stones are used, to the

The garden of the Ninna Temple, Kyoto.

small garden of a tea-ceremony room or Japanese restaurant, and the water running from a bamboo pipe to drive a mini-waterwheel at the entrance to a traditional eating-house. Through the delicate arrangement of form, using only limited space and natural materials but the utmost degree of calculation, these bring a sense of limitless nature, time and space within the concept of something to be looked at. . . .

The genesis of these forms was probably that of the Japanese garden which developed in early times, with artificial miniature hills, ponds, stepping stones and bridges. It shows intelligence to make someone imagine, by the deliberate placing of, say, a bridge which is clearly the work of man, that a man-made pond and stream are by contrast the work of nature. Or there is the 'borrowed landscape' principle, which incorporates into the background the fine shape of a distant mountain, for example, and by making this connection with true nature, strengthens the impression that the garden itself is natural.

The aim of the Japanese garden being to create a natural beauty, it is necessarily made asymmetrical, because the only perfectly symmetrical sights to be seen in nature itself are the full moon and the sun. This is fundamentally different from the western garden designed with geometrical symmetry, as represented by those at Versailles and the Schoenbrunn Palace, and although exhaustive study and calculation were devoted to the creation of both types, they had completely opposite results, asymmetrical and natural in the one case, symmetrical and opposed to nature in the other.—This is something that was raised earlier, when we considered form in Ikebana in connection with the mie in the theatre.

Leaving aside for the moment the question of how such a difference between east and west arose, I would like first to affirm here that there is at work in this kind of 'man-made natural beauty' the same principle as that in the concept of spatial treatment in Nō and Kabuki which we have already seen.

Take, for example, such things as the extension of a time and space severely limited in reality, the attitude which deliberately makes an 'assumption' through the individual's imagination or a theatrical illusion, the device of the evocative 'echo' or symbol, and the 'sense of presence' which makes the onlooker feel that he himself is participating in the environment created around him. So it is with a Bonsai, small though it may be: it can hardly be said to be a good one unless, for a moment, the onlooker loses himself in the same kind of feeling, that he is living within the all-enveloping, age-old nature symbolized by the plant.

In short, the feeling of reassurance that one exists day in day out within nature's secure embrace, and the view that human life in which nature plays no part is inescapably empty. This is the karma of the Japanese mentioned earlier.

Theatre takes innumerable forms, but it goes without saying that in a broad sense it is a projection of human life. If the Japanese have a strong attachment to nature, then it is ·inevitable that it will be reflected in their theatre. We have already seen how extensively and deeply seasonal changes and other phenomena and aspects of beauty in nature are involved in Nō, Kyōgen and Kabuki. I would just like to add here, therefore, a few random thoughts on the way nature is treated on the Kabuki stage and the resourcefulness used in the creation of a Kabuki style of nature.

In discussing *Shunkan* in Chapter 3, I described the method of producing a seashore scene on stage by means of the wave-cloth and wave sounds from the ōdaiko. In certain plays, however, the need can arise for a more literal beating of waves on stage. At such times a stage assistant completely covered in a costume of the same pale blue colour as a wave-cloth appears on the stage to move the cloth up and down or to rock a boat, requiring of course as he does so an 'assumption' of invisibility. He is the *namiko* 'wave man.' In a snow scene, he appears in a pure white costume as a *yukigo* 'snow man.'

Both waves and snow are manifested by means of the ōdaiko, but there are also cases where the idea of a particular season and its natural environment are expressed by more realistic sounds. The noise of insects or birds is a case in point. There are flutes or whistles for producing the sounds of a crow or chicken, as well as a plover on the seashore, a shrike in the mountains, or a bush warbler in springtime. It is the same with insects: there are a great many varieties of *mushibue* 'insect flute' for such things as a bell-ring insect, various kinds of cricket, and grasshopper. When the scene is set on a summer night, particularly when it is against a background of rice-fields receding into the distance, it is absolutely necessary for a chorus of frogs to be heard. A stage assistant hiding right at the back of the stage rubs two clam shells together, and as he does so there comes the croaking of frogs. . . .

In modern times the famous actor Onoe Kikugorō VI was renowned for his dancing among other things, but he displayed a superlative talent in low-life domestic dramas such as *Kami-yui Shinza* and in realistic plays like those newly written for Kabuki. He treasured a vast collection of different kinds of whistles for birds and insects. They are now preserved in the Drama Museum of Waseda University, and are said to have come originally from China. Insects are to be found everywhere in China as well as in Japan, and Kikugorō must have cherished his own private collection with the idea of making use of the individual items on the stage as and when the need arose.

It must surely again be Japan alone that goes to such lengths in its theatre as to show such concern over the sounds of frogs, birds and insects. Again, this is no doubt due not simply to the richness of nature in Japan, but also to the fact that seasonal changes are extensively involved with daily life and aesthetic awareness and that birds and insects in their annual cycle are indispensable as major themes of the changing seasons.

The kind of sensibility which leads a person to hear and distinguish the sounds of birds and, even more, of insects, to give thought to the changing of the seasons and then to be struck by the idea of composing a haiku embodying his feelings certainly does not, I feel, commonly exist in foreign countries. The west too has birdcages, but I have never heard of singing insects being kept in a cage hung on a veranda there.

There is at this point just one small matter of concern, namely, the question of whether the adoption of nature and the creation of man-made natural beauty by the Japanese, true though they are, can be said to be due to a love of nature on their part. The concern arises because there is a view which denies that this is so.

Take, for example, the waterfall found so often in Japanese gardens. Those which incorporate a natural waterfall are another matter, but generally the waterfall is man-made, insofar as the water is simply raised up to a high point by a pump or some such thing and then allowed to fall. Although it is natural enough for the water to flow down from the high point to a lower level, this is the creation of a false show of nature. For the sake of a pleasurable natural illusion, nature itself is distorted and stifled. How can this be done from a sense of love for nature?

This is merely one example of the kind of argument that expresses the negative view. Others could of course be adduced from the use of wire in the making of a Bonsai in order to force the plant into a desired shape, and snipping away at flower stems in an Ikebana arrangement. Indeed, one need go no further than the cultivation of rice, the basis of life for the Japanese, for this has ended up, under the fine-sounding description of improving the strain, by producing prolific top-heavy plants which, if judged by their natural ecology, are nothing more than deformities. What this argument comes to is that, from self-interest, the Japanese have not shown anything like love for nature but have distorted it instead.

In that case, though, Japan is hardly alone in this. The west has also been arranging flowers for ages past and, when it comes to improving strains and breeds, it does not hesitate to alter some of the higher mammals, from cattle and horses to dogs, to improve them as food or entertainment. It is human beings above all else who have emerged from nature to live by eating the fruits of trees, plant roots, birds, animals and fish. It is an accepted fact that all mankind has distorted and sacrificed nature for its own ends. We can only say that this is the provision that nature has made not only for man but for all living things.

If that is so, it seems to me that the attitude of wanting to indulge an affection for nature at close quarters by adding something of oneself and thereby displaying its beauties and blessings in all its forms can after all be described as love. How does the reader see this, I wonder.

To be sure, people differ widely in what they will do to something and the kind of form they want, and it all depends too on the what and where of it. 'Leave wild gorse on the moor,' according to the saying. Even with love between man and woman, there are some people who are not satisfied unless they can fit their loved one into their ideal form, while others see real love as leaving the innate individuality just as it is. No outsider can decide which is true love and which is not.

As I said before, rather than precisely constructed gardens and Bonsai, I prefer nature left untouched at least until trees begin to choke each other. That applies, though, to things around me day by day, partly from a feeling of being shut in when I am constantly surrounded by too precisely finished goods identical in form. When I see a fine Bonsai or a famous garden, I will still give a grunt of appreciation and find satisfaction in it as an example of Japanese beauty. I am put off by a display of bad taste, but if it is a 'manufactured beauty of nature' which really brings nature to life, I am often struck by the warm affection and aesthetic awareness of the creator and lose myself in his work.

For such reasons, I feel that the deep involvement the Japanese have with nature, including man-made nature, is due after all to their attachment to it—but what, then, produced this attachment and what view of nature do the Japanese have?

There is a great difference with the west simply in the matter of symmetry in landscaped gardens, but where does this come from? And what are the differences in nature itself, which is the basis of it all? These are the kinds of question I should like to consider a little more now.

The Spirit of a Natural Cycle

Harmony and Confrontation

When I introduced something of what Zeami said about the Flower, I said that the uniquely Japanese aesthetic sphere variously referred to as wabi, sabi or the beauty of decline was created with the support of the country's climate, with its seasonal changes, and the moderation and richness of nature there; but can the climate and nature in Japan really be said to be moderate and rich?

Here again we are not without problems, because there are people who say that, far from nature in Japan being moderate, it is uncontrollably wild.

The saying has it that 'The things to be feared are an earthquake, thunder, fire and, then, a father,' so first the earthquake and its close cousin the volcano. It is not necessary to bring out topographical or geological maps for this. It is a fact that, in the Great Kantō Earthquake of 1923, 100,000 people died. I was not born at the time, but I have since been told that all the family were driven out of the house in Honjo, the worst-hit area, by the fires raging there, and having scattered in all directions as they fled through the flames, each thought for five days that the others had died. My elder brother, who was then something over a year old, passed into the next world when he was swept out of my mother's arms in the waters of the Sumida River as she nearly drowned in an attempt to escape the flames. . . .

Nowadays the time is coming round again for another big earthquake on the same scale, but volcanoes such as Asama-yama, Sakurajima and Usuzan cannot be ignored either when, to mention just one thing, even Mt. Ontake in the Kiso area has now erupted for the first time in its history. The fact that a mountain such as this is regarded as sacred leaves no doubt that, in olden times, it would not have taken a Nostradamus to see this as a portent of the end of the world.

When it comes to Mt. Fuji, it turns out that it erupted just very recently, in the fourth year of the Hōei era (1707), when it formed Mt. Hōei on its slopes. This was five years after the forty-seven loyal retainers made their attack and the year in which Chikamatsu Monzaemon wrote his fine play *Hori-kawa Nami no Tsuzumi* 'The Drum Echo by the Hori River.' Dormant though it now is, it is a prominent name on the active list, much younger than Mt. Ontake, and there is no telling when it might explode again.

There are other things too, of course—typhoons, for example. Thanks to the advance of science, forecasting them has become possible now that we have the meteorological satel-lite *Himawari* 'Sunflower,' and damage seems to be slightly on the decrease. When the flood damage from a typhoon is also taken into account, however, the disastrous results con-tinue. There are rare occasions, such as that in July 1281 when a massive typhoon completely destroyed the invading Mon-gol army in a single night, when the country benefits; but even an event like that is just more proof of the fury of nature in its attacks on Japan.

When the situation is looked at in this way, it is impossible to deny that Japan is a country which, far from enjoying the mildness of nature, is constantly exposed to its violence. Yet when one leaves Japan and goes to live in Europe, one im-mediately forgets such things as earthquakes and typhoons.

Southern Italy, at least, is a special case. It was an excep-tional occurrence when the cultural city of Pompeii, with its population of 20,000 and a beautiful setting, was suddenly buried in molten lava and hot ash from the volcano Vesuvius in 79 A.D., for London, Paris, Berlin and Vienna all stand on a base of solid rock, with never even a tremor. That is admittedly not absolutely true, though, because extraordinarily there was an earthquake in Vienna a few years ago. To be sure, the tremors were such as would hardly be noticed by the Japanese, but it is said that it threw the Viennese into a great commotion and was reported in the news. This just shows how rare an earthquake is there.

Well, then, if the question now is whether the west, or perhaps foreign countries, are more equable than Japan because they do not have earthquakes and typhoons, I would have to answer no. As I said before, most western countries just have long winters and short summers, with nothing much in the way of four seasonal changes. There is no intermediate spring and autumn, when suitably warm weather, neither hot nor cold, lasts for two or three months. The long winters are bitterly cold, with temperatures of ten or twenty degrees below freezing, and darkness comes at about three o'clock in the afternoon.

I know this harshness of nature in Europe from having lived in Vienna on two occasions to teach there during the winter term. My strongest impression, though, was of the time when I landed at Bergen airport, in Ibsen's country of Norway.

1971—it was already past the middle of March, the time when conversation in Japan would soon turn to the question of whether the cherry blossom would be early or late this year. The National Theatre had been invited to come from Norway for the first time that autumn, and we had arranged for it to give us home-born versions *of A Doll's House* and *Hedda Gabler*. In order to prepare for this, collect material and give some lectures, I was visiting a number of countries, travelling alone as usual.

Having finished my business in Oslo and Ibsen's home town of Skien, I visited the small town of Bergen, on the west coast. It is indeed a place to be remembered, for Ibsen spent several years as a writer and stage manager in the theatre there when he was young. An elegant, beautiful town, on one of the fiords so characteristic of Norway.

No sooner did I alight at the small, almost deserted airport, however, than I saw through the storm of hard powdered snow that whipped against me the white wall of a snow-covered mountain looming up close by. The mountain is said to be only about 1,000 metres high, but since it towers abruptly over the town situated more or less at sea level, it appears extraordinarily high and precipitous. Mountains which seem to have grown directly out of the fiords are everywhere along the northwest coat of Norway.

The pictures of Dahl, who is described as the father of modern Norwegian painting, contain scenes of silver-grey mountains looming behind ships in distress as they are buffeted by storm-driven waves.

Lead-coloured fiords and rockfaced mountains shut in by silver ice—

As I stood amid the steadily falling snow before the silent but intimidating presence of the white wall, I thought of Ibsen's play *Brand*. Brand is a preacher and an idealist by nature, who is true to himself come what may. So excessive is his anger at the corruption of established religion and the degeneration of society that he even sacrifices his family as he goes on with his protests. Finally, claiming to see the true god, he climbs an icy mountain all alone and dies there when he is struck down by an avalanche—the egotistical man who rejects all compromise and carries to the extreme the conviction of all or nothing.

Gazing up there in Bergen at the snowy mountain which towered up to shut off everything else from my gaze, it was brought home to me that this was the mountain that Brand set out to conquer, and that the source of that drama of violent confrontation was here in the stark severity of nature in northern Europe.

Nature is harsh, not only in Norway but in that area gener-ally. Because of this, westerners there certainly do not befriend nature but, instead, are obliged to confront and fight it for the greater part of the year. To take their housing as just one example, it can be nowhere near as simple as in Japan where, with the summer always in mind, there is good ventilation and arrangements are made for a flow of air between the inside and outside of a house by means of wide sliding doors, for instance. There, life could not go on without nature being kept at bay by building thick walls of brick or stone against it, and if there should be no natural barrier to the land to protect it from enemies of a different race, the walls have to be even thicker and everything made thoroughly secure.

Of course this means that, deep down, people long for nature all the more, and so they value the brief summer highly when it does come: sunshades are set up outside along the main streets, and there are even crowds of scantily dressed people ready to bathe in the blessed sunshine. But there is in all this the clear distinction which says that man is man and nature is nature.

While people in the west leave natural wooded areas as far as possible in their natural state, when it comes to creating gardens, they bring in geometry to make them into symmet-rical designs as if to show how clever man is. Could it not be that the reason underlying this is this same irreconcilable 'confrontation'?

It goes without saying that the western drama of confron-tation is not the monopoly of Ibsen but has been a tradition in the west since the time of ancient Greece. I have already said something about its characteristics, but I would add here that Greece, which was its original source, is a poor, harsh kind of land compared with Japan. Having a rough and sandy soil, it grows not cereals but just grapes and olives. Large-scale cattle raising is therefore impossible and, at best, there are only goats and sheep.

Greek tragedy, which began with the stories of the ordeals of Dionysius, the god of the grape, sprang from the soil of nature such as this and from colonial wars to seek richer lands.

The west is not alone in suffering the harshness of nature. I was travelling in Kenya when I became aware of the dreariness of life without the four seasons and was struck all the more by a sense of bleakness and desolation. Having sent for my wife to join me during the Christmas vacation when I was working in Vienna, we spent about three weeks travelling together. We thought we might as well go off to Nairobi, and from there we tried the trip to the foothills of Mt. Kilimanjaro on the usual type of shared microbus.—Here is an extract from a short piece I wrote about the trip for a magazine called *Haiku to Essei* 'Haiku and Essays.'

'—By about the third day we had had our fill of lions, elephants, rhinos, giraffes and buffalo. What remains uppermost in my memory even now is the withered shape of a giant tree lying beside the bones of an unknown animal on the reddish dried-up earth. It was awesome, like the skeleton of a dinosaur. The withered shape of such a huge tree as this would surely never be seen in Japan.

What is more, it was not even summer. In Japan it would have been the middle of winter, but here in Africa just below the equator there are no seasons. The carcasses of giant trees, together with wild animals and human beings, all fall into decay knowing nothing but a parched summer throughout their lives. Summer is only summer when it has a place within the changing seasons of the year. Oh, how keenly I felt what a fine country Japan is.—'

Having made comparisons with such a place in various respects, I feel even now that, although Japan may have earthquakes and typhoons, it is blessed with a climate and nature that more than make up for them. There is no doubt that earthquakes, volcanoes and typhoons are damnable things to those who have suffered from them but, from another viewpoint, they are phenomena which show that active state—the animate breathing form—of the world peculiar to the Pacific basin. Then, too, Japan is such a long archipelago that there are considerable differences between one end and the other, but on average it is mild and fertile.

Even Britain, which is only capable of secondary agriculture in the form of dairy farming, falls far behind Japan in the blessings of nature. I heard somewhere at some time that the reason maps show low-lying areas in green and uplands in brown is because, in the world as a whole, mountain areas are a natural brown colour and the lower parts manage to keep their greenness, and if it seems to be the opposite in Japan, this is because its mountains are particularly green; and I certainly agree with this. As the eighth-century *Kojiki* 'Records of Ancient Matters' says in describing it as the 'Land of Fresh Rice-ears and Abundant Reed-plains of a Thousand Autumns and then Five Hundred More' and 'Land Amid the Reed-plains,' it is indeed a land of rich harvests.

The Japanese have been aware that the blessings of this richness and nature's four seasons far outweigh the negative aspects of earthquakes and typhoons. The fact is that since the transition from one season's weather to the next is never far away, a little patience means that the earthquake subsides, the storm passes and gentler days come round again. This has given rise to appropriate proverbs such as 'Patience brings a fair wind,' 'Even a typhoon passes,' and 'Spring always returns'. . . .

Even a wild climate and an awesome form of nature constitute, not an utterly incompatible opponent as in the west, but one who, if a hand is stretched out at the right moment, responds with a smile. This is the kind of feeling at work here, stemming from a prudent concept of how to deal with reality.

There are fitting assumptions not only of gods on the positive side, as it were, who control farming, the hunt and the fruits of the sea, but often of gods who act negatively, such as those of wind, thunder, water and the sea. By honouring, pleasing and drawing close to them, efforts are made to gain their sympathy and thus to provide a stable life and ensure abundant yields.

Behaviour which assumes that there are within nature supernatural beings in the form of gods or evil spirits and which seeks to obtain beneficial results by identifying with them—that is, shamanism—is a general concept found everywhere including Japan, but it seems to me that, in Japan, these nature gods are particularly numerous and varied.

The folk entertainments which survive in the various parts of the country are no more than expressions first, of simple gratitude for the blessings of the positive sides of nature and, in addition, of the Japanese idea of showing reverence and affection even for its awesome negative sides in an attempt to placate them and, in the last analysis, to bring them into harmony and unity.

The Japanese are said, for better or worse, to set great store by 'harmony.' It is also said that, particularly from the viewpoint of westerners, who have a clear concept of a conflict of opinion and who try to proceed by sorting things out in a logical way, this is a form of compromise that obscures differences and of prevarication that makes a problem hard to grasp. This is surely right. The phrase 'blindly following the opinions of others,' for example, well illustrates this failing of the Japanese.

Nevertheless, although this 'harmony' does contain various failings and weaknesses of this kind, it certainly seems to operate extensively over the entire theatre, culture and psychological framework of the Japanese. Can it not be said that this comes from the stance of 'harmony' and 'concord' identifiable as the instinct behind the traditional way of life, in which climate and nature—in other words, the natural living environment that we have been looking at so far—is seen as being not in opposition but in sympathy, and is counted not as an enemy but as a friend?

In no way do I have it in mind to cut any corners over the matter of nature and climate, nor do I have the slightest intention of giving a forced account of them to fit in with my views, but I do feel that, to say the least, they have without doubt come to be extremely important factors.

This 'harmony' appears in all kinds of forms, but the main one in the field of Japanese culture is the way in which foreign culture was adopted. As was mentioned in the opening chapter, tracing the ancestry of Japanese culture shows that the best parts of it are virtually all imports. They have been adopted with little resistance, and the techniques and skills immediately learned and copies produced. As the Japanese do this, they make incidental improvements by injecting their own tastes, add some originality, and end up by turning what was an import into something of their very own. At times, they produce beautiful objects superior to those from the place of origin.

This is a basic principle of Japan's culture and civilization, from the various types of performing art already discussed to cameras, cars and computers, and the heart of it can be said to be a process in which exotic, foreign things are smoothly introduced, suitably amended, and made to harmonize with their new surroundings. At the present time, the Japanese are making incursions into every part of the world by means of this harmonization strategy and, as a result, are sometimes feared and disliked.

In the field of the performing arts, there is a passage in Zeami's *Kadensho*, quoted previously with reference to the Flower, in which he explains about the harmonization of the conflicting principles of Yin and Yang. It is in a section written in the form of question and answer, and his teaching

in this case is that Nō performances should vary according to
the time and circumstances and that, since the mood of the
audience is likely to become gloomy in the darkness of night,
a colourful programme with warrior plays or other pieces with
plenty of action should be chosen and performed in a more
showy way than usual. He sets out this theory as follows:

> 'This is what our secret teaching says: it must be re-
> alised that, in all things, perfection lies at the point
> where the positive and negative principles are in har-
> mony. . . . Since night, on the other hand, is nega-
> tive, the positive element comes from lifting people's
> spirits by performing fine Nō in a thoroughly lively
> way. This means that perfection is reached by har-
> monizing this positive feeling with the negative one
> of the night. It follows, then, that if a positive feel-
> ing is made more positive or a negative feeling more
> negative, there will be no harmony and therefore no
> perfection—and what interest will there be without
> perfection ?'

It goes without saying that this matter of harmonizing the
negative and positive principles, Yin and Yang respectively,
is a borrowing of the explanation of the five natural elements
according to the principles of Yin and Yang which came from
China in ancient times. This is the dualism theory which
regards everything in nature as being formed from one or more
of the five elements of wood, fire, earth, metal and water, with
the first two as positive, the last two as negative and earth as
intermediate, and sees the 'two spirits of Yin and Yang' as controlling the whole. This Zeami used to give theoretical support to practical methods intended to ensure the success of Nō
performances.

Heaven and earth, sun and moon, day and night, black and
white, male and female, man and woman—the principle of
Yin and Yang was applied to absolutely everything, and the

view that the ideal state is the harmonized unification of dualities is to be found throughout the east. Zeami was explaining the skilful harmonization of nature in the form of night and human activity in the form of performing Nō in order to attain 'perfection'—in other words, complete success—in a thoroughly materialistic sense. This could be said to be a classic example of the Japanese stance of harmony rather than confrontation.

In the previous chapter I wrote that, in contrast to western drama which deals with the logical development and logical resolution of confrontational discord, Japanese theatre ends in catharsis through a mood of grief, lamentation and the like; and I gave the michiyuki, not to be found in the west, as the classic expression of this. The michiyuki has no confrontational discord, but consists simply of a description of human emotions conveyed through nature and a gentle mood of sorrow which invites sympathy and understanding. It seems to me that there is a close involvement here with the different positions of confronting or harmonizing with nature or the conditions of daily life which I touched on in connection with the dramas of Ibsen. When Koharu says "Stay with me, I beg you, whether it be to Heaven or Hell" in the michiyuki from *Shinjū Ten no Amijima*, Jihei replies:

> 'Oh, to be sure, to be sure!
> This body of mine is just base elements,
> And when I die they will return to nothing—
> But the souls of man and wife survive seven exis-
>   tences,
> Proof that we shall never part. . . .'

Man born of nature returning to nature—an unconscious prayer for a harmonious reunion with it. We can perhaps say that this is just a very slight manifestation of a spirit which gains peace of mind in the arms of a warm and beneficent nature.

THE AESTHETICS OF "BEAUTY IS TRUTH"

The Appeal of Devils

Bloody Scenes, East and West

It was Zeami, the main creator of Nō, who compared the beauty of stage art with an ever-changing flower. His *Kadensho* can be said to be a treasure-house of impressive observations which go to the very heart of aesthetic consciousness and the arts in Japan, and one that I particularly like is his statement that "For a devil role to be attractive, it should be like a flower blooming on a rock."

This is the final sentence of his advice on playing devil roles which, together with other sections on such roles as woman, old man, mad person, warrior and god, is given in Part 2 of the work, *Monomane Jōjō*.

For Zeami, devil roles were an important item of performance, because they were a traditional skill associated with the Sarugaku—that is, Nō and Kyōgen—group in the province of Yamato, to which his own troupe belonged. He says, however, that devil Nō are extremely difficult. Why is this?

What makes a devil is the fact that it is strong and fearsome, but for a Nō to be a fine one it must have the Flower. This Flower is another way of referring to audience 'appeal,' and being strong and fearsome is different from being appealing. Nor is this a mere, slight difference, but the same as the one between black and white. They are two utterly incompatible, diametrically opposed elements, and since it is nevertheless necessary to raise them both in order to reconcile them at a higher level, it is certainly an extremely difficult undertaking.

For this reason, Zeami is justified in saying that "An actor who has appeal in devil roles is one who is thoroughly accomplished," and he goes on to say that, in order to be such a player, it is not enough to play these roles alone, for he can only reach the peak of achievement when he excels also in other types of yūgen Nō. It was after he explained this that he concluded the section with his phrase about a flower on a rock.

A great crag towering up from a dark valley deep in the mountains is certainly awesome and daunting enough to make a person keep his distance—and yet, if a single flower were to be blooming there on the bare rockface. . . . The majesty of the crag would be enhanced but, at the same time, the flower would appear even more lovely. The magic of the contrast and the appeal of the combination would, in themselves, create an elegance redolent of poetic emotion. Is this not what an artist could capture in a painting, or a poet in verse?

In making this comparison with 'a flower blooming on a rock,' however, Zeami may have had in mind not a real flower but a capping of snow. The reasons for saying this are that both Zeami and his father Kannami were so well acquainted with poetry collections that the preface to the *Kadensho*, for example, teaches the prime importance of poetry and many of their themes and terms were taken from Japanese *waka*; and the tenth-century *Kokinshū* 'Anthology of Poems Ancient and Modern' has the following verse as the eleventh entry in Book 6 'Winter Poems,' under the heading 'Composed by Ki no Akimine on crossing a mountain at Shiga':

> 'Since the white snow
> Has fallen and settled
> Everywhere,
> It looks for all the world
> Like flowers blooming on the rocks.'

Whatever the source, it is indeed a richly evocative simile, and I feel that it is also a well chosen phrase which captures in a few words the entire ideal form of beauty in Nō and, hence, of beauty in Japan. To raise up and reconcile two things which are, at first glance, contradictory and opposite—this is none other than the principle of harmonizing Yin and Yang seen in the previous chapter but, to be more specific, there is perhaps something uniquely Japanese in the intense urge to create beauty which brings about a transmutation so aesthetic that even a devil appears to be 'like a flower blooming on a rock.'

To exaggerate somewhat, it is what might be called an aesthetic value judgement in the broad sense which believes that, no matter how bad or ugly something may be, it should be changed and can be changed into something of beauty, and which puts beauty before everything else. One only has to compare Nō and Kabuki to make it clear that this beauty is far from having a constant form, but I feel that, in any case, this tendency to concentrate on the beautiful is one of the main characteristics of the Japanese people.

How, then, does this aesthetic tendency appear in Kabuki?

We have already touched at times on the general sense of beauty—of what is called formal beauty—in Kabuki, and we should now take up the blood-stained murder scene as an extreme case of something frightful and ugly being made beautiful. Let us look at *Natsu Matsuri* 'Summer Festival' as a typical example.

Osaka on the eve of the Takatsu festival—the scene a back street in the Nagamachi quarter. The stage is set with a bamboo trellis fence entwined with convolvulus, against a background of a black wooden wall beyond which can be seen the roofs of the houses in the town. In the foreground is a paddy field and in it the lowered big trap (*ōzeri*) is fitted with a container of 'real water' (*honmizu*) known as a 'mud boat' (*dorobune*). Here, the fishmonger Danshichi Kurōbe gets himself into the situation where, in order to rescue the daughter

The murder of Giheiji in the Kabuki *Natsu Matsuri*.

of his former master, he has to cruelly murder Giheiji who, though a grasping, hard-hearted old man, is nevertheless his father-in-law.

It is the famous 'Giheiji murder' scene, staged unhurriedly but to really splendid effect, with the clever use of such things as water and a well. At first Danshichi has no idea of seriously harming Giheiji, but as they scuffle he unintentionally wounds him with his sword. This leads the injured Giheiji to cry "Murder! Murder!," and when he staggers about trying to escape, Danshichi pursues him to and fro around the bamboo fence. As he does so, his thin summer kimono patterned in what are known as 'Danshichi stripes' slips off to leave his upper body bare and reveal, vivid even in the darkness, vermilion tattooing. Threatened by the naked sword, Giheiji falls into the paddy field. As he then crawls out, the sight of him covered in mud and blood from his wound and the colour of Danshichi's tattoos as he glares down with sword held high create a weird contrast but, even amid the horror, a bewitching beauty too.

An evil beauty, perhaps. It would have to be described as a remarkably singular concept of beauty, even within the sphere of Kishida Ryūsei's idea of 'common beauty.' It is a devilish beauty which lures the onlooker into a strange excitement and fascination by means of an 'ultra-modern' stimulus compounded of thrills, sensuality and sado-masochism not found in modern times before the avant-garde arts of the present day.

In addition, this savage murder scene is beautified by several dramatic poses, one using the bucket at the well on the left side of the stage, the 'frog mie' of the mud-covered Giheiji, the mie of Danshichi as he looks first one way and then another before delivering the final blow. . . . This beauty is the very expression of the kind of 'moving plastic form' that had also been used in earlier periods.

What follows is also fine theatre. After the murder, Danshichi pours real water from the well over his head to wash off the blood that has spattered him, finally manages with trembling hand to sheath his sword and push the scabbard through his belt, and then puts his kimono back on. Meanwhile, the rhythmic beat of music from the festival procession has been drawing steadily closer, and now countless lanterns and portable shrines pass by on the other side of the wall. As the sound of the music rises, so also do Danshichi's unease, fear and irritation. Between the noisy festival atmosphere echoing from the night sky and the blood-stained tragedy below, stark contrast.

No longer is the music merely part of the background. With this scene Danshichi finds himself in a desperate situation, cornered there by the realisation of his crime in having murdered his father-in-law and by his instinctive sense of mortal danger to his own life; and I hear the drumbeats of the festival music as the thumping of his heart.

A moment or two later the shrines and all the people accompanying them crowd onto the stage. Tremblingly he goes forward to join the throng as it moves on to the accompaniment of the music and then, unsteadily, he disappears along the hanamichi, bringing to an end a gripping 'bloody scene,' the ultimate in cruel beauty.

If it is now asked whether scenes of devils and cruelty are found only in Japan, this is of course by no means the case. Although, as mentioned before, the classical theatrical tradition, from Greek drama to the French classical theatre and the modern drama of Ibsen, avoids showing blood-filled scenes before the eyes of the spectators, murder scenes abound in the popular theatre, from Shakespeare down.

It is not necessary to quote chapter and verse for murder and death scenes in *Hamlet*, *Macbeth* and other works of his, and there are plenty of more strikingly gory plays among the works of other Elizabethan playwrights.

For example, Thomas Kyd's *The Spanish Tragedy* (1589), which is regarded as a precursor of *Hamlet*, could almost be described as a series of violent acts, with the cruel murder of Horatio, Hieronimo's killing of Erastus, Bel-imperia's killing of Balthazar and her own suicide immediately afterwards, Hieronimo's torture and his biting out his own tongue, his murder of the Duke of Castile and then his suicide. . . . Such works as *The Duchess of Malfi* (1614) by John Webster, who was a little younger than Shakespeare, and *The Revenger's Tragedy* (1607) by Cyril Tourneur are similar and are considered classics of what is known as blood tragedy. These two last works have been staged in Japan in comparatively recent years, when the trend in popular taste was for the erotic and grotesque.

Documentary evidence seems to show that, in England at that time, these plays were staged in a very realistic way. When murders took place, there were, for example, graphic representations of viscera being pulled out from the body, and the blood of calves or sheep is said to have been used on such occasions as being much less likely to congeal than human blood.

Even at the present time there are any number of brutal plays of this kind in the west: the Grand Guignol fringe theatre, for instance, which I saw in Paris on my first visit to Europe in 1958. This had been mentioned as an example of cruel and weird theatre in John van Druten's *Playwright at Work*, which I had translated for publication several years before when I was in my twenties, and so I went to see it with pleasurable expectations. Unfortunately, these were not fulfilled by the four short pieces I saw, but there was a glimpse of what the theatre stood for in the last play, entitled *The Human Torpedo*, in a scene in which a bloodied woman spy was dragged out through the hatch of a warship and, the next moment, there was a great explosion inside the ship.

I am reminded here of an interesting story I heard just recently from a friend of mine, the musician Koizumi Fumio, at one of the regular meetings of the UNESCO East Asia Cultural Research Centre, which have been running for several years. Apparently, a play derived from the great Indian epic poem, the *Mahabharata* (ca. 3rd century), and found extensively in Southeast Asia has a very elaborate murder scene.

A detestable person is not only murdered but also has his chest cut open and his bleeding heart plucked out. Blood flows everywhere. They then very kindly arrange to have veins and arteries of various sizes cling fast to the plucking hand, one after the other, until these are also cut away one by one. All this, he said, takes place before the gaze of the audience with such deliberation that it lasts at least fifteen minutes.

This is further evidence that scenes of cruelty are to be found at all times, east and west, but Koizumi also said that the material used for the blood was obtained from sappanwood. That too I readily accepted, because the dark-red sappan juice obtained by boiling down the heartwood of the tree is the most realistic material used for blood in scenes of murder and wounding in Kabuki.

All kinds of things are used for blood in Kabuki, from the very simple method of employing strips of red cloth to others which involve mixing some red agent with seawood glue or honey but, in so far as sappan juice runs more freely, it gives a much more realistic impression. It seems to have been commonly used around the third quarter of the nineteenth century.

Tsubouchi Shōyō said in his *Tōzai no Senjōteki Higeki* 'Lustful Tragedy East and West' (although short, this is the outstanding essay among his numerous works and one of my favourite pieces) that 'The performance of "blood tragedies" in Japan before 1877 was truly something without parallel,' and he gave 'sappan blood' as a distinctive feature in this. It seems, though, that the countries to the south which produce this sappanwood are well ahead in the use of it in their blood tragedies.

Beautifying Ugliness and Brutality

Japanese 'Cruelty'

Now, it is clear from what we have seen that the genre of bloody scenes and cruel plays is certainly not a unique feature of Kabuki but exists extremely widely and very much as a matter of course in the theatres of races throughout the world. If we accept that cruel plays have a special quality in Kabuki, the question then is what form this takes. In seeking an answer, I think we can go back to the point about there being in it a process of 'beautification,' of the kind we saw earlier in connection with the play *Natsu Matsuri*.

Here I would just like to mention something about a general sense of 'cruelty' pre-dating the theatre, because it seems that dolphins and whales give rise to foreign criticism of the Japanese for being cruel and many Japanese, taking this criticism at face value, worry about it more than they should. I discussed the same kind of thing in the previous chapter in connection with the existence of a love of nature, and I will preempt my conclusion by stating now that there is no reason for saying that the Japanese are especially cruel in comparison with other races.

There is, for instance, a story about a western girl who, on coming to Japan and seeing a small bird cooked whole, cried "Oh, how cruel! And such a sweet little bird!" yet, with child-like naïveté, sat at table and ate with apparent relish meat from a calf that had been roasted whole, complete with head and ears, and carved up before her. Briefly, is this anything more than a difference in customs?

Then again, in Japan one might find carp jerking about as their flesh is crimped to firm it up, or people eating live, twitching prawns, that is, 'dancing sushi.' It is said, however, that in Chinese cookery—never having come across such high-class cuisine, I have no personal experience—people sometimes scoop out and eat the brains of living monkeys, and think very highly of a dish involving forcibly feeding still-blind baby rats with honey to fatten them until they are transparent and then throwing them into their mouths while they are still alive. I myself have seen at an international drama festival in the town of Erlangen in Germany a play in which a philanthropic poet protested against the ill-treatment of monkeys and, as a result, had his head split open when he was used as a sacrifice.

There is no telling which of these is more cruel than any other. I wonder too about the way in which the Japanese feel abashed when they are told that they mistreat cats and dogs and lack concern for the welfare of animals generally. The western attachment to cats and dogs is not because they are accepted and loved at the same level as people but because, as pets, they satisfy a person's tastes and interests or, sometimes, his image of himself and his desire to dominate. When I go to the west, I admire how well these domestic animals are trained but, in order to achieve this, they are given such a hard time when they are young that their natural animal instincts are wiped out. Only if we could ask the animals themselves would we ever know what happiness means for them.

When it comes to cattle and pigs, these are literally disposed of by the convenient reasoning that they were kindly provided by God so that they could be eaten by man. It also goes beyond animals: there can surely be no one who thinks that westerners are more compassionate than the Japanese when they look at the instrument of punishment known as 'The Iron Maiden,' consisting of coffin-like panels with the figure of a beautiful woman on the front and countless projecting spikes on the back, or the method of punishment by dismemberment in which death came from having the limbs tied to four carts and torn from the body by driving the horses in different directions.

There is, on the contrary, the view based on the difference between eating meat and eating fish that the west is more cruel than Japan. A newspaper recently carried an article complete with photographs which said that somewhere in America in just one operation 10,000 rabbits had been enclosed and beaten to death with clubs in order to prevent damage to crops. I have no mind to turn round and ask whether dolphins are more attractive than rabbits, and still less do I claim that westerners or foreigners are more cruel or reprehensible than the Japanese. There is nothing to choose between them, and the first human beings can hardly have had any essential difference of character either. What I do say is that it is strange to make an issue of cruelty in a people's nature on the basis of dolphins and rabbits.

I do, though, feel somewhat irritated at the way in which we Japanese are so undignified, subservient and self-effacing that a foreigner only has to begin to make a point about animal welfare for us—perhaps because of some complex dating from the opening of the country in the nineteenth century—to become apologetic without even getting to the root of the matter.

If I accept that there is nothing to be done about it if I am misunderstood, I will say that there are many of us Japanese who are so heartless that they will throw stones st peaceful animals or catch and eat protected birds. Indiscriminate violence and the pointless taking of life do indeed deserve to be called cruel. They are also crimes, and I feel that a person should guard himself against them by seeing them as expressions of a meanness of spirit and, when a group is involved, as a feeble and childish path to tyranny. People in the west certainly exercise good judgement of time and place with regard to animals, for example, and to that extent they probably are after all more 'adult.'

Now, returning to our subject, in treating this common theme of cruelty there is, in the case of Japan, a process of 'beautification.' It seems to me that, for the Japanese, this is a necessity, while in the west the point of a bloody scene undoubtedly lies in the cruelty itself. I have wondered recently whether this western treatment does not come from the theatrical tradition of 'the encouragement of good and the chastisement of evil,' which has existed since the medieval period. As retribution for a lack of belief in God or of moral virtue, the sufferings of hell and purgatory had to be sufficiently cruel and harsh. Is it not likely that the line of bloody tragedy which has come right down to the present day, in the west had the function, plainly speaking, of providing object lessons to this end?

Perhaps, therefore, scenes of cruelty should simply be thoroughly brutal, ugly and abominable. Drama goes back to the original cause, original sin, which gave rise to scenes of cruelty, and with the leverage provided by such scenes, develops by the pursuit of logic; or these scenes inevitably come in as the conclusions of logical dramas.

Kabuki audiences, however, indulge themselves by not being satisfied with a scene of murder or torture simply as a loathsome situation necessary to the development of the drama as a whole, and by requiring instead 'enjoyment' from the sight and sound of the scene itself. Colour and form, sound and rhythm and, from combinations of these, a sense of total beauty and pleasure. . . .

Natsu Matsuri was put forward earlier as a classic example, but in *Chūshingura* the scenes of the harakiri of the young lord and of Kanpei and the shooting and killing of Sadakurō on the Yamazaki highway, and the murder of the masseur Bunya in *Utsunoya Tōge* all form 'one-act plays' well worthy of appreciation for their artistry in using sight and sound by giving full rein to skills in both performance and production. The elevation of aestheticism and enjoyment can be said to reach its height in these pieces. Japan is surely the only country with this kind of play, in which death, murder and torture scenes each make independent one-act pieces.

When the main character in a murder or torture scene is a woman, the beauty of the cruelty is magnified by a special kind of eroticism. Examples of this—O-Kiku who is hung up and slashed beside the well in *Sara Yashiki*, the tortures in the snow in *Chūjō-hime* 'Princess Chūjō' and *Akegarasu* 'The Morning Crow,' and so on—are too numerous to list in full.

The staging of aragoto and fight scenes could also probably be added to this kind of beautified genre. Something has been said before about the aesthetic sense that underlies the red make-up of the aragoto hero, but the indigo kumadori of the villain, evil though he may be, also excites a certain feeling of awesome beauty. There is also a teaching which says that "Aragoto should be done with the imitation of a boy of six or seven in mind. To imitate a heroic figure is merely vulgar." In talking about his art, Danjūrō II, the great actor who invented kumadori as still used today, is here saying that power alone is not enough for an aragoto role, for this requires a child-like element too. This may be said to express the same spirit as Zeami's teaching that devils should be not only powerful and fearsome but also entertaining.

Originally a violent and murderous brawl, Kabuki fighting has also been raised to the level of a splendid spectacle, in its case by combining set movements, selected and refined over a long period, and musical effects appropriate to them. These fight scenes—for instance, the three-dimensional one in *Ranpei Monogurui* which uses a ladder, roof and lanterns, and the scene of the death of Kokingo in *Yoshitsune Senbonzakura*—again often make by themselves one-act plays which audiences thoroughly enjoy.

Another thing which should stand beside the murder scene

is the weird, spine-chilling one featuring a ghost or revengeful spirit. It should be mentioned here that spirits and ghosts are clearly distinguished in Kabuki. Plays about the supernatural are a tradition of the Onoe house, and Kikugorō III, who could be regarded as its founder, taught that ghosts should be played with a peaceful feeling and spirits with a tormented one because, at their time of death, spirits had lost none of their desire for vengeance. In modern times, Onoe Baikō VI (1870-1934), who took over this artistic tradition from the previous generation, set out this distinction in his *Ume no Shitakaze* 'Wind-blown Plum Blossom [of the Onoe House]' in precise terms, as follows:

> 'When ghosts who have taken the form of foxes or badgers bring their lower arms up, they generally carry the hands on a level with the centre of the chest. Although spirits keep their hands lower, they will look like ghosts if they bring them up even a little too much, and so full attention must be paid to this point. Similarly, spirits have a heavy-eyed look and ghosts have wide-open eyes, and so it is by such things as this that the distinctions between the two are made in performance.'

He has all kinds of other things to say about the playing of spirit roles alone. Parts like those of O-Iwa in *Yotsuya Kaidan* and O-Kiku in *Sara Yashiki* are all made up of such carefully studied artistic devices. I shall discuss 'art' in the theatre further in the concluding chapter but, in any case, there is surely no other country which has built up over hundreds of years such a wealth of concern about the *aesthetic representation* of murder, death, spirits and the like.

In order to beautify scenes featuring revengeful spirits, which should be essentially ugly, weird and frightening, recourse is had not only to the stylization of the spirit itself, but also to the technique of placing them beside completely opposite

O-Iwa in the Kabuki *Yotsuya Kaidan*.

bright and beautiful scenes. For instance, Tsuruya Nanboku's great play *Yotsuya Kaidan*, which could be described as the supreme example of tales of the supernatural. The cruel death of O-Iwa after her torment, the curse scene beside the Onbōbori river, the incest and suicide of a couple tragically wronged by fate . . . there is a series of these frightening, weird or sad scenes. The outcome is a scene showing domination by the spirit of the dead O-Iwa and the capture of the villain Tamiya Iemon, but inserted immediately before this is the strange 'Dream Scene.'

The curtain opens to show, floating in mid-air and made

from silver paper, the character for *kokoro* 'heart,' signifying a scene about what is in the heart, that is, a dream. The stage itself shows a neat, bright farmhouse, and O-Iwa enters in the form of a beautiful country girl. Iemon, dressed as a falconer, happens to come by and begins to be rather flirtatious—whereupon the girl's face immediately changes into the repulsive features of O-Iwa. It is an absurd scene but, brief though this literal 'vision of beauty' is, it is impossible to measure the role it plays in beautifying and taking into a world of romance this long and fantastic play which could well be called the ultimate expression of pain and sorrow.

A more striking scene occurs in Mokuami's *Kagamiyama Gonichi no Iwafuji* 'The Reappearance of Iwafuji at Mt. Kagami.' The Lady Iwafuji having been killed by Onoe, a lady-in-waiting, because of a grudge, her spirit is not at peace. Her bones, scattered in a thicket, reassemble themselves into a skeleton and, in this form, persecute Onoe. The play is therefore commonly known as *Kotsuyose no Iwafuji* 'The Bones of Iwafuji,' but the scene which follows this uncanny one makes a complete change by showing a glorious spring landscape of open countryside. Iwafuji in all her former beauty, dressed for cherry-viewing and carrying a parasol, comes up on the suppon lift on the hanamichi, and as she chases a butterfly, she flies up into the air and disappears over the heads of the audience—a vision of bewitching beauty, or a dream, perhaps? Either way, we can surely describe it as the most widely enjoyed case of Japanese-style aesthetics turning ugliness into beauty.

Just one thing I should like to add here: this kind of theatre of the weird and cruel is by no means the product of savage blood-stained worlds, but is in fact born into ages which, though they may harbour oppression and anxieties, are generally peaceful. The Elizabethan period, for example, was one of peace and national prosperity which arrived immediately after the throne of Elizabeth I had been secured by the execution of Mary Stuart following the bloody disputes about her status as queen, and the greatest national threat, the arrival of the enormous Spanish armada, had been repulsed. Then too, the first three-quarters of the nineteenth century in Japan, which saw the peak in murder scenes and plays about the supernatural, were of course a time of full maturity at the end of a long period of peace.

A world at war, when the lives and property of ordinary people are exposed to danger, has no time to watch make-believe bloody tragedies. Those around them are quite enough: unlike traffic accidents and ordinary murders, they do not occur at random but minute by minute pose a constant threat of high probability.

This was made clear at the height of the Pacific War, for one thing, when casualties on the battlefield were unceasing and everyone was exposed to air raids, and yet bright patriotic plays and comedies starring Enomoto Kenichi and Furukawa Roppa were all the rage. It was a similar situation for a while after the war, when strip-shows and musical films were popular.

In a time when war recedes from people's sense of actuality and the importance of human life tends to be forgotten, bloody plays or pieces about malice begin to flourish, and the real world itself becomes rife with reckless and foolhardy behaviour and murders for no good reason. These are the products of a period in which peace provides idle time day after day and, in addition, there is subconsciously a deep feeling of isolation, anxiety and mistrust. Perhaps present-day Japan since the start of its economic growth can be cited as the classic example of this.

Between the Real and Unreal

Forms of Ideal Beauty

A spirit which seeks to change even negative things such as devils, vengeful spirits and scenes of cruelty into such positive things as beauty and pleasure. This no doubt comes from the view Japanese have of the performing arts, which takes it that they should provide human existence with longevity and happiness. Ultimately, it is probably the same in other countries too, but in the field of drama, at least in the west, the basic process has been to carry out a purging of the emotions by means of the development and resolution of the dramatic content of a play. This has already been mentioned several times, but while in Japan the dramatic content is important, the primary principle is to provide first and foremost a pleasurable aesthetic feeling directly through the senses.

It is Zeami yet again who, in the following sentence from Part 5 *Ōgi ni Iwaku* 'Statements of Inner Secrets' of the *Kaden-sho*, gives the earliest and clearest account of the view that the aim of the performing arts is to contribute to longevity and happiness:

'Now the performing arts affect the feelings of all
men, high and low alike, by softening their hearts,
and they can be a source of increased happiness and
a means of prolonging life.'

Even playing the role of a devil in an entertaining way has as its sole object to soften men's hearts and to move equally both the nobility and the lower orders. One place where he gives an example of this in specific terms is in the introduction to Part 2 *Monomane Jōjō* of the same work. He explains there that although the basic purpose of mimicry is to 'give a close imitation of everything without exception,' there are shades of light and dark in the way an imitation is done according to what is being represented. While such things as the behaviour of the upper classes, especially the nobility and warriors, and movements associated with elegant pursuits like poetry and music should be imitated in every detail, it would not do to imitate too closely and realistically peasants or other rustics. The reason for this is that:

> 'These should not be shown to the gaze of the upper classes. If this were to be done, it would be too vulgar and any interest there might be in it would be lost.'

Zeami and his father Kannami enjoyed the patronage of the military ruler Ashikaga Yoshimitsu, and what most exercised them was naturally to gain the interest of new patrons in the higher levels of society while, at the same time, maintaining the affection of the ordinary people on whom they had previously relied for support. It can be seen from the two quotations above how desperate was the concern to achieve this, and it is clear too that the factor deciding the level of realism in the performance was the question of whether or not something was entertaining for the audience, that is, whether or not in their eyes the Flower was there.

In spite of changes of period, social levels of audiences, and the content and form of drama, this attitude to the performing arts saw no change in Japan. In the world of the Kabuki and puppet theatre centuries later, the following story about

the playwright Chikamatsu Monzaemon appeared as an item
in the introduction to a work called *Naniwa Miyage* 'Gifts from
Naniwa' by a friend of his, the Confucianist and devotee of
Kabuki, Hozumi Koretsura (the father of Chikamatsu Hanji,
the author of *Imoseyama Onna Teikin*).

Someone put it to Chikamatsu that since it was a time when
everything was based on reason and no one would accept anything that was not realistic, even the skill of Kabuki actors was
judged on the extent to which they imitated the 'real thing':
the senior retainer in real life was taken as the model for the
roles of senior retainers, the main consideration in playing the
part of a military lord was seen as making him just like a lord,
and plays of the old kind were shunned as being 'childish.'
What, the man asked, did Chikamatsu think of this tendency ?

He replied that, although the view described appeared
reasonable enough, he rejected it as coming from people who
were ignorant of 'the treatment of truth in art.' He then went
on:

> 'Art lies in the thin membrane between the real and
> the unreal. Because it is indeed the case that nowa-
> days everyone likes faithful copies of the real thing,
> actors playing the part of a lord's retainer will copy
> the actions and speech of a real retainer—but, in that
> case, who ever heard of a retainer of a military lord
> wearing make-up as an actor does ?
> Then, too, if an actor were to appear on the stage
> and play his part with straggling whiskers and bald-
> ing head on the grounds that real retainers do not
> adorn their looks, what entertainment would there
> be in that ? Here there exists no more than the thick-
> ness of what I call a membrane. Unreality without
> being unreal and reality without being real—it is be-
> tween the two that entertainment lies.'

These are Chikamatsu's well-known words 'On the Reality and Unreality Membrane.' As mentioned before, it was he who firmly established drama in Japan through sharp human observation and realistic portrayal which were at least the equal of the western theatre of realism. Even Chikamatsu—or, rather, because he was Chikamatsu, he was well aware of the distinction between a flat realism produced by a simple 'portrayal' and an aesthetically heightened realism. That again was taken further, until whether or not something led to 'entertainment' became the deciding factor in a value judgement. It was simply a matter of this being called the Flower in the medieval warrior culture and 'entertainment' in the popular culture of the Edo period.

Immediately after the passage quoted above, Chikamatsu gives a perceptive example of the limitations of realism, or the difference between reality and art.

A lady in service at court had a lover, but there was no way that the man could be allowed inside the part of the palace where she was. She could only see him occasionally through the rattan blinds and so, 'in her extraordinary longing,' she had an exact replica made of him in wood. However, . . .

> 'She had it made so that, unlike an ordinary doll, the face, for example, showed not the minutest difference from the man himself: the skin colour was of course the same, she had each hair follicle pricked out, and the nostrils, ears and even the number of teeth varied in not the slightest degree. Since it was made with the man alongside, the only difference was that one had the spark of life and the other did not. When the lady put the doll beside her and looked at it, however, it was such a direct copy of the living thing that her pleasure in it faded and she felt only distaste and fear. Even such a love as hers

cooled, and finding it irksome to have the doll beside her, before long she threw it away.'

Chikamatsu then goes on to extend this idea of the membrane between the real and unreal to play texts, and concludes with the words:

> 'While plots too will follow the original in this way, they have a wider sweep and it is when they are finally given artistic form that they provide entertainment for the hearts of men. Texts and the like will also offer much to appreciate if they are given the same consideration.'

Leaving aside the element of beautification, if it is simply a matter of what an art form should be, that is, the gap or 'dimensional difference' between what is reality for the audience and the real thing itself, then it goes without saying that there are those in the west too who well understand the idea behind Chikamatsu's view of the real and unreal.

The famous French actor Benoit C. Coquelin (1841-1909), for example, who made his name in Molière's comedies and had his most successful role in *Cyrano de Bergerac*, is said to have always told the following story from Aesop's *Fables* when he was teaching pupils about the essentials of stage art.

> 'At a fair during a festival, an illusionist imitated the noise of a young pig and received great applause for it. Seeing this, a farmer said that he could do much better, and having hidden a real live piglet under his jacket, he pulled its ears and made it cry out. But the people there went away criticising him, saying "Why, that's nothing like it! The first one was much better."''

After telling this story, he would always go on to say to his pupils, "Do you know why this was? The reason is that the noise the pig made was certainly real enough, but it wasn't done with any artistry."

The point of this story is almost identical to Chikamatsu's view of the dividing line between the real and unreal. I must point out, however, that this story is wholly concerned with the appearance of reality, without any element of the sensuous beautification found in Nō and Kabuki. I feel, though, that there is in it the same difference between 'representation' and 'presentation' that has been raised several times already. Following Aristotle's definition of art as a form of imitation at the beginning of his *Poetics*, through Hamlet's statement that a play holds the mirror up to nature, down to Emile Zola's view of drama as a laboratory of life, as life itself, the principle that has always been at the heart of western drama is that of 'the representation of human existence.' Coquelin's view of his art was in the same tradition, his teaching being intended to achieve this representation to best effect.

In the case of Japan, the aim is not the representation of actuality, but the presentation of an 'ideal image' or 'ideal beauty.' That is fundamentally different. We could perhaps call it the creation of a vision of the way we *want* things to be, which goes beyond the way they *seem* to be. The idea behind this is, I feel, the same as the one we saw earlier in relation to Bonsai and Ikebana. I am not, of course, saying on that account that western drama is not artistic, or that Japanese theatre is superior, and thereby arguing that one is to be valued more highly than the other. Each has its strengths. What I am bringing into question here is the difference in character between the theatres of east and west, by taking into account what their audiences look for in them.

For example, Zeami warned that, when imitating an old man, if the body is hunched up by bending it at the knees and hips in order to make it *seem* old, the Flower will be lost and only the impression of decrepit old age will remain. Since there would be no interest or entertainment in that, what should be done to create the ideal image of an old man? Zeami advised that, for this, one should 'carry oneself gracefully, with absolutely no sense of agitation.'

The essential thing in being an old man is not the outward appearance but unhurried, graceful movements and quiet composure. This is also, he is saying, the desired appearance for an old man. There will be other interpretations, but that is what I consider Zeami had in mind.

Sakata Tōjūrō was a famous player of young male leads in domestic dramas during the Genroku era for whom Chikamatsu is said to have written many of his plays, and on one occasion it was decided that he should take the part of Fujiya Izaemon, a gallant who frequently patronized a well known courtesan called Yūgiri Tayū. New straw sandals were therefore ordered for him from the property man, but when Tōjūrō saw the finished articles, he said that they were too big and asked for them to be remade. The property man pointed out that they could hardly be too big as he had been measured for them before the order was given, but the actor insisted that they were too big and asked for them to be made smaller all round.

There being nothing else for it, they were remade. They were now smaller than his feet, but when it was time for the stage rehearsal he just managed to get the thongs of the sandals between his toes in order to make his entrance. It was the same on the day of the first performance.

Those who saw this thought it odd, and when they asked him the reason, he replied, "I have to take these sandals off in the garden of the assignation house where I wait for Yūgiri. I leave them there on the stage, and if they were too big everyone in the audience would see that I have feet like great shovels, and that would be the end for a play about a great lover like me."

For an audience, a stage lover is the ideal handsome man, who has to be elegant and stylish. They also want him to have small feet and to be pale-complexioned—that is the classic image of a lover. Tōjūrō can perhaps be regarded as the actor who created the most richly realistic style in the history of the traditional theatre, and yet even he had as his final objective this kind of 'manifestation of ideal beauty.'

It goes without saying that the art of the *onnagata* 'male player of women's roles' has been studied, elaborated and refined beyond the mere 'semblance' of a woman, with the aim of creating an ideal feminine beauty. Since the actor is in fact a man, it is only natural that, however much he seeks to take on the 'semblance' of a woman, he immediately runs up against his limitations, whether it be his voice or his large physical frame.

There are female impersonators in the west too, as was mentioned in the opening chapter. From ancient Greece to the end of the medieval period, it was in fact more common to have males playing women's roles. In England this remained unchanged even with the coming of the Renaissance: both Ophelia and Juliet were played by boy actors.

Their stage appearances, however, were limited to the period before their voices broke, and since the text is the main consideration in western theatre, as has been mentioned any number of times, it was enough for them to recite their lines in a high-pitched voice like that of a woman. There was no need, for example, to trouble about depicting feminine beauty by their deportment. All they needed was the charming 'voice and appearance' which Zeami pointed out as being the Flower of a boy of eleven or twelve.

Kabuki audiences, in contrast, were not satisfied with that kind of thing but demanded a striking and yet mature feminine beauty. In Nō, a woman's mask makes clear the sex, nature and age of the character the moment the actor appears on the stage. For the rest, due regard has to be given to the costuming (the choice of robes and the way they are worn) and to maintaining a graceful physical presence; but since there are no masks in Kabuki, its audiences looked for a feminine beauty which was more intrinsic and closer to reality. The reason for this was, I believe, that in the formative period of Kabuki they had become accustomed to a sensual beauty in which arms and legs were exposed to view by women entertainers such as O-Kuni from Izumo.

It was female eroticism on stage, a thing which had never previously existed in the history of the performing arts in Japan. It was, so to speak, forbidden fruit. O-Kuni's creation of 'Kabuki dance' took place in Kyoto in 1603, and even after women performers were banned twenty-six years later on the grounds of bringing disorder to public morals, audiences did not forget the fruit they had tasted. In due course, the female impersonator supplied them with this fruit in an even more complex and richer form.

Yoshizawa Ayame, who was renowned in the Genroku era as the founder of the art of the female impersonator corresponding to Tōjūrō as a young male lead, left many stories about his art in the *Ayamegusa* 'Words from Ayame' section of a work called *Yakusha Rongo* 'The Actors' Analects.' At the start of it, for instance, he states that 'Sensuality is the basis of the onnagata,' and makes a particular point about being 'young':

> 'Even though an onnagata may be forty or more, he will be known as a *waka-onnagata* 'young onnagata.' He could be called simply an onnagata, but the addition of 'young' should ensure that he does not neglect a brightness of spirit. It is a small point, but it should be understood that this word 'young' is important for an onnagata.'

The most fundamental advice from Ayame was that an

onnagata should 'live as a woman all the time.' This was not a matter of simple imitation so that he could 'seem' like a woman. The intention was that, by *living* like a woman from day to day, he would thoroughly absorb the feminine mind and behaviour and *bring them to life* on the stage. He acquired, from within and without, personal experience of the particular features of feminine beauty to be seen from a comparison with men as well as womanish aspects unnoticed by women themselves, and then extended, accentuated and formalized these. By doing this, he created an ideal image of femininity.

The art of the Kabuki onnagata can be said to be the most splendid illustration of what Chikamatsu described as 'unreality without being unreal and reality without being real.'

BEAUTY BEFORE TRUTH

The Flower and Entertainment

The spirit seeking an ideal beauty is the same as the psychology of audiences who say that, no matter what or where the theatre may be, they could not return there unless it made them aware of the Flower and provided them with entertainment. This aestheticism of the Japanese is also, in a broad sense, a spirit of enjoyment; and this spirit means that, when it comes down to it, they would even choose beauty before truth in the ordinary meaning of the word. Or one could say that, in the world of the traditional arts in Japan, 'Beauty is indeed truth.'

The examples already given may be sufficient, but I will give just one more: the portrayal of people living in the lower depths of society. Among the works of Maxim Gorky is a play with that very title, *The Lower Depths*, which was called *Yoru no Yado* 'Lodgings for the Night' when it was first translated and staged in Japan by Osanai Kaoru in 1910. The main characters—locksmith, ex-actor, former baron, tailor, prostitute, tramp, thief, and so on—are all people who have dropped out of society. The cheap basement lodging-house is a set of thorough-going realism, dark and dirty, and the characters too are utterly unlovely, the very epitome of drifters who have turned their backs on reality.

Through these sad lives and its emphasis on humanity, the play is, of course, an indictment of the contradictions in a society at the end of the nineteenth century that had been poisoned by modern capitalism, and so that kind of realistic presentation is absolutely necessary. In a word, the theme in this instance is the 'truth' of society and people, and it is from the picture of this unvarnished truth that the 'beauty' of its humanity shines out.

With Kabuki, the opposite is the case. Both *Benten Kozō* and the riverside scene in *Sannin Kichisa*, discussed in the early part of the book, are similar to Gorky's play in having thieves who are living in the depths, alienated from the conventional world. They, however, are attractively made-up with white face-powder, make their entries stylishly dressed, recite their lines announcing themselves to their popular audiences, and bask in their applause. It might be said that, by sacrificing the everyday reality of the thief and beautifying it in another dimension, it is a eulogy to the pride of the oppressed. In that case, then, we could well say, perhaps, that it is 'beauty' that is 'truth.'

To sum up, while in the west representation is the essence of theatre and verisimilitude its very life-blood and, therefore, 'truth is beauty,' in Japan the Flower and entertainment are its life-blood and 'beauty is truth'—in other words, beauty is given precedence over truth.

To back this, let us bring up an example which, though it is somewhat extreme, is all the more impressive for that. It is the case of murder being committed during a play. It goes without saying that a play is fiction from beginning to end. The audience empathize with the drama, effect a transfer of emotions with the characters on the stage and, by so doing, experience anger, sadness, joy, fear, and so on. Just occasionally, however, the limitations of it as fiction or the conventions that are the major premise are lost to view or broken because the emotional transfer is too powerful.

If it is no more than Kō no Moronō, the persecutor of the young lord in *Chūshingura*, being struck by a piece of orange peel, there is no problem, but unforeseen tragedies become inevitable when it goes much further than that. When this happens, east and west are as one in being made painfully aware of the frightening power of the theatre—but let us look first at an example from the west.

Othello was being performed in a theatre in Chicago in 1909, and a well-known actor called William Butts was playing the part of the villainous Iago. As the performance went on and the cunning Iago gave Othello the idea that his wife Desdemona was being unfaithful to him, until finally Othello became mad with jealousy and determined to kill his poor, innocent and beloved wife—at this point a shot suddenly rang out from a seat in the stalls. Butts, as Iago, collapsed on the stage and died.

The man who had fired the gun came to his senses amid the confusion and, realising that Butts was dead, put the gun to his own temple and killed himself on the spot. A young officer of unblemished character, he had shot the evil stage character forgetting, in the face of his compelling performance, that it was a play.

For an example from Japan, there is the following true story, recorded in Shinoda Kōzō's *Bakumatsu Hyakuwa* 'A Hundred Stories from the Late Edo Period.'

The son of a samurai called Sakurai, who was a morbidly serious young man, fell into a depressed state and shut himself up at home partly because, no doubt, he was over-protected there. Anxious about this, his parents sent him off on a visit to the theatre with a friend. The play was *Tenjiku Tokubei*, but when it came to the part where Tokubei murders his old mother Yae, the dutiful son of the Sakurais changed colour, retrieved the sword that he had deposited at the entrance, and used it to force his way on to the stage as he shouted, "You wicked wretch, Tokubei! How can a son do that to his mother?"

A servant of Ichikawa Ichizō, who was playing Tokubei,

died almost immediately when he had his arm cut off as he was trying to stop him, but Ichizō just managed to save himself by using a piece of stage machinery to hoist himself into the air and make his escape. The young Sakurai was overpowered as he was about to turn his sword on himself, bemoaning the fact that he had failed to kill Ichizō.

These are both exactly the same kind of terrible story, but what I would like to point out here is how different the outcome was in each case.

After the tragedy in Chicago, the young man who had done the shooting and the actor who had been shot were buried in the same grave, and a memorial stone was set up with the following inscription:

> 'To an Ideal Actor and an Ideal Member of the Audience.'

In the Japanese case, Shinmon Tatsugorō, a leading entertainer famous for his dramatic monologues and Naniwa-bushi style recitations (the fifth generation of this line is still active), acted as intermediary and the matter was dealt with privately, in an amicable settlement, by the Sakurai parents making a payment of 100 ryō.

Leaving aside here any question about the morality involved, we must note that although they were both cases of extreme behaviour that transcended the fictional nature of the theatre, there was a great difference in the way they were resolved: in the west, it was a question of how respect could be shown to the reality (truth) of the situation, and in Japan one of how much trouble had been caused by ruining ordinary people's enjoyment of the make-believe and causing a disturbance in the theatre. It is interesting, I think, that this difference should be shown in such stark terms. In Japan the first principle is to sense beauty, appreciate the Flower, and gain enjoyment, over and above truth.

A spirit which prizes the Flower and beauty, even in extreme situations—a spirit based, of course, on the sense of life that existed among the Japanese before the stage was developed because, whatever transformations it may go through, a play is in the end nothing but the faithful reflection of those who create it. Both they and the people who accept and support it are, after all, fundamentally one and the same.

There is an example of this in the matter of food, so necessary for life itself: in Japan, people set great store by the arangement of food on a dish, whenever they have the time to spare. There is an aesthetic feeling about pieces of china with well arranged food on them—and there is no telling how greatly this adds to the enjoyment of the food.

It is the same with the colourful and richly decorated ceremonial aprons in Sumo wrestling. Red, blue and glittery dressing gowns are worn in boxing and pro-wrestling, but these fall far short of the magnificent spectacle of Sumo's decorated aprons and the formal entry into the ring of the procession of top-ranking wrestlers—or is this just a prejudice on my part, as a fan of Sumo? Even the Tosa fighting dogs, though, are decorated with magnificently embroidered sashes.

When it comes to extreme situations, none is more extreme, I suppose, than facing death, as armour-clad warriors did on the battlefield.

In the west, the armour was wholly functional, the very essence of harsh reality. Among the novels of Natsume Sōseki, my favourites are *Kokoro* 'The Heart' and *Rondon-tō* 'The Tower of London,' a place impregnated with the bloody history of an England which, to quote Sōseki, 'cut men down like grass, slaughtered men like chickens, and piled corpses up like dried fish.' Its oldest part, the White Tower, houses countless exhibits from western countries dating from the Middle Ages onwards, from armour, swords, pikes and guns to horse mail, as well as a guillotine and other instruments of punishment.

Japanese armour with white threads, dating from
the Kamakura period.

When I first visited the Tower in 1958, I was captivated—
perhaps because I quite like sharpening steel kitchen knives
and choppers—by the extraordinary coldness of the metal, as
it all gave off the same heavy, dull, silvery lustre. Since then,
whenever I have been to London, I have never missed finding
at least half an hour for a visit to this bloodstained castle.

What, then, of the strikingly different armour of Japan?
I always marvel at its splendour, with the scarlet and black
threads of the body armour and the dragon-crested helmets.
Their beauty is such that nowadays they are put on display
as art objects of the highest quality. Without their colourful

brilliance, there would probably never have been the helmet identification scene at the beginning of *Chūshingura*, in which the helmet of Nitta Yoshisada has to be picked out following his death in battle, and the man-to-man struggle in *Ichinotani Futaba Gunki* would have ended up by being simply a violent fight scene with little or nothing of the Flower in it.

The difference between the cold, all-grey armour of the west and the colourful, resplendent Japanese armour can be compared to that between the glaciers of northern Europe which gave rise to Ibsen and the perfect setting of Mt. Fuji seen through the branches of pine and cherry trees. There is the same kind of difference, I feel, between not only the Tower of London but the castles of the west generally, and Japanese castles, which have left such classic examples for us as the White Heron Castle at Himeji.

Military captains in Japan impregnated with incense the armour made for them by the devoted efforts of master craftsmen, and then went out to face death in battle. The short time they spent on the battlefield, with their lives at stake, was their testimony that they had lived in this world, the supreme hours of their lives. They would announce their names to each other and exchange poems, seeking to beautify, with dignity and colour, the moment that separated them from life or death.

The handsome suits of armour and their fragrant scents were meant to make life into a flower, or death into something equally beautiful.

A teacher called Hasuda Zenmei, who taught me classical Chinese at middle school, shot a wretch of a superior officer in Singapore when defeat came at the end of the war, and then killed himself with the same pistol. He was apparently one of the teachers who influenced the novelist Mishima Yukio, and on one occasion, when he returned home on leave from China where he served first, he was persuaded to take the platform to talk to us. He left with us, as his view of life gained on the field of battle, the thought that 'Death is a poem,' and then went off to war again, never to return.

Wars should, of course, never be allowed to happen, but the spirit he showed was such that, even though he was in the midst of battle on the borderline between life and death, he was ever mindful of poetry and never ceased to look for flowers. This same spirit, it seems to me, underlies the aestheticism of a stage where the love suicide of a man and woman is beautified into a poetic michiyuki scene, and devils, murder scenes, and even vengeful spirits are transformed into objects of entertainment.

Is that not one expression of the spirit of a Japan which, as Zeami and others have said, has such affection for the gentle changing of the seasons as a blessing of nature, and for the beautiful but fleeting flower which awaits its time to bloom?

CHAPTER SEVEN

THE LIVING TRADITION

Fixed Forms, Secret Teachings, and Family Arts

Bloodlines of Tradition

So far we have looked at various aspects of the consciousness of beauty in Japan through Nō, Kabuki and other stage entertainments. These are none other than the world of traditional beauty, which has been nurtured during a lengthy history.

Now I should like to give notice here that such words as 'tradition' and 'the classics' are very different in meaning and content in Japan and in the west, particularly in the case of drama. This is because I cannot help feeling that there is among these differences one special and important aspect which relates not only to Japan's theatre but to her culture as a whole.

This point struck me most forcibly at the time of the UNESCO-sponsored International Symposium on the Theatre in the East and the West, which was held in Tokyo in 1963. This was the first international conference in the world to concern itself only with drama, and it took place in what was then the newly opened circular international conference hall in the Nissei Kaikan building. The president was the former chairman of the Japan Broadcasting Corporation (NHK) and former ambassador to France, Furugaki Tetsurō. There were twenty-one participating countries and these were, in alphabetical order, Australia, Britain, China, Colombia, Czechoslovakia, Egypt, France, Greece, Holland, India, Israel, Italy, Japan,

Korea, Pakistan, the Philippines, Romania, Sri Lanka, Thailand, West Germany, and the United States. It was a truly international gathering, with people coming from all parts of the world, and with the arrival of such figures as the French writer Ionesco, famed for what are called his anti-theatre or theatre of the absurd pieces such as *La Cantatrice Chauve* 'The Bald Prima Donna,' *La Leçon*, and *Le Rhinocéros*, it was a very rewarding week, outstanding even among the many international conferences after the war.

I attended as one of the representatives from Japan, in the wake of more senior people like Kinoshita Junji, Nakagawa Ryūichi, Sugawara Takashi, and Uchimura Naoya, and one of the scenes that remain in my mind as if it were yesterday is the following, concerning Ionesco.

One of the Czech representatives, the actor Walter Taub, attacked Ionesco as a nihilistic and decadent defeatist, and added jokingly, "Above all, his name just won't do ! Ionesco— why, it causes all kinds of confusion with our UNESCO sponsor, doesn't it ?"; whereupon Ionesco left his seat in a huff and went off for a walk.

Now the central theme of the conference was 'The Present State of Traditional Theatre and its Successors, and Attempts at New Experiments' in the various countries, and towards the end of the first day John Dexter from Britain stated, "It is an impossibility to 'preserve' tradition in Britain. Even with Shakespeare, our efforts are directed towards how to destroy the productions of bygone days and create a new stage. That is the path of succession from tradition and the classics." At that time, Dexter was deputy director of the Old Vic and a spirited young man who later produced the film version of a stage production of *Othello* which was released in Japan among other places.

That night, however, he was invited to a performance of Nō in which Umewaka Rokurō played in *Sotoba Komachi*

'Komachi at the Stupa' and, having seen that, he stood up again at the beginning of the next day's session to make an announcement. He said, "I was deeply moved and not a little confused by the performance last night. This is certainly no time for me to discuss the classical performing arts of Japan, but it does seem to me that my ideas are changing. At least I have come to realize that what I said yesterday does not apply to Japan's traditional drama."

In the west, even the very same play has to be kept in constant movement, in a search for new interpretations and new methods of production that goes on day by day, age by age. That is the way that bringing the classics to life for the present day, that is, the inheritance of them, is there; but the Japanese theatre has fixed 'traditional forms' which have continued for hundreds of years and survive intact at the present time. It was this difference that Dexter must have grasped with the intuition of a man concerned with the creative side of drama.

How very special something that Japanese take for granted seems to be when looked at from outside. It is this aspect that foreigners envy most in our theatre, when they see it on coming to Japan for the first time. Where, then, does this difference come from? It seems ultimately to be based on the difference between the west transmitting as its drama classics only the literary texts of plays, and Japan regarding its drama classics or traditions as consisting of the entirety of the performing art, centred on the bodily movements of the actors.

In the Japanese case, it is not simply a matter of the performance of living actors following the traditional forms, but of the performance coming to life as a single, complete stage art by the actors linking up with all the various other components such as costume, make-up, sets, properties, and music, and then by the traditions of all these various elements being assembled into an organic whole, for all the world like the various parts of a living creature. These various traditional elements, whether they be the actors' performances, set designs, musicians, samisen music or even the beating of the clappers, have all been transmitted man to man.

I therefore call the way that tradition exists in Japanese drama a 'physical tradition,' a term covering various meanings. In that case, we should perhaps be led to call tradition in western drama a 'literary tradition.'

There may be no need to give further proof of these different treatments of tradition and the classics, but let us look at just one from each side, east and west.

From the west, let us take *Hamlet*. I will omit details of the changes it has seen in productions, but at different periods and in the hands of different people these have been infinitely varied. In modern times alone, it has been presented in an historically accurate Danish style, in the manner of the Elizabethan court, as a vehicle of realism, and as one of expressionism. In the first half of this century, there was universal acclaim for Tyrone Guthrie's production of *Hamlet* in modern dress with the British actor Alec Guinness in the title role.

I myself have for many years studied the introduction and history of this work in Japan as a topic of research into comparative drama, and this even led me to write a book on the subject called *Nihon no Hamuretto* 'Hamlet in Japan' (1972), but in the course of seeing the plays a great number of times both in Japan and abroad, I have never seen two productions the same. Even the three that I saw while living in Europe for six months in 1965 were all different.

The one in the Soviet Union was a very realistic old-style production in which the ghost itself appeared in the ordinary form of a king. The one by the National Theatre Company of Belgium, which I saw in Paris, had a novel stage arrangement in which a mirror was set high up on blocks at an angle of forty-five degrees to reflect in a symbolic way the labyrinth of passages within the castle, and the ghost, awaited expectantly from one moment to the next, finally never showed itself at all. The interpretation was, no doubt, that it existed only as an illusion to the eyes and ears, or in the heart, of Hamlet himself.

In the production by the Royal Shakespeare Company at home in England, the sets were not particularly unconventional, but the ghost was as black as night, several times the size of a man, and made its appearance by means of some mechanical device. Peter Hall, the producer, said that it symbolized the contradictions, anxieties and sense of crisis that bear down on young people today from every side. . . .

Such are the many and varied forms of the ghost alone, forming as it does an important element in this play. There would be many more still if we were to go back to Shakespeare's time, but not a trace remains of the way in which it was presented on his bare stage in London.

How is it in Japan? Let us take Nō as an illustration. No sooner was the war over than the after-effects of the democratization storm caused voices to be raised demanding the removal of the four corner pillars of both the Nō stage and the earth ring in the Sumo stadium, because they blocked the view and were therefore unfair to some of the audience. This was immediately done in Sumo, where a change was made to a suspended roof and the four-coloured draperies to be seen today. In Nō too—though I did not in fact see it myself but have only heard about it—a stage was built without roof or pillars, I believe in Osaka. It is said to have ended in failure, however, when there was an accident in which an actor fell from it.

The four pillars are not there for decoration. They are an absolute necessity. Nō actors often wear masks when they dance, and they can only see the outside world through the two small holes which form the pupils of the eyes. Some fixed points at eye level are needed to enable them to judge their position on the stage, and these points are the pillars. So vital are they that one is in fact called the *metsuke-bashira* 'eye-fixing pillar' or *mitsuke-bashira* 'sighting pillar.' The three small pine trees standing beside the hashigakari also serve the same purpose. Even when performances abroad do not have a roof over the stage, it is always arranged that pines and pillars of a suitable height are installed. It is therefore wholly plausible that an actor should have fallen from a stage without pillars.

Since Nō is a performing art in which a mask is worn while singing and dancing are performed, the stage has to be constructed in accordance with tradition, from its pillars to the pines. Such things as the singing of the chorus and the musical accompaniment are, of course, very closely linked to the performance—the singing and dancing—of the actors, with the result that no arbitrary variation can be permitted in any of these elements. The living entity, which combines all these elements into an organic whole—a living entity like a physical body, which could be described as 'a whole from separate parts' or 'one out of many'—has developed its traditions within forms which have been refined over a long period of time.

The refined forms of the various elements are what are known as *kata* 'fixed forms.' In Nō, for example, to indicate weeping there is the kata called *shiori* 'sorrow,' in which the actor 'shades' his mask, that is, tilts it downwards a little, slowly raises his hand and holds it just in front of his eyes. There is involved in this the angle of the mask, the time taken to raise the hand, the precise point at which the hand is stopped, the way the fingers are held . . . and so on. A kata can thus be defined as the pattern formed by a 'phase' or position and form in spatial terms, and a judgement of time, that is, the way a time interval is maintained and then brought to an end.

Opera and ballet apart, western theatre may be said not to have kata of this kind in its ordinary spoken drama. In Japan the kata have been created over a long period by the original techniques of famous players and the refining of these as they were passed on from one generation to another. What are called *geidan* 'artistic words' are accounts of this laborious process, and *hiden* 'secret transmissions' refer to the secret transfer of their most vital parts.

They certainly exist in abundance: there is, for example, in Nō what is called Zeami's *Jūrokubushū* 'Collection of Sixteen Essays,' including *Kadensho*, *Kakyō* 'Mirror of the Flower,' and *Nōsakusho* 'Writings on the Composition of Nō,' and Konparu Zenchiku's *Konparu Jūshichibushū* 'Collection of Seventeen Essays by Konparu'; in Kyōgen, Ōkura Toraakira's *Waranbegusa* 'Childish Words'; in the puppet theatre, *Ōmu ga Soma* 'Parrot Mountain' by Takemoto Gidayū I, and *Naniwa Miyage*, which records the artistics views of Chikamatsu; and in Kabuki, *Yakusha Rongo*, which is concerned with famous actors of the Genroku era like Sakata Tōjūrō and Yoshizawa Ayame. Partly as a tribute to my father Shigetoshi on the third anniversary of his death, I introduced and edited quotations from these works in a book called *Geidō Meigen Jiten* 'Dictionary of Sayings from the Arts.'

Together with the *hyōbanki* 'critical writings,' which discussed the appearance and performances of actors from the audience's point of view, these kinds of geidan and hiden have formed the main body of writings on Japanese drama. This is in complete contrast to the west where, since Aristotle's *Poetics*, the mainstream has been the theory of poetic and literary drama, that is, dramaturgy. Here too is clearly shown the difference between the physical and literary traditions. At the same time as the various Japanese forms were giving rise to these geidan and hiden, each of them in its own field was being transmitted from one person to another, and one generation to another, along what might be called the 'bloodlines of tradition.'

It was natural that this should see the establishment of a vertical form of transmission known as the 'house' or 'family.' In Nō at the present time, for example, Motomasa is the present head of the Kanze house, the biggest of the schools of Nō, and he is the twenty-fifth generation. Even in Kabuki, which is much newer, the older houses are of the order of seventeen generations for both the actors Nakamura Kanzaburō and Ichimura Uzaemon, and for Hasegawa Kanpei, who is from a family in charge of stage sets. In the west, there are occasionally cases of three generations all being actors, but there is no kind of transmission of the art of acting, much less anything like a hundredth-generation Sophocles or, Shakespeare having originally been an actor, Shakespeare the Twentieth !

A tendency also arose to transmit secret teachings to one son only—I shall refer to this again later—or, at least, by heredity within the family, and particular forms or styles of acting came to be associated with particular families. For example, the classic Eighteen Kabuki Pieces which include *Kanjinchō, Shibaraku. Sukeroku*, and *Narukami* 'The Monk Narukami,' were originally formulated in 1840 by Danjūrō VII as eighteen kinds of performance which for generations had been a particular feature of the Ichikawa house.

From the Meiji period onwards, imitations of this have followed one after the other, from Danjūrō IX's *Shin Kabuki Jūhachiban* 'The New Eighteen Kabuki Pieces,' Kikugorō V's *Shin-ko Engeki Jusshu* 'Ten Types of Drama, New and Old,' Sadanji II's *Kyōka Gikyoku Jusshu* 'Ten Types of Apricot-blossom Plays,' Kataoka Nizaemon XI's *Kataoka Jūnishū* 'A Collection of Twelve Kataoka Pieces,' and Nakamura Ganjirō I's *Ganjirō Jūnikyoku* 'Twelve Plays for Ganjirō,' to the *En-ō Jusshu* 'Ten Types for Ennosuke' of the past and present players called Ichikawa Ennosuke. Also, although there is no special name in this case, weird ghost plays have been particularly associated with the Onoe house since the noted performances of Kikugorō III (1784-1849) in *Yotsuya Kaidan*.

One indication of the importance attached to physical transmission in the arts is the existence of what is called the 'Human National Treasure.' This title is not restricted to actors, but may be conferred on those possessed of outstanding talent in the traditional arts generally, including singers and accompanists working in the field of theatre music. To be exact, such a person is called a 'Preserver of an Intangible Cultural Property,' a title authorized and awarded by the government. The west has various titles, such as the 'Sir' indicating the knighthood given to Laurence Olivier and that of 'Artist of the People' bestowed on Soviet authors, actors and musicians, but it is perhaps only Japan that has this concept of an 'intangible cultural property.'

How, then, did these fixed forms and 'physical traditions' following vertical lines come to arise? This is a difficult question that needs to be discussed with due care, but the ideas I have on it are the result of long consideration and I shall write about them as they come to mind, as far as possible on the basis of concrete examples.

WHY A PHYSICAL TRADITION?

Song and Dance, Presentation, and Ceremonial Entertainment

First, the characteristic of 'song and dance' or 'comprehensiveness,' which we have mentioned many times as a particular feature of the traditional performing arts of Japan.

If we take just the single example of the lines 'Under a hazy moon, even the flicker of fish / Is dimmed . . .' and the accompanying pose from *Sannin Kichisa* referred to at the beginning of Chapter 3, the rhythm of the spoken lines and the samisen accompaniment, and the appearance of Kichisa as he looks down into the waters of the river are not free and independent of each other but have to form a whole with a balance controlled by precise intervals of time.

Naturally enough, a definite understanding among the various people concerned about the way it all progresses becomes a necessity in such cases. Obviously, this understanding leads in time to fixed forms, as is shown even in the west, for example, by the fact that a certain level of fixed forms is found in classical opera and ballet, which are performed in an integrated way according to the musical score.

The next thing to be considered is the matter of 'presentation,' which has also been discussed a number of times before. Since the essence of western theatre is the re-creation of life, its ideal performance by an actor, say, is a realistic expression of individuality. In *A Doll's House*, Nora is undoubtedly a model of the modern, socially aware woman, but Ibsen's play makes her a unique Nora, specified in a positive way right down to the details of her daily life.

On the other hand, although the main role in the Nō *Aoi no Ue* certainly has the proper name of Rokujō Miyasudokoro, the nature of the stage character is that of the generality of high-born women consumed by jealousy, and of women suffering the punishment of their desire. In Kabuki, the principal female character in *Sendai Hagi*, the nurse Masaoka who sees her own boy Senmatsu die in order to save the young son of her master, is a brave woman for whom loyalty is everything. Only when she is left alone does she hold the body of her child in her arms and weep over it. The scene as she does so is the highlight of the play, but Masaoka is in no way a realistic, re-created character. She is better described as an 'idealized figure' who firmly enhanced and raised to a higher level of beauty the heroism of living while suffering from the conflict between the feudal ethic of loyalty and a mother's love for her child.

Both Lady Rokujō and Masaoka are generalized beings, that is, stereotypes, who have been set up as models of some particular aspect. Naturally, the representation of them consists of common feelings and movements found in such things as jealousy, loyalty and grief, and extracted from individual living sources, which are then built into these model characters. These common elements are none other than fixed forms.

There are any number of artistic observations about these kinds of fixed forms: the aragoto make-up and dramatic pose to show the model form for strength; the way of revealing a loving liaison between a man and a woman by having them stand back to back; the teaching of Danjūrō IX, which stressed the importance of the fingers for a female impersonator and required them, particularly when playing a young woman, to show only four fingers by always hiding the thumb in the palm

A Kabuki female impersonator (*onnagata*): O-Karu
in a scene from *Chūshingura*.

of the hand; another instruction to onnagata, when indicating themselves, to point the index finger up and back from
low down, with the palm turned outwards, when playing a
young woman, and to bend the finger inwards towards the
nose when playing an old woman. . . . Every one of them,
however, came into being to help the presentation of the 'ideal
beauty' associated with each of the various roles, and breathing life into them was the 'beauty is truth' aestheticism peculiar
to the Japanese which we saw in the previous chapter.

There is one more thing, which I call 'ceremonial entertainment.' The special type of four-season nature in Japan is closely bound up with simple beliefs, rites, ceremonies, and annual events in general, and of course the performing arts were born and developed in close conjunction with these. Both Nō and the puppet theatre were originally offertory performances at shrines and temples, or for the gods of the fields, sea, mountains or the dragon god and the like, given for the repose of dead spirits or to offer thanks for past or future blessings. Stories about the wonders worked by the gods and buddhas therefore came into being before anything else and, indeed, in the puppet theatre these are given the special name of *Honji Reigen-mono* 'Pieces about the Miracles of the Original Buddhas.'

Around the fixed points of the spring and autumn festivals, the players travelled about giving performances for the gods and buddhas in shrines, temples and private houses, and the ceremonies which were the reason for giving them came around regularly in step with the seasons. Since the performances were as much offerings for good fortune as any made at, say, the time of the Doll's Festival or the Festival of the Weaving Maid, the same kind of programme tended to be repeated in the same form.

Once something had been a success, it would be repeated several times in succession and improvements and polishing touches added while following the basic line of previous performances. . . . My view is that this practice encouraged the establishment of fixed forms.

'Ceremonial entertainment' is thus music, dance, and other types of performance given as part of ceremonies. An example of it is Bugaku (Gagaku), which has been transmitted from age to age for more than a thousand years down to the present day as a ceremonial court entertainment. Nō was established as an offertory entertainment at shrines and temples in the medieval period, but after Tokugawa Ieyasu set up his government in Edo in 1603 and invited all the provincial lords to Chiyoda Castle for a performance of Nō to celebrate his

Sanbasō in the Nō *Okina*.

imperial appointment as military ruler, Nō became a ceremonial entertainment in his house and in those of the other lords. This led to the establishment of fixed forms which have been passed on down to the present time. Even today, at New Year or important ceremonies such as those held on completion of a new stage or the birth of an heir to the main family of a Nō school, there will be performances of the set of chants and dances known as *Okina* 'Old Man,' the most sacred and auspicious piece in the repertoire.

Kabuki is a performing art which grew up among the very worldly, mercenary common people of the Edo period, and its character as a genuine ceremonial entertainment is very weak. It could almost be said that its first and main consideration is amusement. Even so, the characteristic of 'annual events' which was mentioned earlier runs right through it. On the morning of the first day of the 'face showing,' for instance, while it was still dark, it used to be the custom to hang a small Shinto altar on a wall of the stage in the empty, echoing theatre, to make an offering of rice wine there, and for the head of the troupe to perform before it a Sanbasō dance derived from *Okina* in Nō. In Kabuki the item is known as *Okina-watashi*, and without it there could be no start to the theatrical year.

In addition, Kabuki's cycle of annual theatrical events—the performance of *Shibaraku* at the face showing, of Soga pieces at New Year, of requiem plays with sentiments appropriate to the Bon festival for the spirits of the dead, of ghost plays, of 'farewell plays' about separation from a child in the autumn — could be said to be a very plebeian expression of ceremonial entertainment. Naturally enough, with annual and seasonal cycles, there is a tendency for the fixed forms to become more polished and even more fixed.

Although the Japanese, in this present stage as a modern industrialized society, may be prepared to do without their coccyx or appendix, there is something in them which still prevents them from discarding these ceremonies or ceremonial entertainments. Even when constructing a modern high-rise building, for example, they must still have a Shinto priest come along to carry out a 'ground-pacification' ceremony and then have a ground-breaking ceremony before the work can start. This kind of simple belief on the part of the Japanese lies too at the root of the element of ceremonial entertainment in their theatre, and even deeper, perhaps in their subconscious, lives their very own age-old creed of life which tells them that peace of mind can be gained through harmony and unity with nature.

This kind of ceremonial entertainment can be said to have disappeared in the west at least from the time of the Renaissance when Christian religious drama came to an end because, from then on, theatre was in the service of man alone. In Japan, even though a town-based society was established in the Edo period and there were certainly differences of degree in regard to the aspect of ceremonial entertainment, this remained at the core of all the traditional performing arts and has played a big part in the firm setting of styles and fixed forms.

This setting and fixing of styles and forms is often pointed out by foreigners as a particular feature of Japan extending over the whole of her culture, but my view is that, as far as the theatre is concerned, the causes of it are as set out above.

The Culture of the 'Way'

Transmission and Purification

'Now a person who aims to succeed in this Way of ours [i.e., Nō] should not engage in any other Way. The Way of poetry, however, brings the embellishment of life-enhancing beauties of nature, and so use should certainly be made of this.'

These are lines from the introduction to Zeami's *Kadensho*, which has been mentioned many times before.

Although an exception is made for poetry, they clearly show the ideal of a narrow but intensely profound 'artistic Way' peculiar to the traditional performing arts of Japan. Such an artistic Way created and refined the kinds of styles and fixed forms we have seen already and maintained their 'physical traditions,' but this concept of the 'Way'—*dō* (or, rarely, *tō*) in the Sino-Japanese readings of the character, or *michi* in its Japanese reading—was not limited to the arts performed on stage. One cannot help feeling that it is a thoroughly Japanese thing which has probably remained unchanged from olden times.

For example, I believe that quite some time ago now there used to be a television programme called 'This Way Alone' in which successful and well-known people were invited to come along and talk; and, more recently, in the NHK 'Early Bird' programme I interviewed Tsuji Kaichi, the proprietor of the

Japanese restaurant Tsujidome 'The Crossroad Stop,' for a cookery talk called 'In Search of Good Taste' in a series entitled 'The One-track Way.'

The Japanese certainly like this term 'Way' so much that they seem to apply it to absolutely everything, from *Shintō* 'The Way of the gods,' *butsudō* 'The Way of the Buddha,' *shugendō* 'The Way of the hermit,' *ekidō* 'fortune-telling,' and *Inyōdō* 'The Way of Yin and Yang,' to *budō* 'military arts,' including *Jūdō*, *kendō* 'Japanese fencing,' *kyūdō* 'archery,' *Karatedō* 'Karate,' and the form of unarmed combat known as *Aikidō*. Then there are the Ways of *shodō* 'calligraphy,' *sadō* 'tea ceremony,' *kadō* 'flower arranging,' *kōdō* 'incense-smelling,' *kidō* 'go, Japanese checkers,' *shōdō* 'traditional Japanese dress,' and also *geidō* 'the Way of the arts,' *Bushidō* 'the Way of the warrior,' and even *iro no michi* 'the Way of love.'

There are also many other words and phrases that could be given—*hito no michi* 'the Way of man,' *manabi no michi* 'the Way of learning,' *bunbu ryōdō* 'the dual Ways of pen and sword,' *seidō jadō* 'the Ways of righteousness and evil,' *jōdō* 'the ordinary way,' *chūdō* 'the middle way, golden mean,' *kyūdō* 'seeking the Way,' *shūdō* 'learning the Way,' *shūdō* 'training in the Way,' *tokudō* 'attaining salvation' and, in contrast, *gokudō* 'villainy,' *gedō* 'heresy,' *chikushōdō* 'the realm of beasts' . . . —but there is no end to them. In the world of the theatre, we have hanamichi, michiyuki and the like, and just as there is 'the Way of the arts,' so there is likewise 'the Way of the writer.' Indeed, we could almost say that the whole of Japanese culture is a 'culture of Ways.'

This word 'Way' does not always refer to a simple area of specialization, technique or art, but commonly has within it an element of 'training of the self,' in which one becomes a better person by devoting oneself to the attainment of some accomplishment and, conversely, gains awareness of the very essence of the accomplishment by the character development involved. This nuance can be seen, among other things, in the change from *kenjutsu* 'sword-fighting' to kendō 'fencing,' and from the early *jūjutsu* to the later, more codified Jūdō. It is the ideal of harmonizing and unifying things which appear to be separate and distinct: technique and the mind, the body and the spirit. . . . Here again we can surely see at work the uniquely Japanese motif of the 'harmony' between opposites which was considered above in Chapter 5.

Whatever the origins of this may be, it seems to be held that the establishment of an 'artistic Way' in this sense took place very firmly in the early Edo period, that is, in the first half of the seventeenth century, but it could well be said that the foundations for it were already laid in the fourteenth and fifteenth centuries. This is clear from the lines by Zeami quoted above, but there is an even more important prescription from him in Part 3 *Mondō Jōjō* 'Question and Answer Items,' which can be said to be the heart of this same *Kadensho*. It is the first part of his reply to the question of what is meant by 'knowing the Flower in Nō.'

> 'Answer: One has to go to the very heart of the secrets of this Way of Nō. All that is important in it and all its secrets come down to this one matter of knowing the Flower.'

Furthermore, another of Zeami's essays that has been handed down is entitled *Shikadōsho* 'Writings on the Way of Attaining the Flower,' and in this and other works such as the *Kakyō* he often uses too the word shūdō 'learning the Way.'

Now this artistic Way—profound though it may be in its thought, it is a Way of the arts which creates physical traditions as time goes on—is long and narrow. Its most rigid form is the system of hereditary transmission, which leads to the private transfer of secrets such as those mentioned in the above quotation from Zeami.

It is again Zeami who clearly states the basic approach to

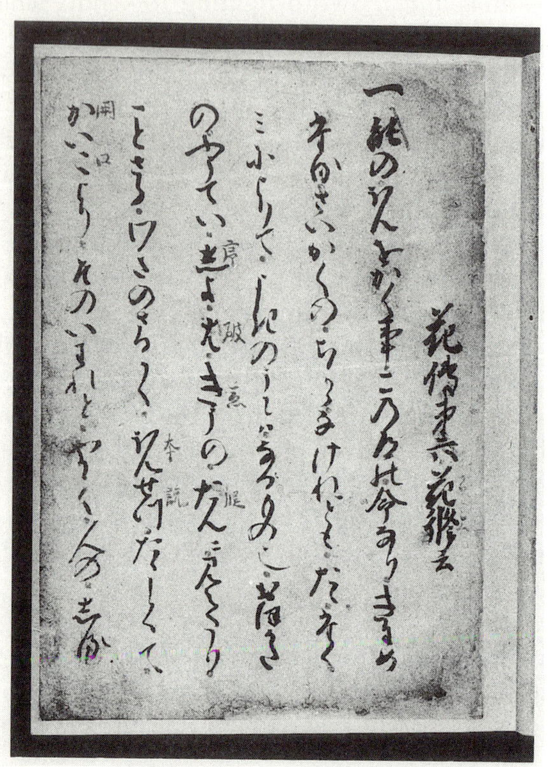

A page of the *Kadensho* in Zeami's own hand.

this, which is the method of transmission to one son only in each generation. He writes as follows at the end of Part 7 *Besshi Kuden* of the *Kadensho*.

'The innermost secrets in this Appendix are matters of importance to our house in this art of Nō, and are for transmission to one person only in each generation. They must not be passed on to anyone whose ability does not warrant it, even though he be an only son. As has been said, "A house is only made a house by what it passes on. A person is only made a person by what he knows.'"

These 'innermost secrets' (*kuden*, literally 'oral transmission,') which he restricted so severely, were the most important secrets of his 'house' and included the now well-known warning that 'With secrecy will come the Flower. Without secrecy there can be no Flower.' There are probably no other words which declare so plainly and positively how tradition should be passed on from one person to another and from one generation to the next.

In fact, the *Kadensho*, which has a section on these innermost secrets, together with other similar essays by Zeami, were kept hidden away in the depths of the Kanze house until the later part of the Edo period, and although a very few parts of them were then copied, they were buried within someone's private library and never shown outside. They only came to be widely available when a scholar called Yoshida Tōgo, having obtained a copy of the *Sarugaku Dangi* 'Talks on Sarugaku' in 1908, annotated and published it and then, in the following year, published it with others of Zeami's writings as *Zeami Jūrokubushū* 'Collection of Sixteen Essays by Zeami.' Since Zeami died in 1443, this meant that what he handed down had indeed been protected as 'secrets among secrets' for 465 years.

Of course, even hereditary transmission did not mean that it was only a true son who could be the 'one person' mentioned in the above quotation. If there was no true son, the secrets would naturally have to be passed on to someone else, but even if there was a son, he was not to be given them if he was unworthy. Such was the severity of the 'artistic Way.'

Similar too was the view that 'A person is only a person by what he knows.' This attitude does not belong to Nō alone, however, but exists too in the seemingly less circumscribed world of the Kabuki actor, for there have been cases of a true son being unable to inherit the family name even in modern times. Conversely, there are many who have become famous actors through their talent and hard work with absolutely no family connection behind them: Nakamura Nakazō I and Ichikawa Kodanji IV, for example. It is this severity that has maintained a world of traditional performing arts which, without it, could not fail to degenerate into a system of lax and purely nominal inheritance.

Be that as it may, what an enormous difference there is between this artistic Way based on transmission to a single person and the method by which the arts develop in the west. On visits to the west, one is often asked what kind of training facilities there are in Nō, Bunraku and Kabuki. Today, to be sure, with the establishment of a training department at the National Theatre, tuition open to the public is now being carried on, but this dates only from the 1960s and while there is in it an element of aspiration for the future, it is still in the experimental stage. The western-style *Shingeki* 'New Drama' theatre is organized on a different basis, but until comparatively recently the traditional drama of Japan was of the hereditary inheritance, apprenticeship, and live-in pupil type, much to the surprise of foreigners when they hear this.

In the west, even if we leave out of the discussion the world-wide spread of the Stanislavsky system in the modern period, there has been from early times a strong trendency in all things not to pass them on exclusively to one person in each generation but to project and disseminate them as widely as possible to the same generation. Even an early example, Aristotle's *Poetics*, was not written in order to transmit his theories on drama secretly to a son or a single individual he looked on as such. His work is the result of his lectures to a large group of students he took with him on walks in the countryside and of the discussions that followed. These disciples of his were therefore known as the Peripatetic school, and the notes made by one of their number survived in Alexandria, were translated in Renaissance Italy, and influenced the whole of Europe as the *Poetics*.

I have long felt that, in terms of quality of content, it is impossible to rank either the *Poetics* or Zeami's writings on his art above the other, and that they are the discussions of the arts which best represent east and west. The ways in which these works have come down to us, however, are thus completely different: in the one case, a single individual treads a narrow path towards self-perfection while, in the other, he begins to speak in a public square, engages in debate with those around him and then moves ahead in a process of self-reform.

Even today, in the west one often sees passers-by who have congregated in city parks to engage in argument and debate. In Japan, there may be noisy, egotistical speeches from politicians, but one hardly ever finds the kind of open-air public discussion seen in the west.

That reminds me that someone once grasped the difference between western and eastern cultures in saying that the one was 'the culture of the public square' and the other 'the culture of the Way.' It slips my mind who and when it was, but I think that it was extremely well put.

This difference between the public square and the Way seems, in the end, to bring us back to the difference between the west, whose strength is in logic and analysis, and Japan, where the way forward depends on the senses and intuition. I will not demonstrate this any further here, but I could perhaps just say that one expression of these characteristics is the conclusion in the geidan and hiden of the performing arts in Japan that, in the last analysis, enlightenment must come naturally from within oneself as a result of solid experience and hard work.

I will turn yet again to the *Kadensho* to illustrate this, for there Zeami takes various different approaches to the question of the Flower and yet ends by saying 'It is not, though, something that can be understood by involved logic.' He goes on to explain that:

'First, you can only know how to stop the Flower

fading when, from the age of six onwards, you have thoroughly absorbed and learned to distinguish the items of training appropriate to each age and the various types of mimicry, and then mastered all aspects of performance and technique. The spirit which leads you to master these aspects will produce the seed of the Flower. If, then, you wish to know the Flower, you must first know its seed.'

As his conclusion, he states that 'The Flower will come from the spirit, and its seed will be the performance.'

The purely physical accomplishments are not by themselves enough for the 'true Flower.' They will be no more than the 'passing Flower.' The true Flower is the character of the person himself, his spirit. In seeking to gain it, however, it is useless to investigate it with 'involved logic,' for it can only be acquired naturally after exhaustive training in all types of performance and to the limit of one's physical capability.

This is the basic attitude running through all the discussions and secrets of the arts in Japan. It could just as well be called, I suppose, the spirit of seeking the Way. Zeami left his teaching on the Flower to be passed on to one son only, but he did not pass on a fixed form of it so much as the 'spirit' underlying it, which would then create an even better form. The British producer Peter Brook, widely known in Japan for his constant quest for a new type of drama, wrote as follows in his book *The Empty Space*.

'I once saw a rehearsal at the Comédie Française—a very young actor stood in front of a very old one and spoke and mimed the role with him like a reflection in a glass. This must not be confused with the great tradition, say, of the Nō actors passing knowledge orally from father to son. There it is meaning that is communicated—and meaning never belongs to the past. It can be checked in each man's own present experience. But to imitate the externals of acting only perpetuates manner—a manner hard to relate to anything at all.'

Just as human bodies live by replacing their cells day after day while apparently preserving their same forms, so Nō and the other traditional performing arts of Japan preserve their fixed forms but, in fact, have lived on right up to the present day by re-creating and renewing themselves through generation after generation of players. Zeami put forward 'novelty' as an element of the Flower, and stressed the tactic of always appearing fresh and new to the audience. In the Meiji period, the Kabuki actor Danjūrō IX is said to have instructed his pupils not to imitate him, but to watch him closely, adopt only the good points, and make the best possible use of their own merits.

This is what is meant by the phrase, 'Go into the fixed forms, but then leave them behind.' As a renowned producer, Brook was keenly sensitive to the creative flame which continues to burn at the heart of the artistic Way.

The small, narrow Ways based on tradition run along over all kinds of buried secret teachings—or, to put it another way, they are closed societies into which outsiders cannot easily tread or look to learn their secrets. One proof of this is that each such society has its own particular customs and taboos.

Take Kyōgen, for example. Like Nō, it puts great weight on the innermost secrets originally designated as being for 'oral transmission' (kuden) only and, according to *Kyōgen no Michi* 'The Way of Kyōgen' by the modern Kyōgen master Nomura Manzō, *Tanuki no Haratsuzumi* 'The Badger's Belly-drum' is treated as a secret play for transmission to one son only, and *Hanago* and *Tsuri-gitsune* 'The Snared Fox' as other secret plays known as *ōnarai* 'major learning pieces.' The form of oral transmission associated with them is said to have prohibited Manzō from even showing his written notes to his own son; and when a player took the role of Sanbasō in the truly religious *Okina* dances, it was necessary for him to purify himself by the practice of using a 'separate fire.' According to Manzō's book,

> 'When taking this role, the player purifies himself and also avoids the slightest defilement. This means that, before the performance, it is necessary for him to follow the type of purification over six nights and seven days known as "separate fire," by which he lives apart from his family and uses his own cooking fire. During these seven days, he himself deals with everything around him, including the cooking, without help from anyone, and on the day of the performance, he cleanses himself by bathing his body with cold water before going into the greenroom. It is also strictly forbidden to speak to members of the opposite sex, and since this applies equally to anyone in mourning, it stands to reason in our Way that a player withdraws of his own accord if he himself goes into mourning.'

The period of this separate living varies according to the school of Kyōgen concerned and it has also become shorter than it used to be, but it is said that the practice is still being carried on as always. Although there may be differences of form and degree, such secrecy and taboos exist in all the traditional performing arts as one aspect of their ceremonial character. They are said to have originated in the secret spells found in the ceremonies of esoteric Buddhism, but it could perhaps be that they were already being practised in a primitive form before Buddhism was introduced into Japan. Then, too, I cannot help feeling that the tendency to form closed societies based on small, narrow bloodlines by making secrets of taboos of this kind resembles in character the secret societies which are much in evidence even today among the races of the regions to the south of Japan.

As this type of society was brought into the islands of Japan by the early Japanese who hailed from the southern regions, and there mixed with other things such as the shamanism of the northern area and the animism of the other early inhabitants, there came to be formed in the natural environment of Japan unique societies which gave all kinds of performances as prayers and offerings to the gods. . . . The people responsible for these had no fixed dwelling-places but were travelling players, and so there is a view which compares the nature of their closed societies and the existence of taboos among them with those of the gypsies. It may be that such a view arose because, coming to Japan as they did from far-away places to offer up prayers and call down blessings by their performances before they disappeared again, it was the custom to welcome their arrival as a visit by guests and to do so with feelings of wonderment and respect.

This does not mean, however, that there is any firm basis to this theory about secret societies from the south, for they are merely part of a romantic world of my own—which we will leave as such. The important thing is that it was the nature of such traditional closed societies, with their narrow 'Ways' and no contact or relationship one with another, which gave birth to their multi-layered character, the main feature of Japanese theatre and other performing arts, which runs through the whole of Japanese culture.

Bugaku took on a standard form as a ceremonial entertainment among the court nobility in the Heian period, and it has had a continuous existence since then right up to the present day. Nō and Kyōgen were formulated for the upper levels of the warrior class in the medieval period, and having developed not as the result of any transfiguration of Bugaku with the passage of time but from the completely separate line of Dengaku and Sarugaku, they were forms which added a new and wholly distinct layer. Still later, in the Edo period, the newly flourishing class of townsmen produced Bunraku and Kabuki, and these too established themselves as forms which added another new layer, quite separate from Nō and Kyōgen in both origin and social appeal.

So it is that, when the Meiji Restoration came in 1868, these four types of traditional performance—Bugaku, Nō and Kyōgen, Bunraku, and Kabuki—were existing together but each forming one of four clear layers without mixing with any other.

If this multi-layered character or coexistence is compared with the situation in the west, I believe that it shows still more clearly what a uniquely Japanese feature it is, because the history of western drama is one of replacement and varying fortunes.

With the downfall of ancient Greece and the accompanying decline of Greek classical drama, Roman drama reached its height. This disappeared in the Middle Ages when it was crushed by the weight of Christian doctrine as being something obscene, and religious drama then monopolized the scene. With the coming of the Renaissance, this too was abandoned on the disappearance of its function as religious entertainment, and as modern states were established, various kinds of national drama came into being. Broadly speaking, however, even these have experienced a common history of replacement and mixed fortunes like one great river, by criticizing, denying or rejecting what has gone before as one period follows another: from the baroque style to classicism; when that was rejected, romanticism; when that itself was rejected, modern realism; and then on again to the present search for anti-realist drama.

In contrast to this is the multi-layered or coexisting character of the Japanese tradition, with any number of streams flowing side by side but with waters of different colours. It does not need to be said that this character is closely bound up with that of society in general.

Japan has never had a history of thorough-going revolutions or varied fortunes that threatened its very existence. The court nobility, the class which supported Bugaku, declined in power but never died out even when the period of military government came, and they remained the highest level of Japanese society. The military class, which nurtured Nō, remained the governing class throughout the Edo period, but during that time the townsman class developed around its core of merchants. This was the situation in which the various traditional performing arts were able to survive by being supported and enveloped by their own particular class of society.

A very important feature of such a layered coexistence was that it naturally brought about a characteristic variety of forms within drama and culture as a whole. The overriding reason which made this situation possible was probably that Japan is an island country in the Far East separated from the rest of the continent by seas. Because of this, Japan was neither destroyed nor made into a multiracial nation, and the diverse classes coexisting within its layered society each guarded the Way of its particular traditions.

Because they were closed worlds, they were small and narrow but, in return, they were completely unalloyed and of high artistic density—having just written this, I was reminded of something I heard when I attended a conference. The National Opera Company from Dresden, which performed in Japan in 1981, is now one of the finest in the world, but it was said that this was the result of it having been cultivated without outside influence, since East Germany was virtually a closed country.

As well as being an island country, Japan was a closed one too for nearly 300 years under the Tokugawa until the Meiji Restoration in 1868. It lost a great deal from this, being late in coming to modern science, for instance, but it can be said to have made a gain by having refined and brought to completion its very own traditional culture.

TRADITIONAL BEAUTY OLD ENOUGH TO BE NEW

Now within the World at Large

There is no doubt that the geographical condition of being an island country and a history of being a closed country until 1868 provided a forcing-house for the special situation in which the traditional performing arts and other forms of traditional culture coexisted and became multi-layered and diverse. It does not necessarily follow, however, that the situation changed completely in the modern period after 1868.

In less than a hundred years since the closed-country policy collapsed and Japan was opened to the outside world, it has succeeded in modernizing itself to such an extent that it has caused feelings of alarm and, finally, even enmity in the west. In spite of this modernization, this feature of 'tradition' in traditional culture remained absolutely unchanged.

This is interesting, or strange perhaps, but if we think about it, there may be in it an indication of general characteristics inherent in the Japanese race.

It goes without saying that, after the Restoration in 1868, the waves of western modernity beat against the world of tradition in Japan as it did against others. By that time, however, Bugaku, Nō, Kyōgen, and Bunraku had all become so completely 'classicized' that there was no scope for creating new works or new forms of production and, hence, no way that they would change.

Ernest Fenollosa, who came to Japan in the last part of the nineteenth century to study Japanese aesthetics, once asked Umewaka Minoru, one of the three great Nō masters of the Meiji period, what Nō was. Umewaka is then said to have replied, "In Nō, all things follow traditions dating from the early Edo period, so we simply have to follow these." This one sentence must surely have explained everything.

This does not mean, of course, that over the course of time there has been a complete absence of new ventures. All kinds of new works, both translated and original, have in fact been staged: in Nō, for instance, *Taka no Izumi* 'At the Hawk's Well,' translated from the work of the Irish dramatist W.B. Yeats, and Takamura Kōtarō's modern Nō *Chieko Shō* 'Notes on Chieko;' in Bunraku, the Meiji-period piece *Tsubosaka Reigenki*, *Hamuretto* 'Hamlet' and *O-Chō Fujin* 'Madame Butterfly' immediately after World War II, Kinoshita Junji's *Urikohime to Amanjaku* 'Princess Melon and the Little Devil,' the UN-sponsored play *Shiroi O-Jizō-san* 'The White Jizō' about a child of mixed blood born during the Occupation. . . . I have seen most of the postwar ones, and they certainly made an indelible impression on me.

They were, however, all confined within the already completed, traditional forms of Nō and Bunraku, and although they certainly added to the repertoires, they did nothing to contribute to any change in the essential nature of their respective lines.

Even today, therefore, these lines consist almost entirely of traditional stagings of programmes as before: in Nō, *Okina*, *Takasago*, *Aoi no Ue* and so on, and in Bunraku, *Chūshingura*, *Ichinotani Futaba Gunki*, *Sonezaki Shinjū*. . . .

Kabuki too, when it comes down to it, is treading the same path, but its situation is somewhat different from those of Nō and Bunraku, and in the twists and turns of the modern period it has suffered setbacks and diversions. Why, now, should this be?

Since I cannot help feeling that the reasons for this provide historical sidelights which should not be overlooked in any consideration of the modern period in Japan, I will just give them in outline.

When the Meiji Restoration came, the great playwright Kawatake Mokuami remained the same powerful author that he had been previously; and energetic and rising actors—including the later Danjūrō IX and Kikugorō V—were giving first performances in a succession of new works by Mokuami at the same rate as they were playing classical pieces.

When a stage art, in the ordinary course of events, ceases to create new works and simple stages repeat of old ones, it is categorized as classical theatre. By the time of the Meiji Restoration, Bugaku, Nō, and Bunraku were already in this position. Kabuki, however, had not yet become wholly classical in that sense. It can be said that at least half of it consisted of 'present day drama' which took on a new face as the world around it changed.

It was only natural, therefore, that Kabuki should be directly exposed to the effects of the Restoration.

The year 1872 saw the beginning of important cultural developments with links to the present day, such as the westernization of theatres involving, trivial though it may be, the provision for the first time of seats and tables, the staging of new western-inspired plays based on the *Saikoku Risshi-hen* 'A Book on Success in the West' (a translation of *Self Help* by Samuel Smiles, which was a best-seller at the time), and administrative reforms like the censorship of plays. It was also in 1872 that there was a complete about-face on the part of the government, with the promulgation of a law stating that "Artistes and actors come under the supervision of the Ministry of Education," and the announcement that Kabuki actors would be given formal educational appointments.

What posed a particularly serious threat to the traditions of Kabuki was the Theatre Reform Movement, which was set up before long through the efforts of academics and people from the political and financial worlds. Its purpose was to give Kabuki an additional function as a social attraction for the upper classes, both Japanese and foreign, by reforming it on western lines.

Behind this, as it was the establishment of the Rokumei-kan, the international social centre so well known in the modern history of Japan, was a policy of Europeanization aimed at gaining the revision of the treaties with the western powers. It was therefore only to be expected that this Theatre Reform Movement should have described a steeply rising curve in the second decade of the Meiji period, a time itself known as the 'Rokumeikan period.' It was brought to a peak by the creation of the Theatre Reform Society in 1886.

This was just at the time of the first cabinet under Itō Hirobumi, the year after the start of the cabinet system in Japan, and the prime mover was Itō's son-in-law Viscount Suematsu Norizumi, counsellor at the Ministry of Home Affairs (and later Minister of Communications).

There were twenty-three members of the Society, including the Foreign Minister Inoue Kaoru from the political field, Yoda Gakkai, Fukuchi Ōchi, Toyama Masakazu, Yatabe Ryōkichi, Wadagaki Kenzō, Hozumi Nobushige, and Kikuchi Dairoku from the academic world, and Shibusawa Eiichi from the world of finance. In addition, there were no fewer than forty-seven official supporters, beginning with Itō, the Prime Minister, and including other public figures such as Ōkuma Shigenobu, Saionji Kinmochi, Mutsu Munemitsu, Mitsui Yōnosuke, and Ōkura Kihachirō.

The main items in the 'improvement' they proposed—the building of a large western-style national theatre modelled on the Opera in Paris or the Scala in Milan; the abolition of onnagata and their replacement by actresses; the promotion of scripts written by men of letters instead of Kabuki playwrights; the complete abolition of the hanamichi, the raised platform for gidayū chanting on stage, and the various types of stage assistants and the like; the establishment of a tasteful, logical type of drama in which the text would be the main element; a recommendation for only one daily performance, in the evening . . . — constituted a through-going reformation.

As is clear at a glance, this arbitrarily assumed the superiority of western literary arts and theatre, and aimed to change Kabuki in order to conform to their standards. It goes without saying that these had virtually no common ground with Kabuki, with its completely different traditions and individual aesthetic expression. Naturally enough, therefore, it came under concerted attack from Tsubouchi Shōyō, Mori Ōgai, Takada Hanpō and other intellectuals of the highest level who stood outside the Reform Society circles. In the Kabuki world too, apart from Danjūrō who belonged to the progressive faction, no one gave the proposals any serious attention.

Since this Reform Society was, moreover, no more than an organization set up to serve the government, as is clear from the names of the members given above, it died a natural death with the fall of the first Itō cabinet in 1888. Such was the sad end of this plan to have Kabuki reform itself.

There is just one thing, though, to be added. It is that, although this Reform Society exposed its own ignorance and lack of understanding of Kabuki reform, was too radical and too direct, and ended in anticlimax, it was by no means without significance if 'modernization' is seen in a broad perspective covering the whole of Japanese drama, and even if it is accepted that there are many pros and cons in this.

There is a view which seeks to deny any value to the Society, on the grounds that it was a government-inspired official organization, but it must surely be said that this is excessively unscientific and biased.

I will not pursue the matter here but leave it to other

writings on the subject, including my own *Kindai Engeki no Tenkai* 'The Development of Modern Drama.' In any case, the western-style remodelling of Kabuki collapsed with the disappearance of the Reform Society, and the road to reform was taken instead by the *Shinpa* 'New School' theatre, which had its origins in 1888 in political plays advocating freedom and popular rights. Furthermore, in 1894-95 at the time of the Sino-Japanese war, Kabuki competed with Shinpa in the production of war plays but suffered a heavy defeat by the new theatre which, though it used amateur actors, was more powerful in terms of its realism and speed of production. It then lost any interest it might have had in continuing in the direction of 'modern plays based on modern life.'

So it was that, as a result of these vicissitudes, Kabuki took a fresh look at itself and settled on a position as a form of traditional drama which, like Nō and Bunraku, put all its trust in the traditional staging of classical works.

Time went on and the year 1909 saw the birth of the Shingeki movement which, having taken root among the modern intelligentsia who wanted something more than was to be found in Shinpa, took as its immediate material translated imports of modern western drama. Associated with this development were the *Bungei Kyōkai* 'Literary Society' of such people as Tsubouchi Shōyō, Shimamura Hōgetsu, and Matsui Sumako, and the *Jiyū Gekijō* 'Free Theatre' formed by Osanai Kaoru and Ichikawa Sadanji II.

Thus, the result was that Bugaku, Nō and Kyōgen, Bunraku, and Kabuki each continued to maintain their respective traditions, and carried above them a new stratum of 'modern drama' in the form of Shinpa and Shingeki.

Since then, this modern drama has itself spawned a diversity of other genres, including opera, operetta, musicals, various kinds of light theatre, and the present avant-garde small-theatre movement, and the extra stratum is becoming ever thicker. A broad view of the situation shows, however, that within this layered coexistence of the two worlds of the traditional performing arts and the modern stage entertainments, the former, characterized by what we can call Japanese beauty, have come through to the present day pure in blood and unchanged in character, with their traditional forms intact.

During the postwar democratization, however, a new awareness was born which extended to the world of traditional drama. The difference was that, this time, the movement came from within, in contrast to the Meiji reform movement which not only came from outside but also from above. What is particularly striking is that, from about 1955, experiments began with the aim of creating a contemporary drama by means of cooperative performances with people from the modern theatre.

The most epoch-making of these was, in my judgement, the 'Evening of Original Drama with Theatre in the Round' devised and produced by Takechi Tetsuji.

'Theatre in the round' is, of course, a modern form of production which uses an ordinary flat stage without any background set and surrounded on four sides by the audience. It is a method used in the search for a contemporary theatre which aims to escape from the picture-frame stage, that is, the 'fourth-wall' type, so characteristic of the modern period, and it was first tried at Washington State University in 1932.

This form of production had already been used experimentally at the Ōkuma Small Hall of Waseda University in Tokyo in 1951. As a new graduate, I took part as a production assistant on that occasion, but what was new about Takechi's venture was, in addition to this new form, the position he took in querying the possibilities for future drama by having Nō and Kyōgen players and people from newer genres perform together.

I can picture the stage very clearly even now. The programme consisted of one of Mishima Yukio's modern Nō plays, *Aya no Tsuzumi* 'The Damask Drum,' and the avant-garde musical piece *Tsuki ni Tsukareta Piero* 'The Moon-struck Pierrot' based on music by Schönberg; and the players from the world of tradition were the two Kanze brothers Hisao and Shizuo (now Tetsunojō) and Sakurama Michio from Nō, and Nomura Mansaku from Kyōgen.

The movement to create a new Japanese theatre by denying the idea of the traditional and the modern and raising them together, so to speak, to a third dimension, has been continued since then. Recent pieces have included *Bakkosu no Shinjo* 'The Bacchae,' a combined work by the Mei-no-kai of Kanze Hisao and others and Suzuki Tadashi's Waseda Small Theatre (which proved to be Hisao's last stage appearance before his death), and Kinoshita Junji's *Shigosen no Matsuri* 'The Meridian Festival' given by Yamamoto Yasue, Takizawa Osamu and other Shingeki players, and Kanze Hideo and Nomura Mansaku from Nō and Kyōgen respectively.

I have mentioned only the most outstanding examples, but it must be said that this kind of development would have been inconceivable before the war, when secret teachings and their transmission were jealously guarded, and the purity of the small and narrow Way was earnestly protected in accordance with Zeami's teaching that one "should not engage in any other Way." In that sense, we could perhaps say that, ten years after the end of the war, the theatre world of Japan finally took a small first step into the modern age.

What I would like to say now, though, is that even at the present time when it has come into this new age, Nō is still Nō, Kyōgen is still Kyōgen, and Kabuki is still Kabuki, as they have always been. While there may be combined performances with other genres and while there may be a quest for a contemporary theatre, their main and true Ways are still Nō, Kyōgen, and Kabuki, and each steadfastly maintains its own traditions.

Here we see again the oft-repeated contrast between Japanese and western traditions. I even find myself feeling that the characteristic of preserving traditions perhaps comes not from the simple situation of Japan being an island country or having been for so long a closed country, but is an inescapable predisposition of the Japanese in whom learning became second nature during their long history of well over a thousand years.

Now there is one more point I should like to make about the connections between tradition and the modern age, including relations with the west. It concerns the question of the value placed on, or the attitude towards, traditional culture.

From the Meiji period onwards, ever since Japan began to pursue western civilization and culture, it has been the fashion among the more impetuous members of the intellectual class in Japan to belittle or disdain their own traditional culture and drama, even at times referring to the latter as 'imbecilic arts.' The radical members of the Theatre Reform Society are just one example of this.

Such impetuosity may, on the one hand, be the driving force which swiftly pushed ahead with Japan's modernization regardless of appearances. On the other hand, however, it is also closely connected with a loss of identity which includes one's traditions. While Japan was thus putting aside its traditional culture in its haste to follow the west into the modern era, the west, in contrast, had its gaze fixed on Japan's inherent wealth—her cultural treasures.

In relation to drama, this meant that when, around 1907, Japan made a direct rush for modern western drama, it was just twenty years after it had been established in the west— where it was already felt that modern realism led into a dead-end and a search was on for a way of escape. There was in this a mutual phase difference. In the eyes of the west, Japan's old traditions shone as something new, transcending mere modernity.

The attention given to Nō by Fenollosa and others, Yeats's contribution of the Nō style to poetic drama, Reinhardt's application of the revolving stage, Meierholid's introduction of the hanamichi. . . . Then, too, since the war, Jean-Louis Barrault's use of the black-clad stage assistant from Bunraku, Brecht's narrative drama which is thought to have perhaps been influenced by Kabuki, and so on. Compared with the influence Japan has had from the west, these things are of course incomparably minor and fragmentary, but Japanese traditions have provided the west with a sharp, fresh stimulus not to be found in its own.

In the last few years particularly, there has been a marked heightening of interest in Edo culture. The great exhibition of Edo arts held in London in the autumn of 1981 was a display of these on a grand scale said to be the biggest ever seen, and this was realised as a result of the enthusiastic demand from the British side. Also, in conjunction with this, more than a hundred events were held to introduce aspects of Japanese culture. One of these was the Kabuki given in London, Berlin, Paris, and elsewhere by Ichikawa Ennosuke's troupe.

I went along with this troupe, and I could physically feel the strength of the interest and reactions generated by its performances. June and July of the following year saw Kabuki performances on what is the largest stage of all at the present time, that of the Metropolitan Opera House in New York, by the biggest group ever assembled, which included Utaemon, Kanzaburō, Ebizō, and Tamasaburō.

Why is the west now interested in the Edo period?—The reason seems to be the realization that a clear understanding of the speed of Japan's modernization and the secrets of her high economic growth is only possible by studying not only the achievements of the Japanese of the Meiji period, but also the many aspects of the culture and social system of the Edo period which immediately preceded it and, hence, also such things as the mental framework and aesthetic consciousness of the Japanese people who created these things.

Within this movement of interest, a boom in research on

Japan is gaining strength all the time, and research institutions concerned with Japan are appearing one after the other in various parts of the world. In the field of drama alone, there were at least two events in 1981 worth recording, in addition to the overseas performances just mentioned.

One was the opening of the first European Kabuki Conference in July in Vienna, and the other the establishment in December of a European Research Centre for Japanese Theatre Arts in the Drama Research Institute of the University of Vienna, as recommended by the summer conference.

Incidentally, this Institute was set up in 1943 and is now the Mecca of drama studies, where research workers gather from all over the world. Its founder was Dr. Heinz Kindermann, best known for his great ten-volume work on the history of European theatre, and although he was in his late eighties when I knew him, he was still hale and hearty. The headship of the Institute he entrusted to his favourite pupil, Professor Margret Dietrich, but he himself was still active as a senior figure in world scholarship.

I have enjoyed exchanges of research material and a continuing friendship with these two scholars since my first visit to Europe in 1958, and their enthusiasm for, and understanding of, Japanese traditional theatre is of no mean order. I myself helped in a very small way with the above conference and Research Centre, but it was these two scholars who first proposed and promoted them.

If we now turn back to Japan, it appears that here too, in step with the west, traditional culture is at present enjoying a quiet boom. According to research surveys carried out by Hayashi Chikio, head of the Statistical and Mathematical Research Institute and a senior of mine at high school, this phenomenon of a return to tradition has shown itself unmistakably in statistical curves since 1973.

Certainly, the numbers of people interested in Nō and Kyōgen, Bunraku, Kabuki and the like are increasing year by year, especially among such groups as students and other young people, and young housewives. It seems to me that, in part, this is because we are at last seeing the results of, for example, the Kabuki classes started immediately after the war by the Shōchiku company and by the Metropolitan Citizens' Theatre and Tokyo Education Committee; the Kabuki classes for students held in recent years at the National Theatre; the popularizing activities of the Cultural Affairs Agency, including the Young People's Arts Theatre and the Mobile Arts Festival; and schools broadcasts and live theatre relays by NHK and other television companies.

It is also a fact, however, that the way people involve themselves with tradition is very different from what it was in pre-war or pre-modern Japan. Until my parents' generation, Kabuki for example would be enjoyed as a part of life in general, as people in Japanese dress sat on mats and cushions in small enclosures eating and drinking. From my time, however, the younger people are, the greater the distance that opens up between them and traditional life and entertainments as modernization advances. This is now an inexorable, inevitable process.

It must therefore be said that it is again understandable for even our own world of Japanese traditional theatre to be one with which our contemporaries cannot immediately identify, unless they have a certain degree of background knowledge or approach it as an object of study. In that respect, there is surely no longer any great difference between the west or foreigners in general and contemporary Japanese.

As Japan's modernization is finally about to catch up with that of the west, we both find ourselves unable to avoid the 'modern sickness' that is already afflicting the west—the human loss in a modern industrialized society, a sense of crisis over nuclear war, anxieties over the destruction of the environment and a time of food shortages, and so on. I wonder whether in fact this present return to tradition in Japan does not have its roots in a desire for a return to human values, a return to nature, and to the source of a beauty which does not exist in present reality or which transcends it and the whole modern age.

Be that as it may, Japanese beauty which lives and breathes within multi-layered diverse traditions has now come to be on a par with the various forms of traditional beauty found in western and other foreign countries, through the closing of the phase difference with world culture in general and the developing activity in mutual exchanges. At the same time, there has been frequent mention lately of the international character of Japanese culture.

To be averaged out and blended in with the rest of the world, however, is of course to lose both past and future. My feeling is that the true Way is for Japan to continue to keep alive her very own *unique* world of beauty, while at the same time not losing sight of the *universality* to be found within her special traditions.

SELECT GLOSSARY

Aoi no Ue   'The Lady Aoi'

aorikaeshi   'backward turn' of a Kabuki set

aragoto   'roughness,' a macho style of Kabuki acting

Benten Kozō   hero of, & alternative name for, *Shiranami Gonin Otoko*

Besshi Kuden   'Appendix on Innermost Secrets'

biwa   a lute-like instrument

bokashi   'shading' of make-up etc.

Bonsai   (the growing of a) miniature tree

Bugaku   ancient court music and dance

Bunraku   the puppet theatre

Chūshingura   'The League of Loyal Retainers'

dō (artistic etc.)   'Way'

Dōjō-ji   'The Dōjō Temple'

Edo   pre-modern name for Tokyo

Edo period   1603–1867

Gagaku   ancient court music

geidan   artistic talk, discussion of the arts

geza   screened music area on left of Kabuki stage

Kezairoku   'A Record of Playful Treasures'

gidayū   puppet-theatre chanting or narration

Hagoromo   'The Robe of Feathers'

hana   the Flower in Nō

hanamichi   raised corridor running through the auditorium to the Kabuki stage

harakiri   ritual disembowelment

hashigakari   passageway leading from the greenroom to the Nō stage

Heike Monogatari 'Tales of the Heike'
hiden 'secret transmission,' secret teaching
Ichinotani Futaba Gunki 'The Tale of Two Young Warriors at the Battle of Ichinotani
Imoseyama Onna Teikin 'An Example of Noble Womanhood'
jo-ha-kyū 'introduction, development, and climax'
jōruri type of musical narration used in the puppet theatre
Jūhachiban = Kabuki Jūhachiban
Kabuki Jūhachiban classic selection of 'Eighteen Kabuki Pieces'
Kadensho 'Writings on the Transmission of the Flower'
Kamiyui Shinza 'Shinza the Hairdresser'
Kanjinchō 'The Subscription List'
keshi-maku 'erasing (= concealing) cloth'
Kojiki 'Records of Ancient Matters'
kōken stage assistant
kuma 'shaded part'
kumadori dramatic type of Kabuki make-up
kurogo black-clad stage assistant
ma 'interval,' timing
Manyōshū 'Collection of Ten Thousand Leaves'
Meiji period 1868–1912
michiyuki 'travel passage'
mie 'dramatic pose'
Mondō Jōjō 'Question and Answer Items'
Monomane Jōjō 'Items on Mimicry'
Musume Dōjō-ji 'The Maiden at the Dōjō Temple'
nagauta type of Kabuki music and singing
Naniwa Miyage 'Gifts from Naniwa'
Natsu Matsuri 'Summer Festival'
ōdaiko 'great drum' used in Kabuki
Okina 'Old Man'; an ancient set of chants and dances
onnagata female impersonator, male player of female roles
oshi-modoshi 'pushing back'; one of the *Kabuki Jūhachiban*
ōzeri 'big trap' used for Kabuki sets
rakugo 'comic monologue'

Rokumeikan   'The Deer-cry Pavilion,' a Meiji-period official social centre

sabi   'tasteful simplicity'

Sannin Kichisa   'Three Robbers Called Kichisa'

Shibai Nenjū Gyōji   'Annual Theatrical Events'

Shibaraku   'Wait!'; one of the *Kabuki Jūhachiban*

shichi-san   the '7–3' point, located three-tenths of the way along the *hanamichi* from the stage

Shinjū Ten no Amijima   'The Love Suicide at Amijima'

shirabyōshi   type of dancing-girl in the medieval period

shōgun   military ruler in medieval and pre-modern Japan

Shōjō   'The Elf'

shōmyō   musical recitation of Buddhist sutras

Sonezaki Shinjū   'The Love Suicide at Sonezaki'

Sugawara Denju Te-narai Kagami   'Sugawara and the Secrets of Calligraphy'

Sumidagawa   'The Sumida River'

suppon   small lift on the *hanamichi*

Tenjiku Tokubei   'Tokubei's Return from India'

Terakoya   'The Village School'

tōmi   'distant view'; a Kabuki stage effect

Tsubosaka Reigenki   'The Miracle at Tsubosaka Temple'

Utsunoya Tōge   'Utsunoya Mountain-pass'

wabi   'quiet taste'

wagoto   'gentleness'; a style of Kabuki acting

yagō   traditional 'house name' of a Kabuki actor, distinct from his usual professional name

Yakusha Rongo   'The Actors' Analects'

yatai   'a building' forming Kabuki stage set

yataikuzushi   'building collapse'; a Kabuki stage effect

yojō   'lingering emotion,' continuing sentiment arising from poem etc.

Yoshitsune Senbonzakura   'Yoshitsune and the Thousand Cherry Trees'

Yotsuya Kaidan   'A Ghostly Tale from Yotsuya'

yūgen   quiet, gentle 'elegant beauty'

BIBLIOGRAPHY

Adachi, Barbara. *The Voices and Hands of Bunraku*. Kōdansha International.

————. *The Living Treasures of Japan*. Kōdansha International.

Araki, J.T. *The Ballad Drama of Medieval Japan*. Tuttle Co.

Bowers, Faubian. *Japanese Theatre*. Tuttle Co.

Brandon, James R. *Theatre Perspective—Asian Theatre, A Study Guide and Annotated Bibliography*. University and College Theatre Association (UCTA), 1980.

————. ed. *Kabuki Plays*. New York: S. French, 1966.

————. trans. *Kabuki: Five Classic Plays*. Cambridge: Harvard University Press, 1975.

Ernst, Earle. *The Kabuki Theatre*. New York: Oxford University Press, 1956.

————. ed. *Three Japanese Plays from the Traditional Theatre*. London, New York: Oxford University Press, 1959.

Fenollosa, Ernest Francisco. *The Classic Noh Theatre of Japan*. Westport, Conn.: Greenwood Press, 1977.

Furukawa, Hisashi. *Kyōgen no Kenkyū*. 'Studies in the Kyōgen' Tokyo: Fukumura Shoten, 1948.

————. *Nō no Sekai*. 'The World of Nō' Tokyo: Shakai Shisō Kenkyū-kai Shuppan-bu, 1959.

Gunji, Masakatsu. *Kabuki*. Kōdansha International.

Hachimonjiya Jisho. ed. *Yakusha Banashi or Yakusha Rongo*. 'Actors' Analects or Discourses on Acting' Kyoto: Hachimonji-ya.

Halford, A.S. and G.M. *The Kabuki Handbook*. Tuttle Co.

Ihara, Toshirō. *Meiji Engeki-shi*. 'History of Theatre in the Meiji Era' Tokyo: Waseda Daigaku Shuppan-bu, 1933.

———. *Kabuki Nenpyō*. 'A Kabuki Chronology' (vol.1 1958, vol.II 1957, vol.III 1958, vol.IV 1959) Tokyo: Iwanami Shoten.

Iizuka, Tomoichirō. *Kabuki Saiken*. 'A Kabuki Guidebook' Tokyo: Dai-ichi Shobō, 1926.

Kawase, Kazuma. *Zeami Nijū-San Bu Shū*. 'Twenty-Three Books of Ze-ami' Tokyo: Nōgaku-sha, 1945.

Kawatake, Shigetoshi. *Kabuki Sakusha no Kenkyū*. 'Studies on the Writers of Kabuki Plays' Tokyo: Tōkyō-dō, 1940.

———. *Kabuki-shi no Kenkyū*. 'A Study on the History of Kabuki' Tokyo: Tōkyō-dō, 1943.

———. *Nihon Engeki Zenshi*. 'A Complete History of Japanese Theatre' Tokyo: Iwanami Shoten, 1959.

———. *Nihon Engeki Zuroku*. 'A Pictorial Synopsis of the Japanese Theatre' Tokyo: Asahi Shimbun.

Kawatake, Toshio. *Nihon no Geinō*. 'The Performing Arts of Japan' Fukumura Shoten, 1953.

———. *Nihon no Engeki*. 'Japanese Drama' Sa-e-ra Shobō, 1955.

———. *Engeki no Zahyō*. 'The Co-ordinates of Drama' Risō-sha, 1958.

———. *Kabuki Sovieto o Iku*. 'Kabuki in the Soviet Union' Engeki Shuppan-sha, 1962.

———. *Hō-ō Kabuki 65: Sono Kiroku to Hankyō*. 'Kabuki's 1965 Visit to Europe: Records and Reactions' KBS, 1966.

———. *Hikaku Engekigaku*. 'Comparative Drama' Nansō-sha, 1967.

———. *Chūshingura*. 'The League of Loyal Retainers' (Photo Library Series) Kōdansha, 1967.

———. *Kabuki no Inochi*. 'The Life of Kabuki' Kōdansha, 1969.

———. *Hō-ō Kabuki 72: Sono Kiroku to Hankyō*. 'Kabuki's 1972 Visit to Europe: Records and Reactions' KBS, 1972.

———. *Nihon no Hamuretto*. 'Hamlet in Japan' Nansō-sha, 1972.

———. *Kabuki—Sono Bi to Rekishi*. 'Kabuki: Its Beauty and History' National Theatre, 1973.

———. *Chikamatsu Monzaemon*. Japanese National Commission for Unesco, Tokyo.

———. *Kabuki no Sekai*. 'The World of Kabuki' Tankō-sha, 1974.

———. *Zoku Hikaku Engekigaku*. 'Comparative Drama Part II' Nansō-sha, 1974.

———. *Dōjō-ji*. 'The Dōjō Temple' (Photographic Anthology) Kōdansha, 1975.

———. *Kabuki Jūhachiban*. 'The Eighteen Kabuki Pieces' (Photographic Anthology) Mainichi Shimbun, 1976.

———. *Kabuki*. Rippū Shobō, 1976.

———. *Kabuki Buyō*. 'Kabuki Dance' (Photographic Anthology) Mainichi Shimbun, 1976,

———. *Engeki Gairon*. 'An Introduction to Drama' University of Tokyo, 1978.

———. *Kabuki-Bi Ron*. 'On Beauty in Kabuki' University of Tokyo, 1989.

———. *Zur Theatergeschichte Japans*. Drama Research Institute, University of Vienna, 1961.

———. *The Traditional Theatre of Japan*. Weatherhill, 1981.

———. *Das Barocke im Kabuki—Das Kabukihafte im Barocktheater*. Austrian Academy of Science, 1981.

———. *Kabuki on the World Stage*. Radio Japan, 1984.

———. supervised. *Kabuki—18 Traditional Dramas*. San Francisco: Chronicle Books, 1985.

Keene, Donald. *Japanese Literature, An Introduction for Western Readers*. Tuttle Co., 1955.

———. *Bunraku*. Kōdansha International.

———. trans. *Four Major Plays of Chikamatsu*. New York, London: Columbia University Press, 1961.

———. trans. *Major Plays of Chikamatsu*. New York: Columbia University Press, 1961.

————. ed. *Twenty Plays of the Nō Theatre*. New York: Columbia University Press, 1970.

————. trans. *Chūshingura: The Treasury of Loyal Retainers: A Puppet Play by Takeda Izumo, Miyoshi Shōraku and Namiki Senryū*. New York: Columbia University Press, 1971.

Kenny, Don. *On Stage in Japan: Kabuki, Bunraku, Noh, Gagaku*. Shufu no Tomo.

Kishibe, Shigeo. *The Traditional Music of Japan*. The Japan Foundation.

Kishida, Ryūsei. *Engeki-Bi Ron*. 'Aesthetics of Theatrical Performances' Tokyo: Tōkō Shoten, 1930.

Konishi, Jin'ichi. *Zeami Jūroku Bu Shū*. 'Zeami's Sixteen Books' Tokyo: Kawade Shobō, 1954.

Malm, William P. *Japanese Music and Musical Intruments*. Tuttle Co.

Maruoka, Daiji and Tatsuo, Yoshikoshi. *Noh*. Hoiku-sha.

Masuda, Shōzō. *Nō to Kyōgen*. 'The Nō and the Kyōgen' Osaka: Daidō Shoin, 1959.

Matsuda, Seifū. *Kabuki no Katsura*. 'Wigs in Kabuki' Tokyo: Engeki Shuppan-sha, 1959.

McKinnon, Richard N. comp. *Selected Plays of Kyōgen*. Tokyo: Uniprint, 1968.

Miyao, Shigeo. *Bunraku Ningyō Zufu*. 'Illustrated Book of Bunraku Puppets' Tokyo: Jidai-sha, 1942.

Nippon Gakujutsu Shinkōkai. ed. *The Noh Drama*. Tuttle Co.

Nishikawa, Kyōtarō. *Bugaku Masks*. Kōdansha International.

Noma, Seiroku. *The Arts of Japan*. (2 vols.) Kōdansha International.

Nomura, Manzō. *Kyōgen Men*. 'Kyōgen Masks' Tokyo: Wan'ya Shoten, 1956.

————. *Kyōgen no Michi*. 'The Way of the Kyōgen' Tokyo: Wan'ya Shoten, 1955.

Nose, Asaji. *Nōgaku Genryū Kō*. 'Studies in the Origins of the Nō' Tokyo: Iwanami Shoten, 1938.

————. *Zeami Jūroku Bu Shū Hyōshaku.* 'Zeami's Sixteen Books Collected and Annotated' (vol.I, 1940. Enlarged ed. 1949, vol.II, 1944) Tokyo: Iwanami Shoten.

Pronko, Leonard C. *Theatre, East and West.* University of California Press, 1967.

Raz, Jacob. *Audience and Actors—A Study of Their Interaction in the Japanese Traditional Theatre.* Leiden: J. Brill, 1983.

Robert, Laurence P. *A Dictionary of Japanese Artists: Painting, Sculpture, Ceramics, Prints, Lacquer.* Weatherhill.

Roggondorf, Joseph. ed. *Studies in Japanese Culture* Tokyo: Sophia University, 1963.

Sakanishi, Shino. *Japanese Folk Plays.* Tuttle Co.

Scott, A.C. *The Puppet Theatre of Japan.* Tuttle Co.

Shuzui, Kenji. *Kabuki Zusetsu.* 'An Illustrated Book of Kabuki' (Co-authored with Akiba, Yoshimi) Tokyo: Man'yōkaku, 1931.

————. *Kabuki Josetsu.* 'An Introduction to Kabuki' Tokyo: Kaizō-sha, 1943.

Sōma, Hiroshi. *Kabuki Ishō to Funsō.* 'Kabuki Costume and Makeup' Tokyo: Yūbenkai Kōdansha, 1957.

Suda, Atsuo. *Nihon Gekijō-shi no Kenkyū.* 'Study on the History of Theatres in Japan' Tokyo: Sagami Shobō, 1957.

Ueno, Tadao. *Kabuki Kumadori Zusetsu.* 'Illustrated Accounts of Kabuki Makeups' Tokyo: Shōkoku-sha, 1943.

Waley, Arthur. *The Nō Plays of Japan.* Tuttle Co., 1976.

Yoshida, Tōgo. *Zeami Jūroku Bu Shū.* 'Zeami's Sixteen Books' Tokyo: Isobe Kōyōdō, 1909.

Index